Issues in British Politics

Chris Green

30 JUN ____

Also by Colin Pilkington

Britain in the European Union Today
Representative Democracy in Britain Today
What is Politics?

Issues in British Politics

Colin Pilkington

First published 1998 by
MACMILLAN PRESS LTD
Houndmills, Basingstoke, Hampshire RG21 6XS
and London
Companies and representatives
throughout the world

ISBN 0–333–65326–2 hardcover
ISBN 0–333–65327–0 paperback

A catalogue record for this book is available
from the British Library.

10   9   8   7   6   5   4   3   2
07   06   05   04   03   02   01   00   99   98

Copy-edited and typeset by Povey–Edmondson
Tavistock and Rochdale, England

Printed in Malaysia

Published in the United States of America 1998 by
ST. MARTIN'S PRESS, INC.,
Scholarly and Reference Division,
175 Fifth Avenue, New York, N.Y. 10010

ISBN 0–312–21381–6 clothbound
ISBN 0–312–21382–4 paperback

Contents

Preface

Issues are the building blocks of the political process. It is issues which drive politicians and political parties; they are the determinants of elections and electoral behaviour; and they are the means by which the general public become involved in political belief and political action.

At the end of the twentieth century the nature of the issues dominating British politics is changing. Partly this is in reaction to world events such as the end of the Cold War and the emergence of an increasingly global market. Partly it is the result of a sea change that has overtaken the political parties, from the neo-liberalism that seized the Conservative Party under Margaret Thatcher, to the social democratic model of New Labour under Tony Blair. Issues such as nuclear weapons which dominated British politics from the 1950s to the 1980s have all but disappeared; others such as devolution or electoral reform also seem set to disappear with the advent of a government dedicated to constitutional reform. This climate of change makes it very timely to take a fresh look at the nature and operation of issues in British politics, with one eye on how we got to the present situation and the other on where we go from here.

To write any political text is rather like writing in the sand, things can change before the ink is dry. Nevertheless, this book is an attempt to capture the issues which surround the political process in the late 1990s, as a new Labour government steers that process in a new direction. I must acknowledge my debt to Dennis Harrigan of Durham, who suggested I write this book and my thanks for their help to my publisher Steven Kennedy, my colleagues in the NEAB examining team and to friends and colleagues in the Politics Association, with a particular word of thanks to Glynis Sandwith of the Politics Association Resource Centre. Above all, however, my thanks and feelings of indebtedness go to the students I have taught, to whom I have lectured, whom I have led in seminars and whom I have examined and assessed. It is they who have made it clear to me what they want to know and how they want to be told about it. I trust they will benefit from this work.

COLIN PILKINGTON

1
Introduction

What is Meant by Issues?

The word 'issue' is much used in politics: indeed, there are those who would say that it is over-used. During election campaigns politicians challenge one another to 'deal with the issues', to 'stick to the issues' and not to be 'diverted from the issues that matter'. Other politicians claim, with more than an air of self-righteousness, that they make a point of dealing in 'issues rather than personalities' and denounce their opponents as 'unable to face the issues'. Voting behaviour is said to have become 'issue-related' and electors are encouraged to choose between competing policies for tackling issues as if they were shoppers searching for the best bargains in their local supermarket. Indeed electors are encouraged to place issues in a rank order of importance and then to choose as their champion the party which they believe might best deal with the issues seen as important: the whole electoral process being treated as if it were a political beauty contest, with issues as the contestants' vital statistics.

Yet, for all the emphasis on political issues, there is a singular lack of agreement as to what the term means, and remarkably few attempts to define it. A typical dictionary definition would be that an issue is a point on the decision of which something depends; a matter in contention or in question. But, perhaps the definition which comes closest to what this book is about, although it is still a view restricted to matters which influence voting behaviour, is the view taken by Dennis Kavanagh in his book on change in British politics (Kavanagh, 1990). According to him, the important political issues have three defining characteristics:

- They are matters over which public opinion is sharply divided.
- They are matters about which voters feel very strongly.
- They are matters for the solution of which voters look to particular political parties.

In fact, it is not surprising that there is no agreed meaning for the term 'political issues' because it is not in itself a homogeneous expression. Issues tend to bunch together into major areas, each with several different levels of specific issues within them. There are at least three of these main issue areas and it would be as well to start this survey by attempting to classify them by type.

A Typology of Political Issues

We can divide issues into three main areas according to whether they are:

- Concerned with the way in which the country and society is run.
- Concerned with the way the country is administered.
- Concerned with the way people live and are treated.

The first of these we can call ideological issues because the points at issue are the different positions adopted by party political ideologies as to how society should be run and what its priorities should be. Included under this heading are major areas of concern such as the economy, social welfare, law and order, defence and foreign affairs. They are the issues which determine voting behaviour because in some degree they affect the daily life and standard of living of every citizen. It is therefore important to the lifestyle and future expectations of those citizens that the party which they believe will best deal with these issues is in power. The issues are not isolated but are inextricably linked through their ideological nature, dependent on patterns of values and belief. Partisan supporters of the Labour Party will define through their membership of the party what their view is on economic issues, welfare matters, the importance of law and order and probably their stance on defence and relations with other countries; their attitudes in one area helping to colour and reinforce their attitudes in another. Problems for the parties begin when the electorate is divided in its loyalties between the various issue areas. During the 1992 election it was shown that Labour was well ahead in public opinion on social issues but trailed the Conservatives badly on the issue of economic competence (Crewe, 1992, p. 2). During the 1997 election campaign, on the other hand, the Conservatives made the mistake of concentrating on one issue – European Monetary Union – over which the electorate was itself no more than lukewarm in its opinions but about which the Conservatives were themselves totally divided.

The second group of issue areas might, quite properly, be called constitutional issues because they are concerned with the way we are governed, rather than with the purpose of government. Included under this heading are the European Union, electoral and constitutional reform, the accountability of government and its agencies, nationalism, devolution and sub-national government. These issues are not so closely linked with the ideological stance of the major parties, they are more the concern of pressure groups and the minor political parties. Within the major parties the approach on such issues might well be bi-partisan or, in certain cases such as Europe the parties are, within themselves, bitterly divided on the matter.

The third group of issues is not so easily labelled but centres on concern about the quality of life for the individual and seeks freedom from discrimination and exploitation. Included are such concerns as the environment, race relations and women's rights. These areas do not involve political parties as a rule, since activism is almost exclusively to be found in pressure and interest groups. On the other hand, both government and opposition parties may well become involved if forced to do so by public opinion; as for example the sudden conversion of politicians by the environmental lobby and the adoption of 'green' policies by all political parties, after the success of the Green Party in the 1989 European elections (Curtice, 1989, pp. 217–30). Sometimes, in responding to public opinion with something like a knee-jerk reaction, the government may well create an issue out of nothing simply through their handling of the matter, as was the case with the BSE crisis over British beef. It is noteworthy that these areas of concern are the fields in which the general public is most likely to become involved in political activity and where people who are not professional politicians have had most effect on the political process.

Within these areas there are clusters of issues, some of general application but others specific and more limited. For example there are many economic issues, but they range from the general such as 'which party is competent to control the country's economy?', to the specific, sometimes known as economic indicators, such as 'unemployment' or 'taxation'. All have their part to play in forming public opinion and electoral attitudes, albeit at different levels of importance.

How Issues are Created

Issues have variable lifespans. Some, particularly the ideological, are always with us although they may fluctuate in importance. Others suddenly appear out of nowhere, become very important for a time, and then fade away again. What then makes an issue, how is it defined and how is it sustained?

As far as most ideological issues are concerned they are defined by the political parties themselves. Parties stress the effectiveness of their own policies for dealing with the problems of the country and denigrate the policies of the opposing party or parties. Their message is reinforced by coverage of the issue by the media, by party publicity on billboards or in newspaper advertisements, through the representations of interest groups like trade unions or employers' organisations, by public relations work carried out by professional lobbyists or by the daily experiences of the electorate who realise that their way of life or standard of living is affected and determined by political actions. Through constant exposure to political argument, whether through the media or by personal experience, the electorate see that there are conflicting views about the problems of society, about which they need to make up their own minds. Most people support a political party and that support, together with the depth and extent of the support, is partially determined by the party's attitude to certain issues.

For issues involving reform or change, where political parties are not directly involved, the issue usually begins with public concern, a feeling that something is wrong or that something needs doing. Sometimes that concern is merely part of a general unease at injustice, unfairness or the way things are going, but in other areas concern may be sparked off by the warnings of experts. Environmental issues are typical of concerns which have increasingly affected people in recent years and which have caused people who hitherto had nothing to do with politics to become involved in political activity. In early 1995 there was so much protest-group activity – especially over the export of veal calves and the extension of motorways – that there was talk of a new militancy appearing in the previously ultra-moderate middle classes and middle-aged. But a tendency for this to be the case had been identified by Michael Moran ten years previously when he saw growing middle-class involvement in pressure group activity as part of a growing disillusionment with the class-based partisanship of the two-party system (Moran, 1985).

Issues are kept alive and amplified by the media. Britain has a strongly partisan press, something like 70 per cent of which is traditionally biased in favour of the Conservatives, despite some strangely convenient and St Paul-like conversions in the run-up to the 1997 election. And that partisan press makes a point of pushing wherever possible those news stories which show their favoured party's policies in a favourable light. Or, as is more often the case, they will sensationalise stories that undermine the opposing party's viewpoint.

Issues and Political Parties

Political parties exist as alliances between politicians who share a common view about where society ought to be going, and who have a common vision of the best way of achieving that goal. The combination of aims, objectives, values and ideas which unites this alliance of individuals represents the party's ideology. And it is the ideological position adopted by the party which predetermines the attitude of the party towards political issues.

During the nineteenth century the ideals of liberty and equality inherited from the French Revolution created the value patterns for two very different, and often opposed, visions of society. Liberty, as an aim, became synonymous with libertarianism or the freedom of the individual; which, in turn, came to represent freedom from government interference, defence of an individual's rights and property, the supremacy of the laws of supply and demand, the desirability of competition, and the maintenance of a country's ancient liberties and independence. Equality, on the other hand, stressed the collective rather than the individual, so that the individual is prepared to surrender some rights for the common good. From this viewpoint there has to be a distribution of property according to the criterion of fairness, the government must intervene when competitive market forces have failed to meet a need, the strong must help the weak, the injustices of the past must be righted and there should be cooperation for the common good both nationally and internationally.

These two positions typify, in very generalised terms, the ideological positions of political parties. The lines are not always clear-cut and party-members can vary in their position relative to the extremes. But, by and large, the parties have their stance on the individual-collective continuum, and it is their position which determines their attitude to issues as they arise. There is a danger, however, for parties which become too closely tied to specific ideological issues when that issue becomes out-dated or irrelevant and the public's perception of the issue radically changes. For example, when the constitution of the Labour Party was written in 1918 the party's commitment to public ownership of the means of production was written into the constitution as Clause IV but, with time, that commitment became an irrelevance and an embarrassment which finally had to be dispensed with by New Labour under Tony Blair.

When serious differences over an issue are not between parties but within a party, the impact of an issue can be to split and possibly destroy that party. In 1846 the Conservative prime minister, Robert Peel, abolished the Corn Laws, a protectionist measure favoured by the farmers and landowners who traditionally supported the Conservatives. Infuriated by his stance on the issue, no fewer than 231 Conservatives voted against their government, which led Peel to join the Liberals and split the party. As a result the Conservative Party was so weakened that there was no majority Conservative government between 1846 and 1874. In 1886 Gladstone's Liberal government attempted to introduce a Home Rule for Ireland Bill and 93 radical Liberals under Joseph Chamberlain voted against the bill, leaving the party and joining the Conservative Party as Unionists. This split removed the Liberals from office between 1886 and 1905, except for a period of little more than two years in 1892–5. This capacity for an issue to split a party and disbar it from office carries an uneasy lesson for a Conservative Party currently so divided over Europe and so spectacularly thrown out of government. Nor do arguments over issues harm only those parties in government. As the Labour politician Roy Hattersley pointed out in 1995, arguments in the Labour Party over the issues which lost them the elections of 1951 and 1979 so weakened and divided the party as to leave them in the wilderness for 13 years in the first instance, and 18 years in the latter (Hattersley, 1995). After the Conservative defeat of 1997 there were many voices ready to warn the party that the length of the Conservatives' stay in opposition would depend upon how quickly they could re-unite behind policies the electorate felt able to support.

Issues and Elections

The political importance of issues is rooted in the effects that they have on voting behaviour. During the 1970s the British electorate became much more volatile than it had been in the past and the strong alignment of partisan support with normative factors such as social class began to break down, reducing automatic support for the two major parties and producing voting behaviour that switched votes between the parties according to voters' perceptions of the issues. As a result of this partisan de-alignment, a new explanation for voting behaviour emerged which divided issues into two types (Jones and Kavanagh, 1983, p. 33):

1. *Position issues* are those to which the parties offer different solutions. The voters' choice of party is determined by their own preferred solution and their perception of which party will best meet that preference. If, for example, voters feel that the most efficient way forward for industry is the removal of state control and regulation, then they are likely to vote Conservative which is widely seen as the party of private enterprise.
2. *Valence issues* are those which all parties agree are important. The choice for voters here is which party they feel will be most competent to deal with that issue. For example, all voters and all parties might well agree on the importance of the National Health Service, but many voters would consider that the Labour Party feels most strongly about the NHS and is therefore the party best able to manage the efficient functioning of the service.

According to this view of voters choosing between parties and issues, voting behaviour can be compared to consumers leafing through *Which* magazine in order to decide which washing machine to buy from the various brands on offer. This is the consumer voting model (Rose and McAllister, 1986) which gained a great deal of prominence during the mid-1980s in an attempt to describe the process of partisan de-alignment.

The link between issues and voting behaviour is perhaps not quite so clear-cut, as has been shown by Ivor Crewe (1992). He distinguishes two factors of importance to voting behaviour. Firstly there is the importance of the issue to the voter, and secondly there is the question of which party is preferred on the issues seen as important. He also mentions as a potential third factor the change in perception of an issue over time. The difficulty with this model is that voters' behaviour does not always seem to agree with their stated perceptions.

During recent general elections the Gallup polling organisation has asked two questions of interviewees. One was 'Which two issues do you consider most important?' and the other was 'Which party do you think would handle the problem best?' In the Gallup post-election survey of the 1992 general election (10–11 April 1992) the issues seen as most important were all social, or economic with social overtones: the National Health Service (41 per cent), Unemployment (36 per cent) and Education (23 per cent), and overwhelmingly the electorate claimed that Labour would be the best party to deal with any social issue. The most highly-rated Conservative issues were well behind in public estimation: control of inflation (11 per cent) and taxation (10 per cent). According to these figures, if the electorate really did vote according to the issues, then Labour should have won with ease in 1992. However, as is well-known, Labour did not win. Commentators on voting behaviour have explained this by dividing the voter's perception of issues into two types:

1. Issues which the voter sees as being important for society as a whole. The voter is likely to tell the interviewer that this issue is important because the voter feels that this is expected and acceptable behaviour that will gain the approval of the interviewer.
2. Issues which voters see as being important for the prosperity and well-being of themselves and their families. Voters are more likely to keep this from the interviewer out of reluctance or embarrassment that their voting behaviour may be seen as dictated by purely selfish motives.

There is therefore a discrepancy between what electors will publicly announce as being an important issue, and thereby which party they intend to support, and what electors will choose to do in the secrecy of the voting booth, when behaviour can be based entirely on personal reasons without the need to consider a public image. After the 1992 debacle the polling organisations re-vamped their techniques to take these factors into consideration. Yet the press and public remained wary of opinion poll results and the immense Labour lead that opened up from 1993 onwards was partially discounted as unreliable. Yet the landslide scale of Labour's victory in 1997 showed that the polls had been right all along. Analysis would seem to show that the electorate's lingering faith in the Conservatives' economic competence had been shattered by the dramatic collapse of the pound against other currencies on Black Wednesday in 1992, while doubts about Labour's ability to handle economic matters without massive rises in taxation had been stilled by New Labour's resolute no-risk strategy under Tony Blair and Gordon Brown.

Summary

Issues are contentious matters which help formulate and polarise public opinion. They can be divided roughly into ideological issues, which are closely associated with political parties, and issues of reform and change, which are more associated with pressure and interest groups. Issues are important in the political process inasmuch as they are involved in the policy-making processes of the political parties, for their effect on voting behaviour, and for the role they play in non-partisan political activity.

2

The Market and the State

Although economic issues are often treated quite separately, it should be said from the start that all issues are economic, in the important sense that all proposed reforms in political life are constrained by their cost and the difficulty of paying for them. Therefore the most general issue which pervades politics, in Britain as elsewhere, is the all-embracing issue of economic competence: as the slogan prominently posted on the wall of Bill Clinton's campaign office during the 1992 US presidential election put it: 'It's the economy, stupid'. Political parties and the governments they form are judged by their economic competence on two levels:

1. **The 'Safe-Hands' Factor.** A government, or a party seeking to become the government, has to be seen as trustworthy in dealing with major economic issues such as international trade, investment and regulation of the financial markets. In the past, financial institutions have regarded the Conservatives as the economically-competent party, with the economy being thought of as being 'safe in their hands'. At the same time – at least prior to 1992 – these same financial institutions have distrusted Labour as 'unsafe', and even the rise and fall of share prices on the stock exchange and the strength of the pound in the money markets have been influenced by the relative positions of the two parties in the opinion polls. A measure of Tony Blair's success in creating New Labour has been the extent to which the City has moderated its doubts about a Labour government's economic competence, to the extent that the FT Index and the pound both rose in value at the news of Labour's victory in May 1997.

2. **The 'Feel-Good' Factor.** To ordinary voters the international economy is an abstract concept. What does concern them is the combination of economic factors enabling them to achieve a secure and comfortable lifestyle. They wish to feel that they have a secure job:

   - which pays a good wage, not too much of which is taken away in taxes;
   - which enables them to acquire a range of possessions to improve their standard of living; and
   - which allows them to save enough give them security in later life.

It is the ability of a political party and its government to deliver this sense of well-being across a variety of economic indicators which determines their economic competence in the eyes of the electorate. The key to economic issues in Britain is the means by which the feel-good factor might be delivered, and in terms of British politics since 1945 the focus has lain in the conflict between government intervention and bureaucratic control on the one hand and free and unregulated market forces on the other. Indeed, the paramount issue in recent years has been the extent to which an interventionist stance has given way to general acceptance of market forces, and the extent therefore to which the classic mixed economy consensus of the postwar period has given way to a new neo-liberal consensus in the post-Thatcher period.

The Reforming Governments of 1945–51

The postwar consensus happened by accident and was born of two factors:

1. The Labour Party's unpreparedness for the 1945 victory which prevented them from introducing a full socialist command economy.
2. The Conservative programme of renewal in the 1945–51 period, under guidance from R. A. Butler, which moved the party perceptibly to the left.

In the general election of July 1945, the Labour Party, to everyone's surprise, won a landslide victory over the Conservatives: winning 393 seats to the Conservatives' 213. Both the country and Labour's supporters expected the new government to put a socialist agenda into place since Clause IV of the Labour Party Constitution aimed for the 'common ownership of the means of production and the best obtainable system of popular administration and control of each industry and service'. But, while it was intended that the party should follow its full socialist agenda, including the common ownership of land, at some time in the future when the time was right, in the immediate postwar period Labour's demands were confined largely to the public utilities. The nationalisations of the Bank of England, Cable and Wireless, the coal mines and civil aviation were all approved in 1946; railways, electricity, road haulage and the waterways followed in 1947; gas in 1948; and the iron and steel industry in 1949, the last being the one act of nationalisation that met with any real opposition from the House of Lords.

It is now commonplace to talk of the Labour government of 1945 as being revolutionary in its achievements. In many ways this is true but, as an application of socialism, it was flawed in its conception:

- Labour was surprised by its own victory; even Attlee and his party had expected that either Churchill would win, out of gratitude for his conduct of the war, or that the result would be like 1929 with Labour as the largest party but without an overall majority.
- Because Labour had not expected to win they had not prepared a proper strategy for the nationalisation programme. George Wigg, a prominent Labour politician, claimed that very little preliminary planning had been done even for the coal mines, the flag-ship of nationalisation. 'The archives were ransacked and revealed two copies of a paper written by Jim Griffiths, one of them a translation into Welsh!' (Childs, 1992, p. 26).
- The parliamentary time required for ten separate nationalisation bills, on top of all the legislation introducing the welfare state plus a mass of routine legislation, meant that no time was available for detailed strategic planning.

The upshot was a programme that transformed Britain in many ways while leaving the nature of Britain's social and political order intact (Hutton, 1995, pp. 46–7). The fact is that the 1945 Labour government did not so much usher in a socialist revolution as begin the process of creating what would become known as the postwar consensus, under which the two main parties were in basic agreement over major political issues and differed only in their approach to specific issues.

Three factors created that consensus. Firstly, despite the impassioned outcry by Conservatives about the evils of nationalisation which Quintin Hogg (later Lord Hailsham) called an evil 'disastrous to the public interest' (Hogg, 1947, p. 286), the Conservatives were not so opposed to nationalised ownership as they proclaimed in public. Hogg himself pointed out in the same book that previous Conservative governments had bought shares in the Suez Canal Company and British Petroleum. What is more, Conservative governments had created the public corporations of the BBC and the Central Electricity Board in 1926; had given their blessing to London Transport in 1933; and took Imperial Airways and British Airways into public ownership in 1939. In a speech to the House of Commons in 1946, and reported in Hansard, Churchill himself admitted to having been in favour of nationalised railways as long ago as 1919 (Childs, 1992, p. 27).

Secondly, the economic policy adopted by the Labour government was not truly socialist in nature, but was in the tradition of liberal democracy as perceived by John Maynard Keynes, who was not even a Labour Party member but a Liberal. Keynes advocated government intervention to promote the creation of wealth and full employment through the use of public investment as a form of demand management, thus creating a mixed economy of both public and private enterprise. 'While Keynes was unhappy with capitalism in the 1930s he did not propose to replace it – merely to modify it' (Jones, 1994, p. 116).

Thirdly, the fact of having been nationalised made very little difference to the structure, organisation and functioning of the enterprises involved. Most of the public utilities had been brought under government control during the war and that control merely continued now, formally confirmed through parliamentary legislation. In the coal industry, for example, the management structure that had run the mines for their private owners was basically transferred as a body to the National Coal Board.

If the general economic issue can be said to be the feel-good factor, then it was that which finally brought down the Labour government in 1951. In order to force through their massive programme of reform in the face of international debts dating from the war, the cost of postwar reconstruction and the emergence of the Cold War, the Labour administration had maintained war-time controls to provide government direction of the economy. The rejection of the Attlee government in 1951 is evidence that the electorate may well appreciate the efforts of government for the general good but will appreciate even more the government which improves their standard of living. It was the aura of bleak austerity about the Attlee administration that has persisted as a negative image for the Labour Party ever since. For a section of the public, albeit an ageing section, the memory of a Labour government was of a time of shortages, rationing and excessive regulation and, over the years, that enduring impression of Labour has worked to the party's electoral disadvantage.

The Postwar Consensus and the Affluent Society

During the Conservative Party's years in opposition, R. A. Butler restructured Conservative ideology, moving the party from the right towards the centre in economic thinking. Churchill then appointed Butler to be Chancellor of the Exchequer in 1951, allowing him to mould and direct economic policy in the first postwar Conservative government. In 1955, Attlee was replaced by Gaitskell as leader of the Labour Party. Gaitskell was a Keynesian social democrat rather than a dogmatic socialist and the Labour Party moved from the left into much the same ground as that towards which the Conservatives were headed. The similar economic stance adopted by the two parties was typified by the use of a portmanteau term constructed out of the names of Butler and Gaitskell. The ideology of the two main parties was said to be neither conservatism nor socialism but rather to be 'Butskellism'.

As a government of the centre, the Conservative administration did very little to overturn Labour measures. The iron and steel industry was de-nationalised, the largely insignificant road haulage fleets were returned to private ownership, but that was that. The Bank of England, the railways, the coal mines and other utilities remained in the public sector and the Conservative government proved itself to be just as committed to a mixed economy as its Labour predecessor had been.

Much Conservative activity was devoted to the restoration of public well-being. Controls and rationing were removed as quickly as possible and standard rates of taxation reduced. Wages increased steadily without there being a massive increase in inflation, while unemployment remained gratifyingly low. Industrial production increased and the terms of international trade improved in Britain's favour. During the 1950s the standard of living rose for all sections of society and many members of the working class acquired a lifestyle that had once been the prerogative of the middle classes. If the so-called feel-good factor is a cliché of the early 1990s, then Harold Macmillan provided a similar phrase for the late 1950s. In July 1957, soon after he became prime minister, Macmillan said, 'Indeed, let's be frank about it; most of our people have never had it so good' (Childs, 1992, p. 106). It was a phrase that was quoted so often, both for and against Macmillan's interests, that it could almost be said that the 1959 general election, which he won, was the 'You've never had it so good' election.

The almost universal feeling of well-being concealed the fact that Britain was doing less well than other countries: in some instances markedly not so. The growth in the British economy during the 1950s was an average 2.5 per cent each year, which was very good by historical standards but the corresponding figures for West Germany and Japan were 7.9 per cent and 7.7 per cent respectively (Jones and Kavanagh, 1983, pp. 137–8).

There were basically three flaws in the consensus which were to create problems in the 1960s, echoes of which have persisted ever since.

- What economists have called short-termism. Shareholders in industry and commerce look for an immediate return for their money in the form of profits and increased share prices. To use Will Hutton's (1995) term, they are looking for 'tomorrow's money today'. But the result of this insistence on profit is a lack of investment. In continental Europe there had to be massive investment because so much of the industrial base had been destroyed by the war. In Britain, owners and management were quite content to continue with old plant and equipment rather than invest in new and, although British industrial output rose briefly in line with world trends, out-dated plant and practices meant that Britain could not keep up with the new technology. For example, when sales of television sets boomed in the late 1950s and early 1960s, British manufacturers were still producing sets based on valve technology. As a result, the British television industry collapsed in the face of the transistorised technology of the Japanese.

- A persistent balance of payments crisis. Growing affluence led to a consumer boom, and spending by British consumers increased considerably. But the money was largely spent on foreign imports, an expenditure that could not be matched by any growth in British exports. Allied to a fixed exchange rate, the balance of payments deficit drained Britain's gold and foreign currency reserves, leading to a major devaluation in 1967 and a running sore of economic crisis which dominated government economic thinking throughout the 1960s.
- Confrontational industrial relations in which neither management nor labour appeared willing to cooperate, leading to perpetual conflict and a series of damaging strikes. At one point the number of strikes, both official and unofficial, were called the 'British disease' by the rest of the world. German industrial relations, in contrast, were harmonious and both managers and workers shared in creating the German economic revival.

During the 1960s and early 1970s both major parties while in government tried to solve these problems but it has to be stressed that differences between the parties were over specific issues such as these and not over the general management of the economy. In that, both parties held to the Keynesian consensus maintaining growth through a mixed economy; attempting to solve economic problems through government intervention and public investment; and spending money to escape from recession. The economy was regulated through fiscal measures, applying and relaxing economic regulators such as credit restrictions and a prices and incomes policy. The alternation of imposing and withdrawing restrictions caused the government to resemble a driver transferring his foot from brake to accelerator and back again, in what became known as 'stop–go' policies.

Collapse of the Postwar Consensus

Whatever success the postwar consensus had in creating the affluent society of the 1950s and 1960s rested on five factors.

- Steady but not excessive inflation, equated in peoples' minds with natural growth.
- Low unemployment levels.
- Exchange rates pegged to a stable American dollar.
- National governments having full control over national economies.
- Cheap supplies of oil for an industry that had become increasingly reliant on oil.

From the 1970s onwards all these five factors began to crumble under international pressure, and the economic problems and issues of the present day are a result of the collapse of the consensus and the response of the British political parties to that collapse.

During the Arab–Israeli War of 1973, Arab oil producers, infuriated by the support given to Israel by the United States and the industrialised West, announced that they would restrict oil supplies to the West until the Israelis withdrew from Arab territory and, as a result, oil prices quadrupled within a year. Being totally dependent on a regular supply of cheap oil for power, heating and transport, the sudden rise in the price of oil meant that industry had to restructure itself in order to retain profitability. Restructuring meant increasing prices – leading to inflation – and reducing wage costs by shedding jobs – leading to higher unemployment.

In 1978 the fixed exchange rate was abandoned and currencies were allowed to float. As a result, financial institutions became increasingly involved with trading in currencies, keeping their investments in offshore funds and moving them from currency to currency in search of the highest interest rates.

In 1979 a further doubling of oil prices produced a worldwide recession, which emphasised the point that there is an international economy within which no national government can retain full control over its own national economy. By the end of the 1970s Britain was suffering from many adverse economic indicators:

- Runaway inflation.
- Rising unemployment that was becoming endemic and structural.
- A declining currency leading to greater balance of payments problems.
- Falling productivity and a declining industrial base.
- High interest rates which deter investment.

- Frequent strikes and other adverse forms of industrial action by trade unionists.

These problems were not unique to Britain, but Britain was more adversely affected by the international recession than most other developed countries. Both main political parties retreated from the consensus of the centre and moved towards the extremes, making the management of the economy far more of an issue than it had been for some time. A vocal section of the Labour Party attempted to move the party to the left, re-asserting the values of true socialism. At the same time the Conservative Party was captured by Mrs Thatcher and the New Right who advocated the replacement of Keynesianism with monetarism.

Monetarism and the New Agenda

Sections of the Conservative Party had never been reconciled to the consensus politics of 'Butskellism' as practiced by Macmillan and which was based on Macmillan's own book, *The Middle Way*, originally published in 1938. In the face of growing economic problems, the Conservative Party under Edward Heath convened a conference at the Selsdon Park Hotel in Croydon which produced a manifesto for the 1970 election that promised a return to older Conservative values:

- a greater commitment to free enterprise;
- a reduction in public spending;
- a restriction of welfare spending to those in greatest need;
- a tougher attitude towards the trade unions;
- a refusal to invest public money in firms and industries in trouble.

This was the first move towards what became known as Thatcherism.

Once in office the Heath government did not find it easy to carry out its promises. At the 1970 party conference the new Minister of Technology, John Davies, former Director-General of the CBI, had told the party: 'I will not bolster up or bail out companies where I can see no end to the process of propping them up' (quoted by Childs, 1992, p. 221). Yet, within two years the government executed a U-turn when it nationalised Rolls-Royce, a name so prestigious that no government could afford to let it go under, despite financial difficulties. The engineering firm was only the first of a series of so-called 'lame ducks' that were given assistance during 1972–3. From this time on the Heath administration reverted to a traditional Keynesian approach, initiating a 'dash-for-growth' which coupled heavy investment with curbs on wage increases. It was the failure of wage control, particularly as applied to the miners, which led to the defeat of the Heath government in 1974.

Heath's reversal of policy, which some saw later as a betrayal, preyed on the mind of a Conservative intellectual, Keith Joseph. He later claimed that he only became a true Conservative after analysing the reasons for defeat in 1974, after which he established the Centre for Policy Studies under the right-wing theorist Sir Alfred Sherman. The Centre adopted and developed the monetarist ideas of the Austrian-born economist Friedrich Hayek, and the American Milton Friedman. Joseph was also very close to Margaret Thatcher and, after her election as leader of the Conservative Party in 1975, she entrusted the task of developing economic policy to the Conservative Party's Advisory Committee on Policy chaired by Keith Joseph and advised by the Centre for Policy Studies.

Under these influences Mrs Thatcher and the Conservative Party moved away from the postwar consensus and fundamentally shifted the issue of economic management onto a new track. The concern of government policy was switched from unemployment, on which Keynesianism had focused, to the problem of high inflation which was seen by monetarists as the main enemy of economecs success. To monetarists, the theories of Keynes were anathema because they saw inflation as largely caused by government interventionism:

- government intervention in order to encourage employment leads to inefficient industry through over-manning and a top-heavy bureaucracy;
- a government-imposed prices and incomes policy leads to inflationary wage settlements that are unrelated to productivity, and it cushions inefficient manufacturers from the realities of the marketplace; and
- government spending that is too high creates a budget deficit that can only be cured by higher taxation which acts as a disincentive to economic growth, or by higher borrowing in the public sector borrowing requirement (PSBR) which is little more than admitting that you are spending money you do not have.

The last years of Labour government between 1975 and 1979 seemed to prove all that the monetary theorists were saying. There was runaway inflation, rising unemployment, large pay increases which were not based on productivity and which were largely negated by inflation, growth was negligible and there was a massive balance of payments crisis.

In 1976 the pound collapsed on the money markets and the then Chancellor, Denis Healey, had to borrow large sums of money from the International Monetary Fund (IMF) in return for which the IMF demanded the right to impose economic advisers on London to oversee the introduction of monetary measures to reduce public expenditure: ironically, the first Chancellor to apply monetarist theories was a Labour Chancellor. Healey tried to mitigate the rigours of monetarism by retaining some Keynesian measures such as wage restraint and public investment in ailing industries. There was a measure of success in that inflation was coming back under control by 1978, but it was the continuation of a Keynesian policy on pay which resulted in the wave of union activity known as the 'winter of discontent' and which led to the victory of Mrs Thatcher in 1979 and the final winding-up of the postwar consensus.

Thatcherism

The whole purpose of Thatcherism was to 'roll back the power of the state', replacing state intervention with the operation of free market forces:

- The structure of British industry would be changed through the privatisation of public enterprises.
- The ability of high-spending local authorities to thwart the economic plans of central government would be curbed by the limitation of local government powers.
- The provision of public services would be taken away from governmental provision, whether national or local, and opened up to private enterprise through competitive tender.
- High unemployment and limited benefit would encourage workers to take lower paid jobs so as to make industry more competitive.
- Taxation would be reduced so as provide incentives for entrepreneurial business.

- Trade unions would be neutralised and have their power to disrupt industry removed or reduced.
- Subsidies to industry would be removed, and inefficient or unprofitable industries forced to reorganise or close.
- High interest rates would limit borrowing to reduce the money supply and bring down inflation.

Based on the experiences of the Heath government very few people expected Mrs Thatcher to sustain her monetarist ideas for very long. Just as Heath had promoted the hard-headed ideas of Selsdon, only to crumble in the face of Rolls-Royce's difficulties, so they expected the Thatcher rhetoric to last until the first problem when she too like Heath would make a U-turn in policy. She soon put an end to any speculation about U-turns: 'You turn if you want to', she told doubters at the Conservative Party Conference in October 1980, 'The lady's not for turning'. Indeed the distinguishing characteristic of Mrs Thatcher's government was the determination with which she pursued her policies despite warnings from her ministers and in the face of unpopularity with the public.

At first it seemed as though this determined non-intervention would lead to disaster. Within two years of being elected, as the country waited for what was seen as the inevitable U-turn, the Thatcher government presided over the largest annual fall in industrial productivity since 1921, the greatest fall in annual output since 1931 and the highest unemployment figures since 1936. These adverse results were achieved by doing nothing, in a hands-off approach which insisted that the state would not intervene to save concerns that could not withstand market forces. While doing nothing to shield industry from recessionary forces, Mrs Thatcher did begin to take action against two sectors of the economy which she saw as restricting the free operation of market forces. Her targets were the trade unions and the nationalised industries:

They were, she thought, two sides of the same debased coinage. The industries . . . were hopelessly distorted and confined by state control and the absence of market competition. The unions were accomplices to the most scandalous of inefficiencies and had to be stripped of their power. (Young, 1989, p. 353)

These issues, the control of the unions and the privatisation of nationalised industries, will be dealt with in Chapter 4.

After Thatcher – a View of Economic Competence

In three successive governments Mrs Thatcher pursued her vision of a regenerated Britain in which the frontiers of the state would be pushed back leading to socialism being defeated and discredited. By the time she was removed from office in 1990 she was able to call on a long list of what she would call successes, which were summed up as four main achievements by Will Hutton (Hutton, 1995, p. 12).

1. The defeat of inflation, pegged at below 4 per cent for a number of years.
2. High productivity and steady industrial growth.
3. Trade union power reduced and strikes virtually eliminated.
4. The public sector made far more efficient and profitable through privatisation and deregulation.

Naturally enough there was a cost for each of these gains. However, whether the Thatcher years are seen as successful or not, they have had a major effect on the general direction of British economic policy. Although there are those who still argue for a return to Keynesian economics, a socialist alternative would seem to be dead. Even the Labour Party has eliminated the commitment to nationalisation from its constitution and distanced itself from the trade unions, while all parties seem to have agreed a new consensus based on a market economy. The new orthodoxy is to talk of the 'stakeholder economy' which seems to bridge the old ideological divisions. Consider three statements about the future economic direction to be taken by Britain and see whether you can distinguish between them:

> The spread of the free market heralds a new age of global competition. That means new markets for British goods and services. If we boldly embrace these new opportunities then we will enter the new millennium with boundless prospects for growth and prosperity. (Conservative Party manifesto, 1997, p. 7)

> Our aim is to end the cycle of boom and bust and equip Britain's economy to compete in the global market-place. Small business, enterprise and self-employment are the engine of a modern dynamic economy. (Liberal Democrat manifesto, 1997, p. 17)

We will leave intact the main changes of the 1980s in industrial relations and enterprise. We see healthy profits as an essential motor of a dynamic market economy. We will improve the competitiveness of British industry for the 21st century, leading to faster growth. (New Labour Party manifesto, 1997, p. 15)

The main economic issue in British politics is no longer a conflict between the individual and the collective as defined by private or public ownership of industry, but a conflict within the market economy between a totally free and unregulated market and a market constrained in some ways by the interests of the people. Such constraints are typified by the Social Chapter of the Treaty for European Union (Maastricht) which is helping to create an alternative form of capitalism in Europe that has been called the 'social market'.

Mention of Europe is a reminder that the British economy can no longer be considered in isolation. Trends and changes in British economics have only mirrored changes that have taken place on a global scale. For example, nowhere have free market policies been adopted so keenly as in the former Soviet Union and everywhere pure socialism seems to have been replaced by revisionist social democracy. As two distinguished political commentators, Michael Moran and Bill Jones, have said:

Across the world governments are, almost regardless of party, introducing economic reforms resembling the Thatcherite programme. This suggests that Thatcherism in Britain was a necessary adjustment to changing patterns in the world economy. (Jones, 1994, p. 564)

In other words, the chances are that a change to a market economy would have happened anyway, with or without Mrs Thatcher. Indeed, to adapt Voltaire's aphorism: if Mrs Thatcher had not existed it would have been necessary to invent her.

The creation of this new post-Thatcher consensus means that there has been a change over the years in the general perception of the best way in which the economy should be run. One factor, however, remained unchanged. Whether the country functioned as a mixed economy or according to market capitalism, the opinion of the public seemed to be that the Conservatives were the most competent party to manage the economy. That competence varied according to the specific indicator involved but overall the feeling seemed to be that the Conservatives could be trusted with the economy where Labour could not. Despite periodic troughs of unpopularity over specific issues such as unemployment, public perception of the Thatcher governments held that she had rescued Britain from the economic troubles of the 1970s.

That confidence in Conservative competence survived the departure of Margaret Thatcher and was a major factor contributing to the surprise Conservative victory in the 1992 general election. Yet within five months that confidence collapsed in the currency speculation and devaluation of 'Black Wednesday' that same September. I have argued above that the first postwar consensus was created partly by the Labour government's failure to introduce full-blooded socialism and partly by the Conservative Party's move from the right into the centre. The second, post-Thatcher consensus was created partly by the rightward move of New Labour and partly by the revelation in 1992 that the Tories could be quite as economically incompetent, through their being forced into the one policy that had previously been unique to Labour: devaluation!

As the electorate's belief in the economic competence of the Conservative Party declined, so did the potential competence of the Labour Party gain acceptability. It is, however, a measure of the success of market economics that New Labour's electoral strategy was predicated on the statement that Labour would not change the general direction of the economy but would continue to operate the system created by the Conservatives, albeit with a higher degree of regulation and moderated by a different scale of values. As Will Hutton put it, New Labour was proposing to 'govern as a nicer group of Conservatives' (Hutton, 1997, p. 17).

This was particularly true of that weathervane of Thatcherite economics, the inflation rate. Control of the inflation rate has become the shibboleth of modern economic planning, with low inflation the guiding star of the German Bundesbank and a sustained period of low inflation being an essential qualification for entry into the European Monetary System. Gordon Brown for New Labour had no difficulty in accepting those Treasury targets for inflation that had been set under the previous Conservative administration. Within days of taking office he had taken action to reinforce the fight against inflation by freeing the Bank of England from the need to consult the Chancellor over the level of interest rates. From here on the Bank would be able to respond automatically to any hint of rising inflation by an increase in the base lending rate, just as the Bundesbank does. This was in direct contrast to the policy of Kenneth Clarke, Brown's predecessor as Chancellor, who had been in conflict with the Bank of England for some months over his refusal to increase the interest rate.

This new insistence on controlling inflation does create a new issue, however. As the economy has recovered since the early 1990s so has consumer confidence returned. In 1997 this was compounded by a series of share flotations on the part of former building societies, in the course of which investors and mortgage-holders with those societies received windfall bonus payments of shares worth thousands of pounds to each investor. The increased amount of money in the economy led to an upturn in consumer spending, and that in turn led to an upturn in inflation triggering an automatic interest rate rise from the Bank of England. High interest rates generate inward investment from overseas and increase the value of the pound. This outcome appears attractive to the public, who can better afford holidays abroad and imported goods, but it is potentially disastrous for industry which not only finds itself having to pay increased interest rates on its borrowing, thus reducing investment, but also being priced out of overseas markets by an overvalued pound. It is the 1990s' equivalent of those balance of payments crises of the 1960s.

3
Taxation, Pay and Devaluation

The competence of a political party to manage the economy may well affect the way in which people vote, but the electorate does not pass judgment on that competence in terms of the general national economy but rather in the context of specific economic issues, such as the level of personal tax paid by the voter or the degree of job security felt by the individual in the face of national employment statistics. These specific issues are linked, and a party's performance in relation to one may well affect its performance in another. On the other hand, an individual will judge each specific issue on its merits and its relevance to his or her priorities, so that a supporter of the Conservative Party may well continue to believe in the Conservatives' overall competence because of their policies on taxation, despite a suspicion that the Conservatives do not make a good showing in other areas of concern.

Taxation

It was the American, Benjamin Franklin, who said that there are only two certainties in life: 'death and taxes'. It is therefore appropriate that we consider taxation before any other economic issue. Taxes represent something to which everyone is reluctantly reconciled but which everyone resents to some degree. There is evidence that fears of high taxation by Labour did much to persuade Conservative waverers to return to the fold in the 1992 general election. 'Only one in ten voters said the tax issue was important to them, but they preferred the Conservatives to Labour on the issue by a massive 72 point margin; and among switchers to the Conservatives 26 per cent cited taxation as influential' (Crewe, 1992, p. 6). The importance of taxation is implied in the way governments of any party have regularly heralded the approach of an election by a tax-cutting 'give-away' budget.

Taxation exists as a means of raising money for necessary government expenditure, but it has also served as a tool of social policy. In Britain the idea was introduced by Lloyd George in his so-called People's Budget of 1909: 'Lloyd George as Chancellor needed to raise £16 million in extra revenue to finance the government's planned social programme . . . [and he] determined that the money should come principally from the rich' (Kingdom, 1991, p. 201). Taxation therefore has a function in the redistribution of wealth, by which money is taken from those with an ability to pay in order to provide services for those in the lower income brackets who cannot afford to pay. In the past the Labour Party became recognised as a party of high taxation, not simply because of Labour's spending policy but because taxation was seen as a weapon in the party's struggle for a more equitable society.

Redistributive taxation is almost always direct taxation, whether income tax for the individual or corporation tax for the firm or business enterprise. A tax on income is a progressive tax in that the more you earn the more you pay. This effect can be heightened by progressively increasing the differential rate at which income tax is levied as an individual's income rises. At the same time, a series of allowances and exemptions reduces the tax of the low-paid. During the last Labour government, in the late 1970s, the standard rate of income tax was set at 33p in the pound while the top tax band reached its peak at 83p in the pound. At the same time, the sum an individual was allowed to earn before paying tax – the personal allowance – was index-linked to rise in line with the cost of living and the general level of earnings.

Direct taxation is a levy on what the taxpayer earns; indirect taxation is a levy on what the taxpayer spends. Here, too, taxation can have a function other than the raising of revenue. Excise duties on tobacco, alcohol, petrol and betting have for some time been known as 'taxes on sin' and the raising of these duties can always be disguised as action against anti-social behaviour, whether it is discouraging cigarette-smoking or providing the incentive for a move from leaded to unleaded petrol: '. . . such taxes on "vice" could even be regarded as slightly morally uplifting' (Childs, 1992,

p. 246). The Green Party goes even further in suggesting that taxes on income and capital should be replaced completely with taxes on energy utilisation such as road tolls, higher prices for air travel, noise-level taxes on lorries, aircraft and motorcycles, taxes on waste and a carbon/energy tax (Hugill, 1995).

The bulk of indirect taxation is, however, a regressive tax, which has little relation to a taxpayer's ability to pay. If the tax on an item is £2, it is a more significant proportion of income for someone earning £60 a week than it would be for someone earning £20 000 a year. When the principal form of indirect taxation was purchase tax, and even in the early days of VAT, there used to be a differential rate of tax so that necessities were taxed at a much lower rate than luxuries. That attempt to mitigate the regressive nature of indirect taxation has largely disappeared, although certain necessities such as food and children's clothing are still zero-rated for VAT.

During the 1980s and the early 1990s, there was a shift in emphasis from direct to indirect taxation. The Conservatives argued that to tax income heavily acts as a disincentive to hard work and enterprise. Moreover, there is no choice as to whether one has to pay or not, since income tax is enforced by law, while a person can choose for themselves whether or not to spend money. Taxation on expenditure rather than on income therefore does not infringe an individual's freedom of choice. Parties opposed to the Conservatives, however, would argue that the logical extension of indirect taxation would end in tax being levied on necessities such as food where there is no choice as to whether the money has to be spent or not. This shift from direct to indirect taxation helps to explain the conflicting evidence between the Conservative government's claim to have cut taxation and the Opposition's counter-claim that taxes rose over the years that the Conservatives were in power; direct taxation was reduced but the reduction was more than compensated for by rises in indirect tax.

From taking power in 1979, Mrs Thatcher's government was committed to reducing income tax, particularly for those in the upper tax brackets. If senior management in industry and commerce were to lead the needed recovery they had to be encouraged by the knowledge that they could keep most of their additional earnings. By 1988 the higher bands of tax had been reduced to just one and this was set at 40 per cent. At the same time the standard rate of tax was gradually reduced from 33 to 25 per cent and a lower band of 20p in the pound was introduced to help the lower paid. Doubts were expressed about the actions of the then Chancellor, Nigel Lawson, in reducing the standard rate by 2 per cent, both in 1987 and then again in 1988, when the country was in the midst of a runaway consumer spending spree.

During the 1980s, however, despite these cuts in tax revenue, the government managed to reduce the cost of public spending and the public sector borrowing requirement (PSBR) dropped from £13.2 billion in the year 1980–81 to £2.5 billion in 19867, and actually went into surplus between 1987 and 1991 (McKie, 1994, p. 48). However:

- These tax cuts had been partly funded by revenue from the North Sea and other British oil fields and partly through the sale of government assets in the privatisation of nationalised industries. In other words, they were financed by one-off contributions rather than any long-term improvement in receipts.
- These tax cuts were not always as generous as they appeared, since there were adjustments to personal allowances and tax thresholds that led to more people paying tax at the lower level than had previously been the case. A Treasury written answer of 21 January 1994 admitted that the freezing of personal allowances in the 1993 budget would mean that an extra 400 000 people would have to pay tax in the forthcoming financial year (McKie, 1994, p. 40).

Another form of direct taxation is National Insurance (NI). Unlike income tax, NI contributions steadily increased after 1979, to reach a peak of 10 per cent in 1993. National Insurance is more regressive than income tax in that, with an upper income limit (no one needed to pay more than £420), low earners always had to pay the increases, while anyone already paying the maximum was exempt from any new increase. And the 1p in the pound increase in NI contributions in 1993 immediately cancelled out all that had been gained by a 1p reduction in the income tax standard rate. This helps explain the anomalous fact that, while most taxpayers were worse off after 15 years of Conservative rule, families belonging to the top 10 per cent of earners were on average £125 a month better off (McKie, 1994, p. 40). Nevertheless, as the *Guardian*'s yearbook quoted John Major as saying in his message for the New Year of 1994, 'The Conservative Party remains the party of the lowest possible tax' (McKie, 1994, p. 48).

As income tax was reduced, the shift to indirect taxation began. In the first Conservative budget of 1979, Geoffrey Howe raised VAT from 8 or 12.5 per cent to a uniform 15 per cent. Later this figure rose again to 17.5 per cent. This more than doubling of indirect taxation, with excise duties also rising faster than the rate of inflation, went largely unnoticed by an electorate seduced by reductions in direct taxation. Yet, the rise in indirect taxation coupled with changes in income tax allowances and increases in National Insurance meant that, by 1993, the average married wage-earner with two children was paying a higher proportion of tax than would have been the case in 1979 under the last Labour government. In 1990–1 both direct and indirect tax were equal at £77 billion. By the tax year 1993/94 direct taxation had dropped back to £74 billion but indirect taxation had risen to £92 billion. Figures prepared by Gordon Brown, the then shadow chancellor, suggested that increased taxes between 1993 and 1995 represented the equivalent of an extra 7p on the standard rate of income tax; figures that later were reluctantly confirmed by Kenneth Clarke.

The role of taxation as an issue working in favour of the Conservatives only lasted until the Budget of 1994. The recession of 1990–91, followed by the crisis of September 1992, hit public spending hard. The PSBR, in surplus since 1987 largely as a result of several large but one-off injections of finance through major privatisations, suddenly went into reverse reaching a total deficit of £38.5 billion in the financial year 1992–3 and showing signs of rising to £50 billion and beyond. One of the remedies put forward by Norman Lamont in his spring budget of 1993 was the introduction of VAT on fuel in the form of gas and electricity, which previously had been zero-rated. The Chancellor proposed to introduce the measure in two stages, VAT at 8 per cent being imposed in 1994, rising to 17.5 per cent in 1995. Efforts were made to disguise the new tax as environmentally friendly; a 'green tax' intended to deter overuse of scarce resources in the form of carbon fuels. But the measure was immediately denounced as the worst form of regressive taxation, since this is not only an example of taxing a necessity, but a case of those who are most in need of heat and light – the old and infirm – being the least likely to be able to afford the increased prices.

The first imposition of 8 per cent VAT passed through parliament but the imposition of tax on fuel became a major issue in by-elections such as that in Christchurch, where a high proportion of retired pensioners in the population, many of them on low fixed incomes and former Conservative supporters, now deserted the party over the issue. When Chancellor Kenneth Clarke attempted to impose the second phase of the tax in the November 1994 budget the measure was voted down but not before considerable damage had been done to the Conservative image. In the public's perception, they had become the party which promised tax cuts before an election and then went back on its promises after the election. This perception of Conservative taxation policy on the part of the electorate was possibly as irrational as their perception of Labour before 1992, but party images are very seldom founded in rationality. The sour taste left by the attempt to levy VAT on fuel enabled the new Labour Chancellor to make an early positive gesture by reducing that VAT from 8 to 5 per cent in his first Budget, helping to create an equally irrational perception of Labour as a tax-cutting party.

The arguments over VAT had mirrored arguments over the poll tax which had plagued the Conservatives in the late 1980s; another regressive tax which penalised the less-well-off and bore no relation to an individual's ability to pay. Both issues show that while the electorate may be willing to go along with increases in indirect taxation in favour of cuts in income tax, they will protest if the taxation is seen to be over-regressive and unfair, especially if it can be shown that increases in indirect taxation outweigh reductions in direct taxation.

In an attempt to retain their reputation as the party of low taxation, the Conservatives argued that any tax increases introduced by Labour if they had won the 1992 election would have been many times higher, because of high-spending promises in Labour's manifesto. In so doing they revealed the true issue over taxation, which is: *Does the electorate want a high level of public services paid for out of high taxation, or do they want low taxes with a consequent low level of public services?* This is particularly relevant as the proportion of dependent population increases; that is to say those who do not work but are supported by those who do, such as students or pensioners. This is what makes the issue of taxation so difficult for a Labour Party that has traditionally always looked after the interests of the poor and needy, by high public expenditure if necessary.

Conventional wisdom states that a majority of the electorate faced with the choice between low taxation and adequate services will always choose low taxation. However, there is an alternative known as hypothecation; the term referring to taxation raised for a specific purpose. In both the 1992 and 1997 election campaigns the Liberal Democrats advocated raising the standard rate of income tax by 1p, specifically for spending on education: the idea finding favour with many people and certainly not losing the party any support. The suggestion would seem to be that, while general and unspecified tax increases might be resented, people are more ready to pay higher taxes,

1.   if they know what the money is being spent on, and
2.   where they approve of the expenditure.

Conscious that fears of Labour as the party of tax increases were primarily responsible for the 1992 defeat, New Labour in the person of its prospective Chancellor, Gordon Brown, was extremely reticent in discussing details of taxation before the 1997 election. Very early in the campaign Brown made it clear that he would make just two pledges on taxation:

- An incoming Labour government would regard itself as bound by the spending programme and economic strategy devised by the outgoing Conservative administration.
- A New Labour government would not raise the basic or top rates of income tax within the lifetime of the parliament elected in 1997. Indeed, there was a new objective put in place through a pledge by Gordon Brown that he would introduce a new lower starting income tax rate of ten per cent – 'as soon as it is prudent to do so'.

Throughout the election campaign Labour consistently refused to discuss taxation proposals beyond a single commitment which was the levying of a windfall tax on the privatised utilities in order to fund a training-for-work scheme for unemployed youngsters. The new consensus between Labour and the Conservatives as to the need for cuts in tax, and income tax in particular, enabled the Liberal Democrats to claim the ideological high ground through their willingness once again to discuss hypothecated tax increases – a 1p increase on the income tax rate to cater for education spending, and rises in duty on tobacco to pay for health service reforms.

The claims of both Labour and the Conservatives that they would not raise taxes led to each accusing the other of having a 'black hole' in their calculations, inferring that the reality of government would require their electoral promises on spending to be paid for by tax increases. In comparison with these doubts about the ability of the major parties to hold their tax-cutting line, the Liberal Democrats gained some credibility for facing the need for tax increases and, by hypothecating these increases appeared to gain acceptance for increased taxation for clearly explained reasons.

Nevertheless, the Liberal Democrats were never going to form a government and a new form of consensus over taxation seems to have been put in place by the parties of government in the latter half of the 1990s. It is now accepted that it is desirable that direct taxation should be as low as possible and the major political issue represented by taxation has become the search to find some way to fund government spending that is neither increased direct taxation nor a regressive form of indirect taxation.

Even despite this growing consensus there was an underlying belief that, once the election was won, the Labour government would increase direct taxation after all – possibly by reducing tax allowances – if only as a way of controlling the consumer boom that was threatening the inflation rate. Yet the first Labour Budget in July 1997 left income tax alone, apart from a policy review into streamlining the tax and benefit system. All the tax-raising measures were aimed at targets acceptable to the majority of the electorate: heavy increases in duties aimed at smokers and drivers; increased stamp duty on top-range housing; reducing tax relief on private medical plans; and, of course, the windfall levy on over-profitable privatised ventures.

The conduct of the Blair government, and his Treasury team in particular, seemed to show that New Labour was willing to follow an essentially middle-class, middle-England agenda on taxation and the economy, forming a new consensus not very distant from the position held by Kenneth Clarke in the last period of the Conservative government and leaving the Liberal Democrats' view of hypothecated taxes isolated as the only radical alternative. Paddy Ashdown, as leader of the Liberal Democrats, was unwilling to let the matter rest. Between the election of 1 May and the start of the summer recess he addressed seven questions to Tony Blair at Prime Minister's Question Time on the theme of a need for increased taxation. Otherwise, he said, 'the crisis in our schools and hospitals this winter will be as bad as, or worse than, any we experienced in the Conservative years' (*The Observer*, 27 July 1997).

Pay

Traditionally, the fear of unemployment controlled the levels of pay demands. While there was full employment and the governing parties held to the Keynesian priority of maintaining full employment, there was little incentive to observe pay restraint. During the boom years of the 1950s and early 1960s the workforce received generous pay settlements, mostly financed by a steady growth of productivity. During the late 1960s and early 1970s the question of pay became a political issue, as increasing inflation raised expectations of larger and more frequent pay increases not covered by growth in the economy. With no government willing to use unemployment to curb excessive pay settlements, there had to be governmental intervention in the pay bargaining process. As early as 1965 Harold Wilson instituted the National Board for Prices and Incomes which was supposed to vet proposed increases in both pay and prices and to prevent increases that were unjustified and inflationary.

After the oil crisis of 1973 inflation and wage demands rose rapidly into double figures, reaching their peak in 1975. The minority Labour government of 1974 was too insecure to enforce the restraints imposed by the Heath government, and both inflation and wage rate increases rose unchallenged to reach and pass increases of 25 per cent a year. The workforce, faced by rapidly rising prices, came to expect annual pay rises above the rate of inflation. And that situation was aggravated by two new elements:

- Leap-frogging was the process by which the first pay settlement of the annual round of pay negotiations set a target which later negotiators felt they had to match if not exceed.
- Maintenance of differentials meant that skilled workers who were paid more than the unskilled insisted on maintaining that differential. A high pay settlement from the lower ranks would be followed by an even higher demand from the better-paid.

Denis Healey, as Labour Chancellor, was required to reinstate a prices and incomes policy as a direct result of the agreement made with the IMF in 1976. The policy succeeded at first and there were two years of restraint helping to drag inflation down below 10 per cent in 1978, but when the government attempted wage restraint for a third successive year the workers and their unions rebelled, producing the 'winter of discontent' which helped defeat Labour in 1979. When Mrs Thatcher took power in 1979 it was made clear that any form of prices and incomes policy would not be acceptable. It was government policy that wage rates should be determined purely by market forces. What was not made clear was the implicit recognition that wage rates would be kept low by the pressures of rising unemployment and government constraints placed upon the trade unions and, during the 1980s, these pressures helped to create a low-wage economy in Britain.

- Many of the jobs created in recent years have been specifically for women; who traditionally are paid less, are not unionised, are very often part-time workers without security of tenure and who will work unsocial hours.
- Many businesses have cut the pay of workers under the pretext that without the cut in pay the firm would have to close.
- Senior staff on higher rates of pay have been encouraged into early retirement to make way for younger staff on much lower salary levels.
- Workers for some enterprises have been dismissed but then re-employed on a self-employed, freelance basis; for less money and without benefits.
- Unlike the 1970s when the majority of workers expected annual pay rises, there were now workers who had to accept a gap of two or even three years between pay rises: workers who accepted the situation quietly for fear of unemployment.

In August 1993 the government abolished the last of the wages councils that were set up to protect workers against wages well below the national average. At the same time the government received approval for its decision to opt out from the Social Chapter of the Maastricht Treaty, in particular from those clauses recommending a minimum wage and protection for part-time workers. A minimum wage for Britain was attacked by government ministers because: 'Rather than hire labour at rates they could not afford, employers would not hire labour at all' (McKie, 1994, pp. 68–9).

Through the creation of a low-wage economy the Conservative government hoped to restore British competitiveness in the world economy: with a certain degree of success. Multinational companies began to shift production to the UK from countries like France, while inward investment in new European Community plant, from

Japan and elsewhere, tended to go to Britain rather than other EC members, all because British wage rates were lower than competing countries in industrialised Europe. Similarly, the government continued to resist the Social Chapter because its provisions on pay would remove what the government saw as Britain's competitive edge. Opposition accusations that Britain was becoming known as the sweat-shop of Europe were disregarded by monetarists who saw the low-wage economy as the easiest way for Britain to escape the recession.

Low pay rates in the private sector were maintained through the fear of unemployment and the growing impotence of the unions. To the monetarists this was the true operation of market forces and there was therefore no need for a pay policy to be enforced by the government. Nevertheless, a pay policy continued to exist for the public sector where the government remained a major employer despite privatisation. In his 1993 Budget the Chancellor made it clear that, unless public sector employers made savings elsewhere, any rise in public sector pay should be below the level of inflation. In the 1995 pay round this was emphasised even in those areas where there was a body awarding statutory pay increases: the government approved a pay rise for teachers but refused to provide funds to local education authorities to pay for the rise, while for nurses who had been awarded 3 per cent rises the government was willing to contribute just 1 per cent, with the rest to be agreed in local pay agreements. The effect of differing pay policies for the private and public sectors could be seen in figures issued in April 1995: in the year to February 1995 average earnings in manufacturing industry grew by 5.25 per cent compared with 2.5 per cent for employees in the service industries, and this at a time when the inflation rate was running at 3.4 per cent.

However, there was one group not affected by market forces. During 1995 increasing resentment was felt by the public not only at the huge pay increases being given to the chief executives of the privatised utilities but at the extremely large bonuses paid out in the form of share options to these men. The case which started the controversy was Cedric Brown of British Gas who was awarded a 75 per cent pay increase in 1995, taking his salary to £475 000 a year. Other cases soon came to light, such as Sir Desmond Pitcher, the chairman of North West Water, who had seen his salary rise by 571 per cent since privatisation, and David Jeffries, appointed chairman of the National Grid on privatisation, paid an annual salary of

£359 000 and making a potential £1.78 million in share options (*The Guardian*, 1 March 1995).

To dismiss opposition protests as 'the politics of envy', as many ministers did, was to misunderstand the true nature of the issue. People may resent large salaries earned by a few but mostly accept them as a fact of life. What does antagonise the public is:

1. a sense of unfairness in that these executives are being paid so much more than those who ran the utilities under public ownership;
2. the unfairness implicit in the fact that they are being paid extremely large salaries when their employees are having to manage on far less; and
3. that the utilities they head to such personal profit are not necessarily more efficient as a result, even though charges to the consumer are increasing.

As a newspaper editorial of the time said: 'It is curious how, when "market forces" are invoked to settle levels of remuneration those at the top are always aligned upwards while those at the bottom go down' (The *Guardian*, 1 March 1995). In this instance the newspaper was pointing the finger at Cedric Brown whose 75 per cent increase was announced on the same day as 2600 staff in British Gas showrooms faced 16 per cent cuts in average salaries of £13 000 a year.

In response to the constant criticism of these large awards to top executives, criticism led in parliament by Tony Blair, John Major was forced to retreat on the issue and condemn such payments as undesirable. The same newspaper as above found a significance in this policy reversal for the economic management of Britain as a whole: 'There is a plausible case for saying that this was the precise moment when the 16 years of Thatcherite revolution finally went into reverse' (*The Guardian*, 11 April 1995).

Nevertheless, the anomaly of executive pay rises did not go away simply because John Major had noticed it. The Labour Party also got itself into difficulties over the extent to which it was committed to the Social Chapter, how far it would go in imposing a minimum wage and to what extent they would listen to the trade unions. In an attempt to distance itself from its old reputation of pay free-for-alls and being in the pocket of the unions, spokespersons for Labour such as Gordon Brown refused to set a figure on the proposed minimum wage and moves were set in motion to curb union powers at the Labour Conference.

The reticence on economic policy displayed by New Labour during the 1997 election campaign extended to pay policy. There was a commitment to a minimum wage but the figure at which that minimum would be set was left vague and was, it was suggested, likely to be rather less than the absolute minimum requested by the unions. Policy on public sector pay was equally restricted by Gordon Brown's acceptance of economic guidelines laid down by the outgoing Conservative government. Despite long-standing Labour hostility to the idea of rate-capping being used for any local authority which breached the ceiling on spending targets, the new Labour government rate-capped a number of local authorities, most notably Somerset and Oxfordshire, in July 1997. In the case of Oxfordshire, where capping threatened to lead to 140 teachers being sacked and schools being left unrepaired, the Labour group was especially bitter in claiming that the programme which was being capped was based on policies included in the Labour manifesto, on which both the councillors and the parliamentary party had fought and won on 1 May. At the same time, local councils who were celebrating the Labour government's freeing of capital receipts for council house sales – funds blocked by consecutive Tory governments – discovered that they might have to use those funds to make good the shortfall in government grants.

Devaluation

Perhaps above all other economic issues, devaluation is seen as a matter of national pride and prestige. In the political world it was seen to be as important for Britain to have a strong currency as it was for the country to have a strong army. The two major devaluations of the postwar period, those of 1949 and 1967, were executed by Labour governments, and it also fell to Labour to defend the massive run on the pound in 1976, the Labour Party thereby acquiring the label of 'the party of devaluation'. Fear that Labour would not be able to defend the value of the pound was a contributory element to the 'fear factor' which is the mirror image of the feel-good factor, and which denied Labour victory in four consecutive general elections between 1979 and 1992. It is therefore ironic that the latest – and what appeared at the time to be the most damaging – devaluation happened under a Conservative government, in September 1992.

Yet, despite its central role in the economy, devaluation is seen as a personal matter and, like taxation, is one of the criteria by which individual citizens judge the economic competence of governments. In 1967 Harold Wilson made it a priority after devaluation to speak to the country on radio and television, assuring them in the now famous phrase that 'the pound in your purse or pocket' had not lost any value domestically.

The important thing about the 1949 and 1967 devaluations was that sterling was then a reserve currency with a fixed exchange value against the price of gold and the dollar. Many countries, most of them former members of the British Empire, operated within the sterling area using the pound for their international business transactions and holding their currency reserves in sterling with British banks. To devalue the pound in those circumstances was to break faith with foreign investors by slashing the value of their bank accounts. The effective devaluations of the 1970s and 1980s were less important because the pound had ceased to be a reserve currency and exchange rates were allowed to float against one another within fairly loosely defined limits. Then came the European Exchange Rate Mechanism (ERM), placing the pound within fixed exchange rates again and once more making devaluation a potential issue.

Mrs Thatcher, as prime minister, was totally opposed to Britain re-entering fixed exchange rates, especially a system like the ERM which carried connotations of European monetary union. Her Chancellor, Nigel Lawson, had no such fears and, even though forbidden to take Britain into the ERM, he unofficially set a fixed rate by manipulating the value of the pound against the German currency so that it maintained a parity of three marks to the pound. When Britain finally joined the ERM in the autumn of 1990 that sort of rate against the deutschmark was maintained; and it was too high. In 1990 the German economy was suffering adverse effects from the reunification of the country and German interest rates were forced to keep on rising. Other countries within the ERM were obliged to raise interest rates in line with the Germans in order to maintain their currencies in line with the mark. All Europe slid into recession but those countries with a sensible rate pegged against the mark suffered less than those which had difficulty in maintaining their exchange rates. Britain, with an over-valued pound, not only suffered a worse recession than most other countries in Europe but attracted the attention of currency speculators.

The condition of sterling in 1992 was tailor-made for the speculators: the exchange rate against the mark was over-valued by about 15 per cent and the economy was remarkably weak. The prime minister, John Major, had, when Chancellor, been the man who had taken Britain into the ERM and he had been the person who chose the rate at which the pound was valued on entry. Together with his Chancellor, Norman Lamont, John Major felt obliged to defend the value of the pound within the ERM in the face of heavy speculation against sterling, and despite evidence that the exchange rate was ultimately indefensible. Black Wednesday (16 September 1992) saw interest rates rise twice to an all-time high of 15 per cent, and then fall again, all within the one day. It also saw vast sums of money, estimated at £5 billion in just one day, paid out by the Bank of England to support the value of the pound, only to result in a substantial devaluation (*The Guardian*, 27 February 1993).

Before this it was Labour that had been branded as the party of devaluation and the Conservatives who were known for their successful defences of the pound. Ironically enough, the effects of this devaluation were entirely beneficial, with the prices of British goods on the export market and the labour costs of British industry once more extremely competitive internationally. As a result of the devaluation Britain was the first European country to emerge from recession, exports boomed, unemployment figures began a steady decrease and interest rates dropped from that high of 15 per cent to 6 per cent in just four months. Yet the public did not see it that way and the events of 1992 meant that the issue of devaluation no longer represented an adverse factor for Labour but added to the inability of the Conservatives to re-create the feel-good factor. As a *Guardian* survey of public opinion on economic issues said:

> Until Black Wednesday the Conservatives were always ahead of Labour on the economy question, even when Labour was ahead on voting intention. . . [but] . . .that confidence has now evaporated and the Tory economy record is now, for the first time, a liability. (*The Guardian*, 13 April 1995)

- For the first time it had been a Conservative rather than a Labour government that had devalued. And maintaining the value of the pound was seen as a fundamental measure of the economic competence of the Conservatives.

- The panic measures undertaken on Black Wednesday, and the vast sums of money paid out in vain, gave the impression of incompetent and ineffectual ministers who did not know what they were doing.
- The fault was seen to lie with an error of judgment concerning the value of the pound *vis-à-vis* the mark at which the pound was pegged on entry into the ERM. And that judgment, seen as another measure of incompetence, had been made by John Major as Chancellor.

The doubts over competence introduced by Black Wednesday were later compounded by revelations over taxation increases under the Conservatives. These doubts did not necessarily promote Labour as the party best able to deal with the economy, but it did mean that, in comparison with the Conservatives, Labour was no longer disadvantaged on the issue of competence. Psychological analysis after the 1997 election showed that the huge opinion-poll lead built up by Labour, which was later to be translated into their landslide majority, began to build up in 1992 in the immediate aftermath of Black Wednesday and never thereafter slipped back to any significant extent. On the other hand, the new confidence engendered by the Blair government was one of the elements leading to the pound regaining all that it lost in 1992, returning to a parity of three marks to the pound, opening up the pound to external speculation and damaging the competitiveness of British industry.

Summary

Perhaps there is a new realism which recognises that a government should have priorities other than making people feel good in the short term. There is an American expression to explain unpopular measures: 'No pain, no gain,' they say. When he was Chancellor, John Major came up with a variant on this: 'If it isn't hurting, it isn't working,' he said. The main economic issue facing politicians and the political parties in the late 1990s is probably a recognition that 'feeling good' should be seen as a long-term rather than as a short-term aim. None of the factors mentioned in this chapter is in itself going to make the electorate feel any better in the immediate future, but the critical issue facing politicians is to find solutions that will ultimately produce that feel-good factor. And that means evolving effective economic policies. The problem with John Major's statement was that, in the perception of the electorate when they came to judge him in 1997, the policies were hurting quite badly, but they were not working.

4

Employment, the Unions and Privatisation

The economic competence of a governing political party is reflected, as has been said, in the ability of a government to engender the feel-good factor among the electorate and this is measured not only through such specific economic issues as the level of personal tax paid by the voter but by the way in which the various parties manage or propose to manage those aspects of the economic infrastructure which most affect the electorate, such as the issue of employment, the role of the trade unions and the increased privatisation of public utilities.

Employment and Unemployment

If high taxation has often proved to be the Achilles' heel of the Labour Party, then the reputation of being 'the party of high unemployment', earned in the 1930s, has just as persistently dogged the Conservatives. During the years of the postwar consensus the Conservatives adhered to the Keynesian ideal of full employment in an attempt to lose their reputation on this matter. This they had almost succeeded in doing, until the monetarist policies of the first Thatcher government once again forced up the unemployment figures to a peak above even that of the 1930s. In every general election between 1979 and 1992 the issue of unemployment was at or near the top of a list of voters' concerns, and it is a paradox that the Conservatives won the elections of 1983, 1987 and 1992 despite the natural advantage Labour has on the issue.

It is easy to misunderstand the concept of full employment as advocated by Beveridge in support of Keynes' theories (Beveridge, 1944). The term 'full employment' never did mean 100 per cent employment of the workforce, since the pattern of work is not static and at any one moment there has to be a certain number who have either just left a job or are about to go into one: nor should we forget that there are those who are, by any criterion, unemployable. Keynes himself was prepared to accept unemployment figures of up to 6 per cent within his definition of full employment, while Beveridge preferred a lower figure of 3 per cent. To understand the relationship between employment and unemployment, it is necessary to look at three categories into which unemployment may be divided, as formulated by John McIlroy (Jones, 1989, p. 165):

- *Frictional or temporary* unemployment is a pause between jobs; a break of anything from a few days to a few months for a person who has completed one period of employment and is waiting to commence another. It can include *seasonal* work where workers taken on to meet a period of high demand are laid off at the end of the busy season until demand picks up again.
- *Cyclical* unemployment is created by the general ebb and flow of the economy. During a period of low economic activity industry will go into recession and workers will be laid off because of a lack of demand for their services. When there is an economic recovery there is an upturn in activity and workers are re-employed.
- *Structural* unemployment is the most serious because it is a product of changes, both in the nature of industry and in the patterns of employment. The changes are permanent and once jobs are lost there is little chance of recreating them. Two major factors contribute to this:

  1. De-industrialisation in which entire industries decline or die, as has happened for example to coal-mining, ship-building and the iron and steel industry. Or where industries are undermined by competition from elsewhere, as with the British textile industry which suffered as a result of cheap imports from the Indian sub-continent.
  2. Technological change in which human employees are replaced by machines. At first this largely affected manufacturing industry where automated plant replaced production line

workers, but more recently it has increasingly affected white-collar activities like banking, where employees have been replaced by computers and electronic transactions.

To these categories of the true unemployed we can add quite large numbers who are best described as economically inactive. These are adults of working age who nevertheless are not gainfully employed. They include those who have taken early retirement; the chronically ill or disabled; those withdrawn from work for training or re-training; women who are classified as housewives; and single parents and others who fear that employment would mean a loss of their social security benefits. They are not actually earning and they are often a charge on the public purse through social security payments, but they have been removed, or have removed them-selves, from the labour market. In 1995 it was estimated by Paul Gregg and Jonathan Wadsworth of the Centre for Economic Performance at the London School of Economics, that 19.8 per cent of the potential workforce fell into this category (*The Guardian*, 3 April 1995).

For the first twenty years after 1945 a combination of government policies and postwar boom created what was, in effect, full employ-ment, at levels even better than either Beveridge or Keynes had envisaged. During the Labour government of 1945–50 unemploy-ment ran at, or below, the 2 per cent level. After 1951, during the years of economic boom, there was often a labour shortage and unemployment rarely rose above 1 per cent, the average unemploy-ment figure for the period 1945–68 being 1.7 per cent (McIlroy, in Jones, 1994, p. 164). There was a point just before the 1959 election when unemployment rose to nearly 500 000 and there was talk of this losing the election for the Conservatives. However, they recov-ered and it was not until Wilson's second government after 1966 that unemployment rose above 2 per cent and stayed there. Ironically, it was the Labour Party which first broke with the ideal of full employment: the Labour Chancellors of the 1966–70 government, James Callaghan and Roy Jenkins, both using the threat of un-employment to curb inflationary wage demands from the unions.

Under the Heath government of 1970–74 hopes of continued full employment faded. Elected on the Selsdon programme of non-interventionism the Heath government saw unemployment rise to 4 per cent by 1972, breaking the psychological barrier of one million in the process. The U-turn by Heath and the dash-for-growth policy in the second half of that government improved matters slightly, but when Labour took over in 1974 nearly 600 000 were out of work. When Callaghan replaced Wilson as prime minister he stated quite frankly from the start that the option of spending one's way out of recession no longer existed. The monetarist policies introduced by Denis Healey under the tutelage of the IMF produced unemployment levels that grew to one and a half million by 1978, leading to the famous Saatchi and Saatchi poster for the 1979 election campaign which showed a long queue of dole claimants under the heading 'Labour isn't working' – a poster which was later seen as being distinctly ironic.

The Thatcher government took over in a time of recession engendered by the oil crisis and immediately introduced anti-inflationary measures, simultaneously raising taxes, increasing interest rates and massively cutting public spending. The impact on employment was explosive. From 1.25 million at the time of the election, unemployment rose to top two million by October 1980 and reached 2.67 million by the start of 1982. Beginning with Mrs Thatcher's second term in 1983 the unemployment figures rose yet again over three years, surpassing the highest figure recorded in the 1930s, to reach a postwar peak of 3.4 million, or 14 per cent of the working population by 1986. After that the minor boom of the late 1980s saw a slow recovery in employment until unemployment returned to the level it had reached in 1979, bottoming out at 1.59 million, or 5.6 per cent, in April 1990. After that, recession intervened once more and unemployment figures climbed until they almost reached the three million mark again, peaking at 2 992 300, or 10.6 per cent, in January 1993 (McKie, 1994, p. 40). After that the situation once more improved, with the government-massaged official figures for those seeking work retreating to near the two million mark by the time of the 1997 election.

However, unemployment statistics do not reflect the true number of workers who are unemployed. Between 1979 and 1988 there were no fewer than 19 changes in the way government defines unemployment. Excluded from the figures, at one time or another, have been married women who leave work but do not claim benefit; all those on training schemes or re-training; men over 60 or under 18 and, indeed, anyone else not 'actively seeking employment'. In the run up to the 1987 election, when official unemployment figures were running at well over three million, Labour estimated that the true figure for those out of work was nearer four and a half million. In

1995 a survey of what Will Hutton calls the 'marginalised working population' showed that 19.8 per cent were economically inactive, 1.1 per cent were on government schemes of one kind or another and 8.1 per cent were unemployed, placing 29 per cent of the population outside the active work force (Gregg and Wadsworth, 1995). The final step in manipulating official statistics came when the Conservative government replaced unemployment benefit with the Job Seekers Allowance, only recognising as unemployed those who were available for, and actively seeking, work.

In the 1990s the whole structure of employment has changed. Figures published in April 1995 (Gregg and Wadsworth, 1995) showed that only 35.9 per cent of the working population had full-time jobs, compared to a figure of 55.5 per cent in 1975: a drop of 35 per cent over 20 years. There has been a slight increase in those calling themselves self-employed, from 5.5 to 7.5 per cent, but the major change has been those working part-time or on temporary short-term contracts. More and more men in their fifties are leaving the labour market through early retirement. The length of time a person spends in a job is also less, the average man's job lasting 6.4 years and the average woman's 4.3. The old ideal of people leaving school and getting a job for life has gone for good and the short-term, part-time nature of so much work, often without rights over things like sick, holiday and redundancy pay, leads to a lack of security among even the employed. Another crucial element is the role of women. In 1995 women were poised to take over from men as more likely to be in work; the figures for April 1995 showing that 49.4 per cent of all employees were women. Unemployment is increasingly a male phenomenon: the same set of statistics showed that with a national unemployment figure of 8.4 per cent, 11.3 per cent of the male working population was unemployed, as against only 4.5 per cent of women.

The years of Conservative government created what Will Hutton calls the 'thirty, thirty, forty society', with the population divided into three groups according to their place in the country's pattern of employment (Hutton, 1995, pp. 105–10):

- One-third of the population is the disadvantaged, being those who are out of work, or are economically inactive for one reason or another.
- A second third is the marginalised or insecure whose work is insecure, unprotected and without benefits such as paid holidays.

They include part-time and casual workers as well as many of the self-employed and those on fixed-term contracts.
- Just 40 per cent of society make up those privileged to have a full-time job or a part-time job that has lasted more than five years.

The issue over employment is therefore no longer a simple one of being in or out of work, it is increasingly a question of which groups of people are likely to be in work, the type of work they do and the conditions attached to their employment. The Conservatives have refused to acknowledge that such a problem as job insecurity actually exists, while New Labour and the Liberal Democrats are unable to escape the consequences of the social change that has made career flexibility and job mobility the norm. The response of both the left-of-centre parties has been to stress the need for constant training and re-training to allow individuals to cope in a world that has lost the stability of long-term job security. Labour's policy of a compulsory levy on firms to pay for training programmes was abandoned in 1996 as a potential 'burden on business', but was retained as Liberal Democrat policy.

The response of the Blair government to the issue of unemployment was well signalled in the run-up to the election and immediately put into effect by Gordon Brown in his first budget as Chancellor. New Labour labelled its policies as a 'New Deal' for the unemployed and proposed to use the £3.5 billion expected from the windfall tax on privatised utilities to pay for a three-pronged attack on the long-term unemployed, especially the young (*The Guardian*, 3 July 1997):

1. The first part of the New Deal is aimed at 18–24 year olds who have been out of work for more than six months. The unemployed will be offered four choices – a job with an employer, a job on a voluntary scheme, a place on one of the government's environmental task forces or full-time education and training. As part of the carrot-and-stick approach to this Welfare-to-Work programme, those unemployed who turn down all four of these options may well have their benefit cut.
2. The second part of the New Deal is an offer to pay employers a subsidy of £75 a week for six months if they take on anyone who has been unemployed for two years or more.
3. The third arm of the Deal was unheralded until the Budget and consists of £200 million to provide help for the million single

parents who are unable to work and are on benefit. Those single parents who want to work will be offered help and training to find work, the most useful help coming in the form of assistance to provide child care while the parent is at work. Allied to this was the promise that 50 000 of the under-25s being offered training would be trained as child care assistants.

It is significant that the proposals of New Labour follow the direction tentatively advanced by the Conservatives. The stress is now essentially on the 'out of welfare into work' aspects of government proposals, making the programme for reducing unemployment part of a wider attack on what is seen as the dependency culture.

Taming the Unions

Elected as she was in the aftermath of the 'winter of discontent' it could be said that Mrs Thatcher had a mandate to 'do something' about the unions: indeed she came to power apparently spoiling for a fight. In 1979, when she was asked in a radio interview with Jimmy Young whether her approach might not lead to confrontation with the unions, she said, 'My God, I'll confront them' (Jones, 1989, p. 5). The unions were seen as obstacles to all the reforms wanted by the Conservatives, and as defenders of everything that Thatcherism defined as the failed policies of the consensus:

- Unions caused wage inflation.
- Unions obstructed the introduction of new technology.
- Unions were responsible for poor productivity.
- Unions would not let managers manage.
- Unions, in the form of the National Union of Mineworkers, had brought down the Conservative government in 1974.

Mrs Thatcher was particularly opposed to the form of corporatism represented by the National Economic Development Council (NEDC) which had been set up by the Macmillan government and gradually known as 'Neddy', wherein the TUC participated in discussions and decision-making with the CBI and the government in an attempt to secure agreement on measures to encourage economic growth. Unlike European countries, which had a formalised corporate structure, the normal pattern of industrial relations in Britain was based on confrontation, with an 'us and them' attitude towards negotiation on both sides.

On the one hand, employers wished to keep the labour market deregulated: '. . . to share profits or decisions with unions in the interests of better industrial relations was anathema, inhibiting managerial options and freedoms. Similarly, but on the other hand, 'It was none of the unions' business or interest to solve employers' problems for them by exercising wage restraint, participating in decision-making or sharing in profits' (Hutton, 1995, pp. 83–4). During the boom years of the late 1950s and early 1960s this attitude led to the unions taking as much as they could in pay increases, extracted through strikes if necessary, and to the employers giving way to wage demands for the sake of industrial peace and continued production. Even after the Labour victory of 1964 when the government was urging restraint on the unions, this was countered by an army of powerful shop stewards like the notorious 'Red Robbo' at the British Leyland motor plant. By 1970 there were 350 000 shop stewards in the union movement, very few as militant as Robinson but with considerable autonomy from their national leadership and with the ability to call unofficial or wild-cat strikes.

Between 1969 and 1979 there were three attempts to regulate the unions:

- The Labour White Paper *In Place of Strife*, based on the Donovan Report and sponsored by Barbara Castle. This was killed off by the unions with help from a section of the Parliamentary Labour Party led by James Callaghan.
- The Industrial Relations Act of 1971, which met with massive resistance from the unions and which fell when the Heath government was brought down in 1974 following the miners' strike.
- The Social Contract of the 1974–9 Labour government, a largely voluntary agreement by the unions which ended in the 'winter of discontent' and the election of Mrs Thatcher on an anti-union platform.

Thatcherite action to limit trade union power succeeded where its predecessors had failed for a number of reasons:

1. Mrs Thatcher put James Prior in charge of union legislation. He was not supported by his prime minister and indeed she some-

times appeared to undermine his authority, but Prior's reputation as a 'wet' Tory and his non-confrontational approach, even the fact that he was disliked by the prime minister, all helped the unions to accept things from Prior that they would have rejected outright if they had come from a more right-wing minister,

2.   The government did not try to do everything at once but introduced legislation bit by bit, in what was known as the 'softly, softly' approach. Unpopular union practices like secondary picketing were attacked first, with support from a public still reeling from the winter of discontent. Only when the first measures had been accepted and consolidated did the government make the next move. In the end, it took nine separate pieces of legislation between 1979 and 1993 to bring in all the government's proposed reforms.

3.   In a series of showpiece strikes, of which the Miners' strike of 1984–5 was the most famous, the government faced down the unions showing that they would not give way and were willing to sit out even the most damaging of confrontations. And what the government could do, so could the commercial world. A year after the miners' strike collapsed, News International, the newspaper group owned by Rupert Murdoch, sat out a similar damaging strike to ensure a union-free production plant in Wapping, East London.

Additional factors reinforced government action:

- Increasing unemployment proved a double-edged weapon in both reducing the membership of trade unions and in making the unions more reluctant to take industrial action. Between 1979 and 1993 union membership dropped from 13.3 million to 9 million.
- Unions were refused recognition, with 9 per cent of workplaces de-recognising unions that previously had had the right of consultation in those places.
- Unions were offered recognition and sole representation in new plants in return for no-strike agreements. This was particularly favoured by Japanese firms setting up assembly and manufacturing plants in Britain.
- Labour-intensive traditional industries which had once formed the élite of the union movement, such as mining, iron and steel

and ship-building, were in decline, with a consequent decline in union influence and power.

- During the 1980s the nature of employment was shifting from the traditional heavy manufacturing industries to service industries like the retail trade, catering and financial services. Service industries had the tradition of having a part-time, casual, largely female and non-unionised work force.
- Technological advances enabled unskilled, or differently-skilled, workers to do the work of previously powerful skilled tradesmen, as for example newspaper reporters who could type in their own stories to the computerised printers instead of needing hot-metal typesetters.
- Whole industry collective bargaining was replaced by thousands of local, in-house agreements and deals. The concept of workers combining for mutual support and collective strength was lost in a fragmentation of the unions.

On 25 January 1984, the Foreign Secretary announced that no employee of the Government Communications Headquarters (GCHQ), an intelligence listening-post, would be allowed to belong to a trade union. GCHQ had suffered a number of strikes between 1979 and 1981 and the government, backed by the American CIA, had decided that union membership at GCHQ was detrimental to the security of the western alliance. Protests followed and, although 95 per cent of GCHQ employees accepted the decision, legal arguments with the remaining 5 per cent were pursued as far as the Court of Appeal and actions were still being brought in the courts as late as 1988. The final straw came at a meeting between Len Murray and the prime minister at which the TUC leader was told that union membership was incompatible with a citizen's patriotic duties. Within a year of the GCHQ decision the government was locked in its struggle with the miners, the unions were characterised as 'the enemy within', the power of the police was mobilised against union pickets, generous concessions were granted to strike-breaking miners and the power of the unions was effectively smashed (Young, 1989, pp. 354–7).

The Thatcher governments dealt with the unions without significant disruption largely because there was public endorsement of that policy. Partly alienated by events such as the winter of discontent and partly conditioned by a largely anti-union press, the public had come to believe that the unions were a disruptive and over-powerful force in society whose power needed to be curbed. This public perception of the unions and the nature of their links with the Labour Party meant that for many years the unions represented an electoral negative for Labour.

The modernising leaders of the Labour Party, beginning with Neil Kinnock, saw the need to distance the party from the unions. The most significant move, undertaken successfully under John Smith's leadership, was to rescue the party conference from domination by the union block vote through the introduction of one-member-one-vote (OMOV). This, however, was seen by Smith, with his allies in the party and the unions, as a move to re-vitalise the Labour–Union link rather than any desire to cut it. '. . . the GMB general secretary, John Edmonds, believed that the introduction of OMOV was crucial to modernisation, the involvement of union members as individuals would strengthen the link with the party' (Joy Johnson, 31 January 1997, pp. 12–13).

Yet the modernisers of New Labour have gone much further than OMOV to remove union influence. Direct sponsorship of MPs was replaced by more general funding at constituency level, while union representation on the National Executive Committee was also reduced. Despite this, the unions have remained major paymasters of New Labour: over the 1992–7 parliament the TGWU made regular payments to Labour amounting to £2 million while, in the election year 1997, large sums for the war chest were provided by the major unions – £2 million from the GMB, and £1.25 million from Unison (Joy Johnson, 1997).

The continuing financial links between New Labour and the unions enabled the Conservatives to use the threat of union power in electioneering. In 1997 the voters were told that the unions would demand a return for their money by returning to their old ways if Labour were elected. This fear-mongering was assisted by a strike of fire brigade crews in Essex during the 1997 election, together with vague mumblings about industrial action from unions such as the transport workers and the NUT. On the whole, however, Labour's commitments to the unions in 1997 were seen as very modest – the restoration of union rights at GCHQ, the right of all workers to union representation if more than 50 per cent of employees wanted it, acceptance of the 48-hour working week, adherence to the EU Social Chapter, and the introduction of a minimum wage.

The fact is that twenty years after the industrial turmoil of the 1970s, with trade union power much reduced and unused, the public's fears of the unions have largely disappeared. As a political issue the unions no longer have any potency. Instead, the issue at the turn of the century concerns what role the unions might have left to them in what has become an increasingly non-unionised market economy, staffed by employees who are non-permanent, often part-time and for the most part female.

Privatisation

Any mention of privatisation before the 1979 general election was taken as meaning that nationalised industries would be returned to private enterprise, as iron and steel had been denationalised after 1951. Serious privatisation did not begin until Mrs Thatcher's second term but, when the pattern became clear, it was very obvious that the government was aiming for more than the mere return of state industries to private ownership. Nationalised industries had a popular reputation for abusing their monopoly position; being inefficient, expensive and unenterprising, and there was therefore a groundswell of public support for action against them. Yet the government wished to go far beyond mere denationalisation, and included within the umbrella term 'privatisation' have been a number of different processes:

1. The selling-off of state-owned industry in the name of efficiency and customer service. This process began slowly with the sale of state shares in otherwise private companies such as BP or Jaguar Cars, moved on to public corporations like British Telecom and British Airways, and was extended to public utilities such as British Gas, Electricity and Water. Finally the government was ready to tackle the major nationalised industries such as British Coal, British Rail and, ultimately perhaps, the Post Office.
2. The deregulation of government-controlled activities. As early as 1986 this was applied to the running of bus companies but other areas followed in an attempt to remove government barriers to free commercial competition.
3. The contracting-out of services previously provided by national or local government workforces to private contractors. Contracting-out began with obvious services like catering or clean-

ing in the education, local government or health sectors. School meals, hospital cleaning or dustbin collection were handled by private concerns who obtained the contracts through competitive tendering. Later, other services were contracted out, including professional services such as accountancy, training programmes and computer technology.

4. Opening up the public sector to market forces. This included the transfer of control from the civil service to government agencies and has encompassed, for example, the private provision of prison places.

Originally the privatisation process was introduced to make the formerly nationalised industries more efficient, but there were other benefits. Very early in the process the government found that allowing anyone to purchase shares in the privatised industries, creating millions of small shareholders who had never owned shares before, was very popular. The popularity was increased by the number of sales where shares were offered at below market price, allowing purchasers to re-sell their shares for a substantial profit after only a short time. In mid-1995 it was estimated that someone who had bought 1000 shares in Northumbrian Water for £2400 at the time of privatisation in 1989, now had shares worth £9280, as well as having received a total of £1141 from annual dividend payments (*The Observer*, 13 August 1995). This ability to make money from privatisation created an entirely new class of people who became involved in capitalism. Privatisation also provided a useful source of revenue for the government. It was revenue from the major privatisations, running into many billions of pounds, which allowed the budget to run at a surplus for so many years in the mid-1980s, eliminating the PSBR and allowing wide-ranging tax cuts.

Despite the economic and political reasons for privatisation, the principal argument rapidly became ideological. Margaret Thatcher believed she had been elected to diminish the power of the state, and every industry privatised was a further diminution of state power. Privatisation which began on a small scale became a political imperative, until most enterprises had been returned to the private sector and the government seemed to be casting around for whatever they could privatise next.

From the start privatisation has had its critics, for a variety of reasons and not only among the opposition parties:

- *Waste of assets.* There were many people who regarded enterprises in public ownership as valuable assets. Lord Stockton (the former Conservative Prime Minister Harold Macmillan) made a famous speech in the House of Lords in which he compared the sale of nationally owned enterprises to 'selling off the family silver' in terms both of the loss of the asset value of these enterprise and of the revenue from those that made a profit.
- *Against national interests.* Long before the nationalisation programme of the 1940s the government had invested in industry: the strategic importance of oil led to the government's purchase of BP shares in the early years of this century. Privatisation, however, could lead to the sale of strategically important industries to foreign concerns. At one stage Kuwait acquired over 20 per cent of Britoil; and American, French and German companies acquired large stakes in the motor industry and public utilities like electricity and water.
- *Security of provision.* Many utilities had been nationalised to ensure the continued provision to the entire population of necessities like water and waste disposal. Could uneconomic provision of these services, in remote rural areas for example, survive when the providing companies were driven by the profit motive rather than the ideal of public service?
- *Transfer of monopoly.* It was claimed that privatisation would increase competition, but very often it only resulted in the transfer of a monopoly from public to private hands. For most consumers there was still no choice as to who would provide their water, electricity, gas or telephone line. Moreover, there was no guarantee that private management would be any more efficient than it had been in the public sector, since in most cases it largely consisted of the same people.
- *Loss-making deals and sweeteners.* Public enterprises were often made 'suitable' for privatisation at great cost and then sold off for a great deal less than they were worth, as was made clear in Geoffrey Lee's study of privatisation (Jones, 1989, p. 157). In 1988 British Aerospace bought Rover Cars and Royal Ordnance for a total of £340 million, after the government had written-off Rover's debts of £2.7 billion. Once BA had bought the two, surplus land they owned was sold off for a total of £1 billion resulting in a substantial profit of over £650 million for BA.
- *Massive windfall profits and public loss.* Vast sums of money were transferred from the public purse to the pockets of private

shareholders thanks to shares in the public utilities being under-valued at the time of privatisation. A survey in 1995 compiled by the financial information company Datastream, following concern over speculative take-over bids for electricity companies, compared the price the government obtained at privatisation with the value of the privatised company's shares just one month later. Total estimates were that shares in privatised utilities were sold off by the government for £7.6bn less than their market value only weeks later; the equivalent of a loss to government revenue of 4p in income tax. The biggest loss was in the shares of British Telecom which were sold for £8bn but which were trading at £12.8bn within a month (*The Observer*, 3 September 1995).

- *Public service or private profit?* One of the benefits of public enterprises, particularly in the case of public utilities, is that necessary services can be supplied to everyone regardless of the financial consequences. An example often quoted is the Post Office, which charges the same to send a letter to someone in a remote Scottish farmhouse as it does to someone in a crowded city. The fear is that private investors purchasing a public utility will only be interested in the profit-making sections of the enterprise and the remainder will either cease to exist or be provided with a much inferior service. This was seen at the time of bus de-regulation when city streets were crowded with many different competing bus companies while rural areas received a much reduced service, if they received one at all.

The resumption of the privatisation programme under John Major was beset by difficulties, as though the entire issue had run out of steam. This was particularly true when attention turned to two areas even Margaret Thatcher had not dared to touch: the Post Office and British Rail. Attempts by Michael Heseltine to privatise the Post Office were vetoed by a parliament in which many Conservative MPs represented marginal seats containing irate voters keen to defend their rural sub-post offices, scheduled for closure under privatisation.

Rail privatisation went ahead but during the privatisation process there were so many changes and reversals of policy forced by parliamentary defeats and the sheer weight of public opinion that critics began to speak of the railways as being 'a failed privatisation', and led many people to believe that the delays forced on the programme would leave the process unfinished when a Labour government dedicated to reversing the process took over. In fact this did not happen but the chaotic nature of rail privatisation did leave the way free for Labour to bring in a much harsher regulatory regime for the privatised utilities, leading to substantial fines being imposed for poor performance in both the rail network and the water supply industry.

As time went by the possibility of undoing privatisation became more difficult and more expensive. Quite early on Labour abandoned hope of reversing the early privatisations such as British Telecom or British Gas and confined themselves to the less acceptable privatisations such as water and the railways. Even on these, statements on the subject were increasingly qualified by the proviso that it depended and on how far the process had progressed when Labour came into power.

Just as the Conservatives failed to reverse nationalisation after 1951 because the party had moved to the left, so it rapidly became clear that New Labour was unlikely to reverse privatisation not only because the process had gone too far but because the party itself had moved somewhat to the right of centre and no longer had the same ideological objection to privatisation. Indeed, during the 1997 election campaign the party created quite a stir by stating that it was ready to consider a continuing programme of privatisation, taking in air traffic control for example. As Tony Blair said at an election press briefing on 7 April 1997:

> We believe there is a third way between state control of industry and laissez faire. Where there is no overriding reason for preferring the public provision of goods and services, particularly where those services operate in a competitive market, then the presumption should be that economic activity is best left to the private sector, with market forces being fully encouraged to operate.

The issue of privatisation has therefore moved from being one of 'for and against' to one involving a greater control of the process. Labour moved from simple opposition and renationalisation to a programme of greater regulation for the services provided by the privatised companies and, above all, argued for a high level of taxation levied on the vast profits made by the privatised utilities. Stockbrokers for the electricity and water companies concluded in 1995 that the industries could absorb a one-off windfall tax of £10 billion without it affecting their dividend pay-outs (*The Guardian*, 10

April 1995). Gordon Brown focused on this as the main factor that he could use in raising the funds for some of the spending programmes in the Labour election manifesto, particularly for his training plan for getting the young unemployed back into work.

Brown also mentioned the possibility of an audit of government assets, particularly property owned by Whitehall, as a result of which non-essential parts of the state-owned structure could be sold off or contracted out. The position adopted by the newly-elected Labour government was that nothing could be ruled out, however much it seems to go against Labour's traditional standpoint.

Summary

As the political approach to general economic issues has shifted from Keynesianism to market forces so the attitude of the political parties in general, and the attitude of New Labour in particular, towards specific economic issues has been forced to change. Part of the pragmatism of New Labour lies in a recognition that certain things have changed permanently and that the party must face new issues as they arise and not revert through some knee-jerk reaction to issues that are no longer relevant.

- The issue of trade union power has changed in that the unions can no longer rely on the Labour Party to act as their political arm, nor can they maintain their controlling influence over the party. The issue now is the role of the unions under New Labour.
- The days of full employment and the prospect of a job for life have probably gone for good, and the issue is now the means of handling a labour market which has endemic structural unemployment built into it, managing the ups and downs of job insecurity and employment flexibility.
- The issue over pay is no longer one of maintaining annual pay rises for all, but one in which the distribution of income must be seen to be carried out on a fairer basis than has previously been the case, and where employers do not use the threat of unemployment to exploit the workforce through paying wages that are below the poverty level leaving the state to pay the bill through social security support for the low-paid.
- Taxation cannot be decreased indefinitely without services suffering. Either a cut in services is recognised as politically desirable or

some means such as hypothecation has to be found to make tax increases palatable to the electorate.

- After decades in which the conflict between public and private provision was resolved by the consensual mixed economy the balance has finally tilted towards private provision, even in the eyes of the Labour Party in its guise of New Labour.

5

Social Welfare

In a phrase first used soon after the publication of the Beveridge Report, in a broadcast made by Churchill to announce that the government accepted the proposals of the Report for implementation after the war, the founders of the welfare state proudly announced that their intention was to provide care for all, 'from the cradle to the grave'. The view that this provision is desirable has been accepted by the generations who have grown up with the welfare state, until it is seen as part of the natural order that governments should look after the needs of all members of society, but particularly the young, the old and the disadvantaged.

Social and welfare issues are important because, inevitably, at one time or another during the course of their lives, each and every citizen is likely to require the help of the state, whether it is for medical or surgical assistance, the provision of education, help with housing, care of family members, or as a safeguard against disability or unemployment. The political decisions which implement these services affect the daily lives of everyone, and it is therefore only natural that the issues surrounding those decisions should be of paramount importance to every person in the community; party policies towards these issues are obviously a major determining factor at election time.

As far as social and welfare issues are concerned, there is one general issue that overrides all others across the whole social field; whether we are talking about health provision, old age pensions, education, unemployment benefit or social security. That is about whether welfare provision should be universal or selective, and subsumed within that argument is the question of what the cost of welfare might be and who is to pay for it. The whole point of the welfare state on its foundation was that it may have been minimalist and often defective in its provision, but it was universal and available to all without distinction or discrimination. On the other hand, those arguing for selective provision put forward an entire menu of sub-issues, which included such questions as the role of the state, the disincentive effect of benefit provision, the changing nature of family values and the possibility of social dependence.

Arguments over these are amongst the oldest in English politics: the first legislation on welfare provision was included in an Act in 1598, while the first draconian regulation of that provision followed almost immediately, in the Poor Law Act of 1601. Arguments over the Poor Law led to the nineteenth-century ideological division between *laissez-faire* liberalism and Disraeli's 'one-nation' Conservatism, and it was administration of the Poor Law that was one of the prime factors in the creation of local government in England and Wales.

The Cost of Welfare

In 1572 a compulsory rate was levied on the residents of all English and Welsh parishes in order to provide relief for the poor of the parish and, from that point on, the provision of welfare and who exactly might be entitled to that welfare became a political and economic issue which persists today. Ratepayers objected to paying what they saw as excessive charges for poor relief, particularly if they had a suspicion that money was being given to those who were not eligible, or who were undeserving in some way. From 1601 onwards there was repeated legislation against vagrants, intended to deter people from begging relief from parishes in which they were not normally resident. Much of this legislation has never been repealed and the underlying sentiment of distrust which motivated these suspicions persists in the belief, widespread in the tabloid press and sections of the Tory Party, that there are people from all over the world attempting to enter Britain simply in order to get welfare handouts from the state and make free use of the National Health Service.

Allied to the idea of the 'outsider' who wanted relief to which he or she was not entitled, reluctance to pay their rates led citizens to develop the concept of the 'idle', 'shiftless' or 'undeserving' poor. According to this view there was an entire segment of society which did not want to work and which was quite ready to live off handouts from other people. In the 1830s Jeremy Bentham denounced the Speenhamland system of poor relief as 'a bounty to indolence and vice', and that view helped to usher in the workhouse system which aimed to make the receipt of poor relief as unpleasant as possible, thus in effect punishing people for being poor. The harsh workhouse regime is discredited now but exactly the same attitude towards the poor can be seen when today's tabloid press launches one of its periodic campaigns against what it calls 'social security scroungers' and 'welfare fraud'. These critics of the cost of the welfare state are particularly concerned, they say, by the possibility that what they call the 'nanny state' is responsible for a culture of dependency; destroying people's liberties though the erosion of initiative, self-respect and healthy competition.

The fundamental problem underlying the cost of the welfare state, which makes it such an apparently insoluble issue, is that such a state, as envisaged by Beveridge, was predicated on the economic conditions prevailing in the late 1940s and 1950s rather than the conditions pertaining to the 1990s:

1. That period was one of near full employment, meaning that there was a sound base of taxation to pay for the service. While the economy continued to grow there was no problem because the tax-take grew with it. With the decline in the economy, and the growth of unemployment, the problems began, not only because the tax-take was lower, but because people who had previously been contributors became recipients of assistance.

2. In the 1940s people had lower expectations of an acceptable standard of living. What was not appreciated in the establishment of the welfare state was a rise in the overall standard of living that would lead items that were regarded as luxuries in the 1940s to be seen as necessities by the end of the century. Welfare benefit is supposed to insure against want by providing basic essentials such as food, housing and clothing. But what can be done with those who believe that the quality of life goes beyond mere existence? Is the welfare state intended to free people from *relative* poverty as well as *absolute* poverty?

3. By the same token, the success of the welfare state produced its own problems through a steadily increasing dependent population of young and old. A growing number of students in full-time education and a greater expectation of life for old people, all contributed to the number of people outside the working

population making demands on a public provision, which in turn became ever more expensive as a result of social and technological change. At its crudest this problem can be expressed in terms of the disabled and chronically sick who are unable to work and therefore unable to pay tax or make National Insurance contributions. At one time these people would have died before they had received overmuch in benefit: today they are living far longer due to medical advances and thereby become a long-term charge on the social security budget.

4.   Although the welfare state was introduced to help those in real need, the main beneficiaries ultimately were the middle classes, particularly in the fields of health and education. In prewar Britain the middle-class family, with too much money to qualify for any relief that was available, had to devote a considerable portion of their income to insuring against ill-health and paying for their children's education. The National Health Service and free secondary education allowed a rise in the amount of disposable income that the middle class had to spend on other things. The growth in home ownership and the consumer boom in things like cars, refrigerators and television sets which characterised the 1950s and 1960s for the middle classes and the skilled working class, was largely financed by the provisions of the welfare state. This is why the welfare state was supported by successive Conservative governments between 1951 and 1974, every bit as enthusiastically as it was by Labour. It is also the reason why, when the need arose to cut back spending on the welfare state, it was seldom the health or education budgets that were threatened but rather the social security budget for those, like unmarried mothers, who could be portrayed as the 'undeserving' poor.

5.   The role of women has changed dramatically since the institution of the welfare state in 1948. Beveridge was very much the product of his class and times in his attitude to women. He assumed that once the war was over all those women who had been in employment while the men were in the forces would return cheerfully to being simply housewives. His assumption was that, as had been the case before the war, the average woman would give up work when she married and that she would be supported for the rest of her life by her husband, with her social security entitlement arrived at through her husband's

contributions. Beveridge just did not make provision in his Report for the place in society that would be played by women, particularly single women, by the end of the century. No more than any other man at that time could he foresee the extent of social changes which mean that in the 1990s women represent virtually 50 per cent of the workforce. Even less could he foresee the number of divorces there would be by the end of the century, nor the proportion of couples living together outside marriage, nor the increase in the numbers of unmarried mothers and single-parent families.

6. Mentioning the role of women emphasises the point that the provision of welfare in Britain is based on the household rather than the individual. For their purposes, the legislators of 1945 envisaged the idealised average nuclear family of two married adults, only one of whom worked, and their 2.4 children. For the purpose of assessing benefit it was assumed that any income earned by an individual formed part of a joint household income for mutual support.

The Beveridge Report

On 10 June 1941, William Beveridge, a Liberal who had been involved in the reforms of 1908–11 which introduced old age pensions and National Insurance, was asked by the Minister of Labour, Arthur Greenwood, to chair a committee examining the issue of social insurance in the postwar period. The terms of reference were 'to undertake, with special reference to the inter-relations of the schemes, a survey of the existing schemes of social insurance and allied services, and to make recommendations'. The problem was that the embryonic welfare system set up before the First World War had become chaotic as a result of emergency measures introduced during the depressions of the 1920s and 1930s, and restructuring was required if social conditions after the war were to recover from the problems that had afflicted the country right up to 1939. It was not a particularly interesting brief and really required little more than some bureaucratic tinkering to tidy up the services offered by government. Beveridge, however, set out to do far more than that and set himself the task of totally rebuilding the various welfare systems into a radically new and comprehensive structure that could properly be called the welfare state.

The Report compiled by Beveridge's Committee, called quite simply Social Insurance and Allied Services, was published on 1 December 1942 at a cost of two shillings (10p), although a 20-page summary was available for threepence. Between them, the full report and summary sold over 600 000 copies. It was received with wild enthusiasm by the public and, coming as it did only two weeks after the victory of El Alamein, was treated by the government propaganda machine as yet another sign that the end of the war was in sight and that this time it could be seen that the country had been fighting for a better world once the war was over. The public policy editor of the *Independent* newspaper, Nicholas Timmins, ranks the Beveridge Report alongside Stephen Hawking's *A Brief History of Time* as '. . . one of the most bought but least read books ever published in Britain'. But the report was very important for wartime morale in that it described the sort of society for which Britain was fighting. Copies were even dropped as propaganda over Germany and favourable reviews were found in Hitler's bunker after the war (Timmins, 1995).

Beveridge having gone far beyond his original brief produced an interlocking system of social welfare, health and education provision within a full proposal for national insurance that did, as Churchill said, cover the lives of every citizen 'from the cradle to the grave'. In his introduction, Beveridge claimed that his main enemy was the giant Want, but there were four other giants to be attacked. The whole thrust of the Report was to identify these five giants and to describe the ways in which they would be attacked by five corresponding freedoms:

- Freedom from Want   social security and National Insurance
- Freedom from Disease   a free national health service
- Freedom from Ignorance   improved free secondary education
- Freedom from Squalor   housing and town planning
- Freedom from Idleness   a programme for full employment

Many of the proposals in the Report upset Conservative members of the war-time coalition government. Kingsley Wood, the Chancellor of the Exchequer, was particularly scathing, deriding Beveridge's universalism by conjuring up the vision of millionaires queuing in the post office to receive their pensions. More seriously, he was the first of many to say that the country could not afford the proposals, claiming that they would raise taxes by 30 per cent.

Nevertheless, there was all-party acceptance of Beveridge's ideas, meaning that no matter which party formed the government after the war the Beveridge Report would be made operational. Only two measures – the Butler Education Act of 1944 and the Family Allowances Act of 1945 – were enacted by the war-time government but there had been White Papers on all the other recommendations and all the legislation was in place, waiting only for peace before it was put into practice. It is so common to think of the creation of the welfare state as being peculiarly the achievement of the Labour government of 1945 that it is worth stressing the point that we should still have had a welfare state if the Conservatives had won the 1945 election. It would not necessarily have been the same and it may not have been quite so comprehensive, but it would have existed.

Earlier in this book mention was made of the postwar consensus on economic matters, known as Butskellism. Much the same consensus existed on social issues, again centred on Butler, supported by the small but influential Tory Reform Group whose ideas were taken from Harold Macmillan's *The Middle Way*, and who became increasingly influential as the party cast around for new ideas after the defeat of 1945.

Social Security

The social security aspects of the Beveridge Plan included:

1. A number of universal, flat-rate benefits paid for on the insurance principle through National Insurance, which in effect insured the citizen against loss of income through inability to work – these consisted of unemployment benefit, sickness benefit and retirement benefit.
2. A number of other flat-rate and universal benefits against eventualities such as death or the arrival of children – these being a maternity grant, death grant and family allowances.
3. A safety net of assistance from public funds for those whose income fell below subsistence level, this assistance being means-tested and therefore selective in its provision. In effect National Assistance replaced the old Poor Law, taking the provision of relief out of the hands of local bodies like the parishes and centralising that provision nationally.

The social security provisions, apart from the family allowances which were already in place, were introduced as rapidly as possible after Labour took office in 1945. Their implementation was very expensive, especially the old age pension which was paid in full despite the majority of recipients not having made any National Insurance contributions to pay for it. With the economy still suffering from the effects of the war it is doubtful as to whether the Attlee government could have afforded the implementation of Beveridge if it had not been for a loan of $3.5 billion from the American government. Even then the cost of the welfare state was predicated upon the government maintaining full employment, defined by Beveridge as an average unemployment figure of no more than 3 per cent. In the end that was no problem because, in fact, it was the 1970s before unemployment even rose as high as 3 per cent (Timmins, 1995, p. 133).

The social security system proposed by the Beveridge Report flourished during the boom years of the 1950s and 1960s because it was largely paid for out of growth in the economy, and continuing full employment ensured that no great demands were made upon it. During the 1960s, however, despite general agreement over the success of the system, disquiet was expressed in three areas:

1. A strand of thinking in the Conservative Party felt that, although it was right to help people in real need, a flat-rate universal benefit also paid money out of state funds into the pockets of those who did not need it. A similar line of thought claimed that universal provision of benefit encouraged people to be lazy, feeling no need to provide for themselves or their families while they knew that the state would provide. The worries of these reformers within the Conservative Party were originally expressed by Geoffrey Howe in a study paper he wrote in 1961 (Howe, 1961). Ironically, since he would later be able to put his ideas into practice as Mrs Thatcher's first Chancellor, Howe foreshadowed all the sentiments later associated with Thatcherism, writing about 'rolling back the role of the state' and replacing the 'dependency culture' with the 'self-help state' in which individuals would be encouraged to care for themselves and their families, thereby reducing the burden on the taxpayer. For the time being this viewpoint, which would have means-tested all benefits, got no further but it was a view

that would re-emerge in the late 1970s as growing unemployment meant that the social security budget took an ever-greater share of public expenditure.

2. The flat-rate contributions to national insurance, as recommended by Beveridge, had to be set low so that the poorly-paid could afford them. Yet, in time, this meant that the pool of money in the insurance fund was too small to pay more than a minimal flat-rate benefit. This low level of benefits in turn meant that there was an abrupt drop in living standards for previously high-earning individuals when they retired, especially if they did not have an occupational pension scheme. In continental Europe most state pension schemes were related to earnings, and therefore paid different rates of benefit, unlike the flat-rate British system.

    Rumblings of discontent over this led to the introduction of a graduated scheme in 1961, with the stated intention of working towards the day when everyone would receive a pension equivalent to half their final salary on retirement. At first employers objected to paying higher National Insurance contributions when they were increasingly paying towards occupational pension schemes for their employees. The graduated pension scheme therefore included the principle that those already contributing towards an employer's scheme could opt out of the graduated element. The State Earnings Related Pension Scheme (SERPS) which the graduated system became, established one principle which undermined the universality of the welfare state. In allowing individuals to opt out of a state scheme, the way was opened for others to opt out of the state health service and educational provision.

3. The third area of concern was over what has been dismissively called 'the rediscovery of poverty'. In the 1960s two academics in the Social Administration department of the London School of Economics, Brian Abel-Smith and Peter Townsend, attempted to relate the concept of poverty to the subsistence level defined by Beveridge, expecting to find that the welfare state had abolished absolute poverty. Not only did they find that this was not the case, but they also discovered that the means-tested supplementary benefit paid to the low-paid or unemployed actually made people worse off if they obtained work or better-paid employment. Abel-Smith and Townsend reported

a very high persistence of poverty, especially affecting children, and defined what became known as 'the poverty trap' which actually militated against people seeking work (Abel-Smith and Townsend, 1965).

Poverty and the 'Why Work?' Issue

Beveridge himself did not use the term poverty but always spoke instead about want. He was well aware that there is a difference between absolute poverty and relative poverty. Absolute poverty means not having sufficient money to maintain an acceptable quality of life in terms of food and shelter, and the concept of the poverty line therefore presupposes a subsistence level, a minimal standard of living beneath which someone lapses into absolute poverty. There still remains the problem of defining subsistence because, as the general standard of living rises, so too do the expectations of even the poorest.

Beveridge had been very clear that unemployment or sickness benefit should be set at subsistence level so that everyone would have the minimum essential provision. Unfortunately, those framing the necessary legislation, afraid of the cost, fudged the figures and the benefits fixed in 1948 were only 70 per cent of what Beveridge had considered to be the subsistence level. Because of this far more people than anticipated fell into the safety net of national assistance, or supplementary benefit as it was known later. The numbers in receipt of national assistance had reached two million by the mid-1960s.

Abel-Smith and Townsend measured the poverty level by two criteria. In the first they took the basic rate of supplementary benefit as being the bare subsistence level below which existence would be difficult. But, because the original figures proposed by Beveridge had been blurred in their implementation they believed the basic rate to have been fixed at well below the poverty line, and they considered a figure of 140 per cent higher would be more realistic. This greater, but still minimal, income was made up of the basic supplementary benefit together with small one-off grants for things like clothing or fuel, plus whatever income a claimant might be allowed to earn without suffering a cut in benefit. When these criteria were applied to the situation in 1960 it was found that less than 5 per cent of the population were actually living at or below the 'official' poverty line. But when the figure of 140 per cent of supplementary benefit was taken it was found that 14 per cent of the population – 7.5 million – were living on the margins of poverty, even if not in actual absolute poverty. Significantly large numbers of those living in poverty were children, and a high proportion of these were living in families where the father was working but earning less than he would have received in benefit if he were out of work.

The report by Abel-Smith and Townsend made family poverty into a major political issue that has persisted ever since, helping to create pressure groups such as the Child Poverty Action Group (CPAG) and Shelter. It also created what is known as the 'Why Work?' issue, as it became evident that many individuals, and particularly single parents, were caught in a trap whereby any efforts on their part to break out of poverty often had the effect of making them even poorer. This can clearly be seen in the impact of a measure introduced as a result of the CPAG's activities. Family Income Support (FIS) was introduced in 1971 by Keith Joseph as mean-tested benefit for families of the poorly-paid, intended to top-up earnings to a reasonable level of income. However, if recipients of FIS increased their earnings, 50p was deducted from FIS for every extra pound earned. As income increased the employee, while still receiving FIS, could start paying income tax and increased national insurance contributions, and families could lose out on relief payments like rent rebates or free school meals. As a former director of the CPAG, Frank Field, said,

> It is now a fact that for millions of low paid workers very substantial pay increases have the absurd effect of increasing only marginally their family's net income and in some cases actually make the family worse off. (*New Statesman*, 3 December 1971, pp. 772–3)

The Changing Attitude to Welfare

The Labour government of 1974–9 was the last to make major reforms of the social security system for the benefit of its recipients:

- Annual increases in benefit were made official and the amount by which they were increased was linked to either the rise in the cost of living or the rise in average earnings, whichever was the greater of the two.

- Tax allowances for all children and family allowances for the second and subsequent children, paid through the breadwinner's earnings, were scrapped in favour of child benefit. This was a fixed sum paid on all children including the first and it was paid in cash direct to the mother, while fathers who were the breadwinners for the family lost their entitlement to tax relief. This was an important stage in recognising that women had more than a subsidiary role in the receipt of welfare.

Despite these developments in social security, the position of the social security budget in the light of galloping inflation and rising unemployment was becoming serious. By the late 1970s five million people were receiving supplementary benefit and even a Labour prime minister like James Callaghan was forced to concede that Britain had seen the end of full employment as a realistic goal and that this in turn would mean the end of a welfare system paid for by taxes from a fully employed nation. Some Conservatives, backed by the more vociferous sections of the Tory press, gave voice to the old concept of the 'deserving' and 'undeserving' poor and began to argue that taxpayers' money was being wasted in paying benefit to those who did not deserve it. These attacks began when the Conservatives were still in opposition but they continued after the 1979 election. Because their numbers had increased so much in recent years, unmarried mothers were made a prime target for attacks on the 'undeserving'. Their receipt of social security benefit, it was implied, was like rewarding them for their immorality. In a series of well-publicised attacks, Conservative ministers like Michael Howard and John Redwood accused unmarried mothers of deliberately becoming pregnant in order to extract child and housing benefit and other allowances from the state. Alongside this categorisation of the undeserving recipients of benefit ran the usual stories of 'shirkers' and 'scroungers' which implied that there was a substantial proportion of the population who, rather than work, were lying and cheating to get money out of social security.

The Thatcher and Post-Thatcher Agenda for Social Security

When the Thatcher administration came to power in 1979 it was known that the prime minister, like many of her supporters, was opposed to the universal, tax-funded social and welfare system. She was largely in favour of an insurance style approach to welfare provision but, according to her, that insurance should be privately funded as far as possible rather than represent a charge on the Treasury.

The first Thatcher government moved immediately to cut certain provisions:

- The link between the annual raising of benefit levels and average earnings was cut, the level by which benefit would be raised in the spring was determined by the rise in the retail price index the previous October, and this became the sole criterion.
- Benefits were cut for certain classes the government could categorise as 'undeserving', such as strikers.
- Child benefit was frozen.

The reductions were mild enough but Mrs Thatcher, like her ministers, was well aware that the middle classes were every bit as supportive of the welfare state as Labour, and it was known that deep cuts in any area other than in contentious provisions like strikers' benefit would be very unpopular with the electorate. The freezing of child benefit was part of a long-term strategy because if a benefit is frozen until it loses its value it can be abolished without anyone noticing. A death grant of £30 fixed in the 1940s when it would just about pay for a simple funeral, and a maternity grant of £25 to help with the costs of baby clothes and expenses, were neither of them increased and, by the 1980s, were laughably inadequate for their stated purpose. They were such a minor consideration that no one even thought to protest when they were abolished in 1984.

In 1982 the Central Policy Review Staff (the Think Tank) was asked to look at the problem of ever-increasing public expenditure that could well represent 47 per cent of GDP by 1990. The resulting report was nothing less than a plan to dismantle the welfare state, including the freezing of any cost of living increases in welfare benefits. The report was greeted with horror by government ministers who could see the damage these suggestions would do to public opinion, and with the help of a judicious leak to the *Economist*, carried out by Peter Walker according to Hugo Young, the plan was abandoned. The prime minister's press office issued a denial that Mrs Thatcher had had anything to do with the plan and reassured everyone that the welfare state was safe in the government's hands.

But no one ever quite trusted the Thatcher government's commitment to the welfare state after that time (Young, 1989, pp. 300–1). The review of social security began in 1984, when:

- Supplementary benefit became Income Support.
- FIS changed its nature to become Family Credit in an attempt to merge the tax and benefit systems in order to solve the 'Why Work?' issue.
- There were cuts in SERPS coupled with heavy incentives to encourage individuals to opt out of the state scheme in order to take out private pension plans. This was very successful, with over five million people having opted out by 1993. Unfortunately, the government faced additional expenditure when some form of compensation had to be devised for the 500 000 or so people who had opted-out of occupational pension schemes as a result of faulty advice.
- Sick pay was funded by the state for only the first three days of absence from work, after that it became the responsibility of the employer.
- One-off payments from the Social Fund – clothing and bedding grants and so on – were scrapped and replaced with repayable loans.
- The maternity grant and death grant payments were abolished.

The changes of 1984 merely represented the start of a steady programme of cuts which stressed the importance placed by the Treasury on the need for cuts in public spending. The process accelerated after 1987 when Mrs Thatcher, having won her third successive election, decided that it was time to 'dismantle the dependency culture'. 'There is no such thing as society', she said, in an interview given to the magazine, *Woman's Own*, on 31 October 1987, 'And no government can do anything except through people, and people must look after themselves first'. To emphasise the point a politician of the right, John Moore, was appointed as Secretary of State for Health and Social Security. He followed his leader's train of thought by saying in repeated speeches that 'welfare recipients must be moved away from dependence and towards independence'.

Throughout the 1980s the government definition of unemployment was changed at least 19 times and the rules for claiming unemployment benefit were also changed in line with the new definitions. The contribution of John Moore was to withdraw the right to Income Support from 16- and 17-year-olds. He claimed that it was not necessary since all school-leavers were guaranteed either a job or a training scheme. There was some merit in his arguments but they failed to take account of teenagers who had run away from home and those who had failed, for good or bad reasons, to get or keep a job or training place. Whatever the government might argue, the public perception was that Moore's alterations were the start of youngsters sleeping in cardboard boxes on the streets and the cause of increasing numbers of beggars in our major cities.

There was a time when people believed that John Major would look more favourably on the social security system than his predecessor. However, the recession into which the country was plunged ensured that the government continued to look for reform of social security in order to cut public spending. Under John Major the Department of Social Security got two of the most right-wing Secretaries of State since John Moore – Michael Portillo and Peter Lilley. It was Peter Lilley, in the Mais Lecture to the City University on 23 June 1993, who signalled the end of universal, tax-funded benefit in a defining statement, 'The structural reform of social security must involve either better targeting or more self-provision, or both'. Michael Portillo on the other hand was prepared to dispose of unemployment benefit as such, replacing it with what was known as the Job Seekers Allowance in order to stress that benefit would not be paid unless the recipient signed an agreement stating that work was actively being sought.

The Thatcherite approach to poverty had avoided direct help to the poor. Instead the free market ideology had claimed that tax cuts and other help given to the entrepreneurial classes would create growth which would, in turn, mean that a share of the new wealth would 'trickle down' to benefit all groups in society. Even the government's own figures from the 'households below average income' (HBAI) survey published in early 1997, showed that this policy did not work (*The Guardian*, 28 April 1997). The number of people living below the poverty line (below half average income) rose from 5 million in 1979 to 14.1 million in 1993. After 1993 there was a move in the other direction but it meant little more than that the numbers of poor dropped from 14.1 million to 13.7 million in 1997: it still meant more than 20 per cent of the population living below the poverty line.

The Labour Response

For some time after 1979 the only response of Labour to cuts made by the Conservative government was to state that all the cuts would be restored. Once Neil Kinnock became leader, however, it became clear that many factors including the nature of unemployment had changed since 1979 and that a major rethink of Labour's welfare policy was called for, as a result of which one of many policy reviews was set up. By the time of the 1987 general election the review had not made much progress and the main thrust of Labour policy was simply to restore the value of child benefit and pensions, and also to restore the link with earnings rather than the cost of living as the measuring-stick for benefit rises. Another policy adopted by Labour which was to have a lasting influence was the suggested imposition of a national minimum wage.

This idea was to counteract the abolition of wage councils by the Conservative government and what was seen in some circles as the deliberate establishment in Britain of a low-wage economy. Faced with competition from Pacific Rim countries like Korea or Malaysia where labour costs were always low, British manufacturers were making themselves competitive by paying low wages and recruiting a largely female, part-time and non-unionised workforce that would accept low wages. The Conservative government was very much in favour of these moves which they saw as 'restoring Britain's competitiveness', as well as being a true application of market forces. Labour, however, recognised that a minimum wage was a vital element in social security provision because, increasingly, the claimants for Income Support were less those who were unemployed than those who were in work but receiving less than the subsistence level in wages. One of the key factors in the 'Why Work?' issue was that many jobs that were available were so low-paid that an individual was better-off remaining unemployed and on benefit.

The minimum wage was one element that caused the Labour Party to change its attitude towards the European Community. In 1988 the President of the European Commission, Jacques Delors, came to Britain and addressed the TUC on the subject of those social policies he and the Commission were proposing for Europe, proposals that would form the Social Chapter of the Maastricht Treaty for European Union. These policies regulated matters such as workers' health and safety, the rights of women in the workplace and a statutory minimum wage:

This was so much in line with Labour thinking that the party enthusiastically endorsed the direction being taken by Delors and the Commission . . . Europe seemed a logical way by which, indirectly, the social policies desired by Labour could be introduced into Britain, despite a Conservative government. (Pilkington, 1995, p. 215)

The Conservative government was totally opposed to the Social Chapter and negotiated an opt-out from its provisions at Maastricht largely because of the minimum wage requirement. The governments position was laid out by one of its right-wing exponents Michael Portillo who, as Employment Secretary, was speaking on 27 July 1994 about the social policies announced for the incoming new Commission. 'The government will not tolerate unwarranted interference in people's lives from Brussels which would put extra costs on employers, make firms less competitive and reduce the number of jobs'. The opposition parties fought the government over the Social Chapter opt-out during the ratification of Maastricht but lost the argument, although many social issues such as equality of the sexes in pension entitlement have nevertheless been introduced into Britain through decisions of the European Courts. The implementation of the Social Chapter, including the question of a minimum wage, remains a commitment for New Labour although to the despair of the trade union movement the party as led by Tony Blair was reluctant to put a figure on what that minimum wage might be even after the victory of 1997, the figure of £3.40 an hour proposed in the 1992 manifesto having been jettisoned before 1997.

Under the leadership of John Smith the Labour Party had set up an even more involved policy review in the Commission on Social Justice under the guidance of Sir Gordon Borrie. For the first time the Labour Party moved away from the simple reversal of Conservative policies and – finally prepared to think the unthinkable – agreed that social change demanded a re-structuring of the welfare state, promising to look again at the universal versus selective argument. The report, published by Borrie in 1994, rejected both the integration of the tax and benefit systems and an extension of means tested benefits. It did recommend raising benefits and pensions as well as introducing unemployment benefit for part-time workers, but it also recommended the taxing of child benefit and other universal benefits for higher rate taxpayers.

Only a year after publication of the Borrie Report, hailed at the time as a 'New Beveridge Report', Tony Blair told his shadow social security secretary, Chris Smith, to spend another six months in rethinking Labour's welfare policy yet again. In so doing he seemed to confirm Roy Hattersley's accusation that New Labour under Blair was too preoccupied with the problems of the middle classes at the expense of the disadvantaged. In November 1995 the shadow chancellor, Gordon Brown, laid out a new policy for the young unemployed under which young people who had been out of work for more than six months would be offered the choice of employment subsidised by the government, or voluntary work, or full-time education, or work on an environmental task force. Anyone refusing all four alternatives would lose 40 per cent of their income support entitlement. The plan was widely criticised as a variant of the American Workfare, in which people are forced to work for their benefit.

The Brown plan and the Smith re-think of Labour policy were taken as evidence that the Labour Party was beginning to acknowledge that welfare spending was out of hand and that measures would have to be taken to restructure the social security system for the future. The left was also suspicious that in their campaign to win the votes of Middle England the modernisers of New Labour had accepted a little too readily the middle-class view of welfare claimants as being 'shirkers' and 'scroungers'. Compare, for example, policies on welfare payments as stated in the 1997 manifestoes. There is nothing remarkable about the Conservative statement that 'we will crack down on benefit cheats', but it is remarkable to find an uncanny echo of that statement in New Labour's 'we must crack down on dishonesty in the benefit system' (*The Observer*, 13 April 1997).

Conclusions

There is little doubt that the social security system is in difficulties. It was expressed by Frank Field, Labour chairman of the Parliamentary Select Committee on Social Security, as essentially being about increasingly scarce resources being asked to meet increasingly heavy demands, 'We live in a world where increasingly people work fewer years and yet live longer in retirement. There is simply no way in which the welfare bills can be cut and yet each and every one can have an adequate pension' (Field, 1995). The way in which costs are rising is indicated by the fact that government spending on social security benefits in 1949, the first full year of the welfare state, was 4.7 per cent of GDP; but by 1992 that had risen to 12.3 per cent of GDP (McKie, 1994, p. 107).

The issues surrounding social security, therefore, all arise from the cost of welfare and how that cost might be met. These issues have thrown up a variety of scenarios for future action:

1. To do nothing, but allow the demands made on social security to continue to rise, with a consequent rise in taxes and national insurance contributions to pay for it. This is not a serious option because it is not electorally possible for a political party to continue advocating indefinitely that taxes should be increased. Indeed the opposite is so much the case that, by late 1995, the Conservative government was desperately looking for ways to cut welfare spending for no other reason than to finance tax cuts in the run-up to the next election.

2. To cut welfare benefits. Again not a popular electoral move. Many benefits on the insurance principle, such as old age pensions, are granted as of right because of contributions made over many years and it would be legally dubious to deprive people of what is theirs by right of their having paid into the scheme over many years. The only option here is to continue to trim benefits to persons who can be represented as 'undeserving'. This was the principle adopted in the spending round leading up to the 1995 Budget when the Treasury asked Peter Lilley, as Social Security Secretary, to freeze single parent benefit, and abolish it for new claimants. Even a rightwinger such as Lilley felt the need to protest about the scale of cuts in a letter to William Waldegrave at the Treasury on 9 November 1995, saying that 'the impact on operations will be devastating'.

3. Dismantle the welfare state and the social security system for all but the very needy. This is the solution put forward by the Tory Right. The 'No Turning Back' group of Thatcherite MPs, with close links to Michael Portillo and John Redwood, proposed that child benefit should be scrapped along with state pensions for those already possessing an occupational pension. The various National Insurance schemes would be phased out to be replaced by private schemes to insure against sickness, unemployment and retirement. At the very start of the 1997

election campaign the Conservatives came up with a plan for the complete reform of pension provision in Britain and for phasing in a replacement of the state pension by personal private schemes. *The Guardian* called it the most 'radical pension plan since Lloyd George's People's Budget introduced pensions in 1909. There would be no state pensions except for the poor, unemployed or long-term sick. . . Everybody else would be on their own' (*The Guardian*, 14 April 1997).

4.   If the universal flat-rate provisions of the National Insurance scheme were abolished, social security would become no more than a safety-net for the really needy and any benefits under this could be rigorously means-tested. However, there is doubt as to the effectiveness of means-testing. The Borrie Commission dismissed means-testing as counterproductive and Frank Field listed three main faults in the process. According to him (Field, 1995), means-tests:

- penalise effort by withdrawing benefit from anyone who earns a little extra;
- discourage savings when to have them disqualifies a person from benefit;
- encourage dishonesty in declaring tax and savings and create a 'black' economy.

One possibility remaining is that there should be a shift towards in-work benefit, so that family credit benefit would be paid to those forced to take low-paid work. The risk in such a strategy would be that government money would be subsidising low-paying employers.

5.   Reduce the number of benefits given as of right and increase the number of benefits that are conditional. Beveridge's original intention was that benefits should not be paid automatically but that the recipient should be seen to have obligations as well as rights. As far as unemployment benefit was concerned Beveridge originally proposed that, after a given period, someone on unemployment benefit should only continue to receive benefit if they agreed to a course of training or re-training. It is a proposal not unlike that put forward by Gordon Brown 50 years later. This last point reinforces the suggestion that a new element has been introduced, or re-introduced, into the welfare debate by the emergence of New Labour. Since 1945 it has been accepted

that, whatever the stance of the Conservatives, Labour would remain true to the model of a universal, flat-rate, tax-funded, non-means-tested social security system. Yet Beveridge was a Liberal rather than a Labour supporter who wanted little more than a minimal provision to guard against absolute poverty, while preserving a Liberal respect for individual effort to improve on the minimalist position. It is possible to detect signs that New Labour, as it has moved from socialism to a more social democratic stance, is coming closer to Beveridge's original intentions.

6. A recognition that social security provision is still rooted in the social structures of 1945 means that no modification of the details of the system will be worth anything until the basic foundations themselves are reformed. In Australia there has been something of a revolution in that the social security system has moved its focus from the family unit or household to concentrate on the individual. Rather than the household receiving income support each unemployed partner is paid a separate benefit – unemployment benefit if seeking work or parenting benefit if looking after children. If one partner obtains work their benefit is reduced according to their earnings but, unlike the situation in Britain, the partner's benefit is not touched. This removes the threat that to re-enter employment can reduce the household income and thereby removes the 'Why Work?' issue.

All these arguments bear witness to the way in which neo-liberalism has taken over the political agenda in the 1990s. The underlying assumption is that Britain's spending on social security is excessive and growing out of control. In fact growth in social spending is modest, and in comparison with other industrialised countries the social security budget is quite small, ranking about eighteenth in the world order when considered as a percentage of GDP. Only Portugal in Western Europe spends less on its welfare provision than does the UK, while the Benelux and Scandinavian countries spend a third as much again. As Will Hutton put it in a newspaper article, the question of spending on the welfare state is only a political issue if the creation of a low-tax state is a priority (*The Guardian*, 18 September 1995). The appointment to ministerial rank in Tony Blair's first government team of New Labour's most innovative thinker in the social and welfare sphere, Frank Field, seemed to be indicative of the intention by New Labour to under-take a root-and-branch reform of the welfare system, given the new realities of the late twentieth century.

Yet the first actions of the new Labour government seemed to suggest that Blair's cabinet saw some merit in the post-Thatcherite neo-liberalism that John Major's government had been following – an expressed intention to move towards private provision of pensions; the threat that unemployment benefit will be withdrawn if applicants do not accept what work is on offer; the withdrawal of free tertiary education in the universities; and suggestions by Frank Dobson that the Health Service will not rule out any option, including 'hotel charges' for hospital beds and the need to pay for doctors' home visits. All these measures, or potential measures, seemed to be carrying New Labour further and further away from the old ideals of free universal provision.

Gordon Brown's budget of 2 July 1997 was said to be the first step in the creation of a new welfare state. It has to be said that the welfare state will not, and cannot, be like the one established by the Beveridge Report. In a newspaper debate with Roy Hattersley (*The Guardian*, 26 July and 2 August 1997), Gordon Brown made it clear that the debate over poverty at the end of the century centres on rival interpretations of the meaning of 'equality'. On the one hand it is possible to strive for equality of outcome through some form of redistributive taxation, or society should aim for equality of opportunity whereby education and employment offer advancement to each and everyone.

6

Education, Health and Housing

The Beveridge Report was essentially about the elimination of want, and that was basically dealt with through National Insurance and social security. The other 'giants' against which Beveridge pitted himself – those of ignorance, disease, idleness and squalor – were dealt with by measures about which it was much more difficult to arrive at a consensus. While everyone could agree about the need to tackle poverty, there were distinct ideological barriers against reaching agreement over education, health and housing, not so much over the need to provide them as over the nature and form taken by that provision.

The divide was between Labour's emphasis on egalitarianism and the Conservatives' aspiration to the 'opportunity state', in other words it is an echo of the divide between universal and selective provision. For Labour the overriding value was that of fairness and equality of treatment, for the Conservatives it was allowing freedom of choice to the individual and providing the opportunities for personal achievement. For the Conservatives the egalitarianism of Labour is about the 'politics of envy', with the object of reducing everyone and everything to the lowest common denominator; while for Labour the Conservative model allows achievement only for an élite, lavishing resources on a favoured few at the expense of the many, leading to first and second class provision for first and second-class citizens.

As far as the individual–collective divide is concerned, Beveridge was a Liberal allowing both sides to claim his ideas as their own. The reality in the equation was provided by the Treasury whose consistent imperative is a reluctance to spend public money. The

83

more selective approach to spending adopted by Conservative administrations matched Treasury policy much more closely than did Labour's. This is why Conservative reforms in social policy have always proceeded more smoothly than reforms under Labour (Timmins, 1995). It is also the reason why repeated calls over the years for party politics to be kept out of the debate over education, health or housing have been in vain. These policy areas are key political issues simply because attitudes towards them are intensely party political.

Education

Education helps to form attitudes and values and therefore underpins the foundations of society; it trains and prepares the bureaucrats, executives, technocrats and scientists who will manage the future existence of the state; and it helps mould the form society will take. As a result, education as an issue poses certain questions for the political process:

1. How is education to be organised, and for whose benefit?
2. Is education meant to facilitate equality or is it to exploit inequalities to the full?
3. Is education to be regarded as a form of improvement for the individual, or is it strictly utilitarian in terms of training workers?
4. What form should the curriculum take? What is to be taught, how is it to be taught and what is the hidden curriculum implied in those decisions?

The development of education as a political issue hinges upon the way answers were sought for these four questions. For 30 years after 1945, arguments centred on the first two questions as the political parties fought over the rival merits of comprehensive or selective schools for the provision of secondary education; this period coinciding with expansion both in education itself and in the funding for education. After 1974, however, the emphasis switched to arguments over the nature of the curriculum and what were perceived as declining standards; this phase coinciding with retrenchment in funding and ultimately combining with the Thatcherite ideology of market forces to bring the argument back to selectivity.

Overall, the main argument in education and one which has maintained it as a major political issue is the way in which the British education system has been seen, and continues to be seen, as failing in comparison with other countries, especially our main industrial and commercial rivals. That failure has long since been identified as due to Britain giving, 'far too much attention to traditional liberal educational ideas, which favoured the arts against scientific and technical education' (Coxall and Robins, 1995, p. 25). The result has been what Hutton has called a three-tiered education system in which grammar schools modelled themselves on public schools and modern and comprehensive secondary schools modelled themselves on grammar schools (Hutton, 1995, pp. 213–17). It is a system where academic achievement as measured in examination results is everything. As Coxall and Robins have pointed out, this is the wrong way round: 'Educational planners in the 1940s should have devoted more effort to consideration of the content of educa- tion rather than focusing almost exclusively on questions of orga- nisation' (Coxall and Robins, 1995).

The Butler Education Act of 1944

Work on reforming state secondary education had begun even before Beveridge had reported, because a series of uncodified changes and reforms since 1900 had left a fragmented and divisive structure. The school system was dominated by a typically British preoccupation with class, which meant that success at school was for a select few, with very rare exceptions. In 1938, out of the entire school population, only 19 000 students stayed on at school until they were 18; only 8000 obtained their Higher School Certificate (the equivalent of A-levels) and a mere 4000 got into university. Of those entering university only one in every 150 came from elemen- tary schools, as against one in eight from public schools. Compared with the adult population in other countries, one in a thousand went to university as against one in 125 in the United States (Barnett, 1986).

Before Beveridge reported, a parliamentary committee under Lord Fleming had been set up to enquire into opening up the entry requirements into public schools through offering scholarship places for non-fee payers. The scheme had failed because not enough public schools were willing to make that many free places available.

Failure to reform the public schools was a major shortcoming of the postwar settlement. A true reform of the school system was never possible while the top 5 per cent of society were able to keep their children out of the public sector. Pleas for extra resources for state education fell on deaf ears when children of the people responsible for providing those resources were not themselves affected by improvements in the state sector.

When he first became president of the Board of Education, Butler was tempted by the idea of comprehensive schools – or multilateral schools as they were then known. However, a long argument over the place of church schools in the state system sidelined all other organisational issues. Ultimately Butler chose the tripartite system in preference to comprehensive schooling, except where comprehensive schools existed as tripartite schools on one site. Proposals for a more technically orientated education were thwarted by lack of funds.

Significant provisions of the 1944 Act were:

- Overall control of education was in the hands of the newly-established Ministry of Education, while day-to-day decisions were kept firmly in the hands of local education authorities.
- Elementary schools were abolished and education divided into three stages of primary, secondary and further education.
- Free secondary education was to be provided for all children up to the age of 15, with pupils divided by aptitude and intelligence tests at the age of 11 into the three strands of the tripartite system, suggested in 1943 by a committee led by Sir Cyril Norwood:

    (i)   Grammar schools for the academically minded.
    (ii) Technical schools for those interested in applied science and technology.
    (iii) Secondary Modern Schools for the practical rather than academic pupil.

- There should be an 'ease of transfer' between strands of the tripartite system, with a review of the pupils placement at the age of 13.
- There should be parity of esteem and parity of provision across all strands of secondary education.
- The school leaving age was to be raised to 15 immediately, and to 16 as soon as was practically possible.

- Means-tested grants would be available to enable all students who wished to do so to continue their education at college or university.
- Nursery education should be available for all children aged between three and five.

Failures of Implementation

Although the Education Act was passed by the coalition government in 1944, its implementation was left to the Labour government after 1945 and difficulties faced by that government meant that many critical parts of the Act were never put in place.

- There was a massive increase in the numbers of children born in the latter years of the war; the five-year period 1942–7 seeing a million more children than there had been in the preceding five years: the phenomenon was later characterised as 'the postwar baby boom'.
- There was a growing number of children about to enter primary education.
- There were increased numbers in secondary schools thanks to the raising of the school-leaving age from 14 to 15.
- There was a lack of suitable premises since building had largely been suspended during the war.
- There was a drastic shortage of trained teachers, again through the suspension of many training courses for the duration of the war.

There was an economic crisis in 1947–8 and a demand for funds by other parts of the government programme such as emergency housing, the National Health Service and nationalisation. Cuts had therefore to be made in the education programme before it had even started. As a result:

- Raising of the school-leaving age to 16 was postponed indefinitely (it was not to be achieved until 1972).
- The proposed provision of nursery education was also postponed until circumstances were right (universal provision of nursery education was still being proposed in the 1990s).

- Proposals for compulsory part-time education to the age of 18 were scrapped.
- The creation of technical schools as an important part of the tripartite system was left to the discretion of local education authorities. The majority of these authorities either did not care or could not afford it. Without government compulsion no more than 2 per cent of secondary pupils received a technical education!

The most serious economy was that which failed to provide technical schools and thereby reduced the proposed *tripartite* system to a *bipartite* system. The whole ethos put forward in the Butler Act was that there should be equality of opportunity, while recognising that there was not equality of ability. The 11-plus test was intended to define children by their ability and aptitude and then to place them in the kind of school that best suited that aptitude. The three types of school intended for post-11 education were meant to have parity of esteem, and the test which children sat was meant to be a tool for accurate selection, not an examination to be passed or failed. If there were only two possible outcomes of that test and, of those two, one led on to the new GCE examinations and a possible university entrance, while the other led to no qualifications and leaving school at 15, then it soon became obvious that a grammar school place was to be regarded as a pass and a secondary modern place as a failure.

The Comprehensive Debate

Despite being proposed at the time of the Butler Act, the idea of comprehensive schools did not catch on even with the Labour government and Labour councils; only 20 such schools had been opened by 1951. Labour was content that the provision of free secondary education meant that academic opportunities were now open to the working class, and for that purpose they were content with the grammar schools.

Doubts about the selective system began in the 1950s as faults in the selection process became apparent:

- Parents believed that a child who had not got into grammar school had failed but, since there were only enough grammar schools to take 20 per cent of the school population, 80 per cent of schoolchildren were branded as failures at 11 and many parents were disappointed, including a significant number of middle-class parents.

- In many local authority areas the provision of grammar school places was even less than 20 per cent and the possibility of a grammar school education was a matter of luck dependent on where you lived. In an influential report made to the National Federation for Educational Research in 1957, many children did not get the education for which they were suited. The report spoke of more than 10 per cent of children ending up in the wrong sort of school.
- Teachers, parents and the pupils themselves had limited expectations of those who had 'failed' the 11-plus and performed accordingly. When the time came to review 13-year-olds for possible transfer into grammar schools it was found that two years of secondary modern education had widened the ability gap to the point where it could not be bridged. Moreover, the IQ tests on which the 11-plus was based were found to be unreliable and it was shown that primary school children could be coached into overachieving, even on supposedly objective tests.

The arguments began at a time when education was beginning to expand in the boom years of the 1950s. The Conservative government which took power in 1951 saw itself as providing the 'opportunity state' and, under Sir David Eccles, who was Minister of Education from 1954 to 1962, spending on schools was greatly increased. Many new primary and secondary schools were built and secondary modern schools acquired the CSE examination in an attempt to restore the 'parity of esteem' that even Eccles admitted had not been achieved. As a result of the Robbins Report, more than 10 new universities were created or planned in a massive expansion of higher education for all.

The Robbins Report was only one of several important reports into educational provision which began to provide proof that selection at 11 was educationally bad. Two other reports which addressed the comprehensive debate were *15–18* (the Crowther Report of 1959) and *Half our Future* (the Newsom Report of 1963). Eccles accepted most criticisms of selection but refused to do anything about it in case change harmed the grammar schools. In 1962, however, Eccles was sacked in Macmillan's 'Night of the Long Knives' and was succeeded by Edward Boyle, a left-wing Tory who said in the foreword to the Newsom Report that 'The essential point is that all children should have an equal opportunity of acquiring intelligence and developing their talents and abilities to the full.' Under guidance from Boyle, 90 out of 164 local education authorities (LEAs) drew up plans to go comprehensive.

When the Labour government took over in 1964, Tony Crosland as Secretary of State for Education was determined to make all secondary education comprehensive 'if it is the last thing I do' (Timmins, 1995). In 1965 the Department issued Circular 10/65 requesting local education authorities to produce plans to make their schools comprehensive. Crosland wanted to make the circular compulsory but Harold Wilson was an ex-grammar schoolboy and he did not want to see grammar schools swept away. A section of the Labour Party persuaded Crosland to 'request' rather than 'demand' compliance. Nevertheless, by 1970 32 per cent of secondary pupils were in comprehensive schools even though many were makeshift 'shot-gun marriages' of grammar and secondary modern on split sites. Only 8 per cent of local education authorities had not drawn up plans to go comprehensive.

In 1970 Ted Heath appointed Margaret Thatcher as Secretary of State for Education. Within 10 minutes of arriving at the Department of Education and Science, Mrs Thatcher had cancelled Crosland's circular, initiating three years of argument in the Tory Party. Yet the irony is that however she may have preferred grammar schools herself, Margaret Thatcher closed more grammar schools and created more comprehensives than any other secretary of state, including Tony Crosland and Shirley Williams. When Mrs Thatcher took over in 1970 32 per cent of children were in comprehensives, by 1974 that figure had risen to 62 per cent. She also saved the Open University from closure, raised the school leaving age to 16 and made yet another promise about nursery places for all.

The Labour government which took over in 1974 more or less finished the comprehensive programme. Eight Conservative authorities fought to preserve their grammar schools and, by playing the system, 150 grammar schools managed to survive until 1979 when the arrival of Mrs Thatcher as prime minister got them off the hook. Labour had also abolished direct grant grammar schools which, in 1975, were offered the choice of either transferring to the public sector or becoming fully independent and fee-paying. For the moment it was an end to the argument over selection and the issue moved to being one about educational standards.

The Issue of Standards

In 1968 two educational theorists brought out the first *Black Papers*, a collection of essays dealing with what were perceived as declining standards in education (Cox and Dyson, 1971). The essays themselves were disparate but were largely anti-egalitarian, often élitist and all deplored the way in which standards had fallen, particularly in maths and English. They called for a return to grammar schools in secondary education and for an end to experiments with progressive methods of teaching in the primary schools. The *Black Papers* caught the attention of right-wing figures in the Conservative Party and, after 1974, as Labour moved towards compulsory comprehensive education, the Conservative right adopted the debate over standards as their own, moving the main educational issue from the question of organisation to one of curriculum.

Since 1945 issues of the curriculum had been kept out of the government's hands. Overall supervision of curricular matters had been given to the Schools Council in 1964, supposedly an independent body but one very much dominated by teachers and the teaching unions. A strong feeling emerged that people other than teachers, particularly parents, should have a say in what was taught in schools. The perceived problems were that progressive education had gone too far in primary schools, while secondary education had been virtually swamped by the problems of going comprehensive, the raising of the school leaving age and the feeding through of the 'baby boom'. According to a semi-official report, known as the 'Yellow Book' from the colour of its cover, the answer was to revert to traditional methods and a traditional curriculum. The 'Yellow Book' was never published but leaked details were given in the *Times Educational Supplement* of 15 October 1976, pp. 1–3.

In 1976 the prime minister, James Callaghan, called for the involvement of parents, teachers, professional bodies, higher education, both sides of industry and the government in what he labelled 'The Great Debate'. In 1978 the debate produced a somewhat feeble bill which legislated for:

1. Parent governors.
2. Parental right to information in school files.
3. Parental right to choice of school.

The 1978 Education Act failed to cope with certain issues brought up in the 'Great Debate' – which had called for a centralisation of educational control, with a national curriculum and testing. But these issues thrown up by Labour's great debate provided the agenda for the Conservative government after 1979. When Keith Joseph became Education Secretary in 1981 he was the first Thatcherite to control a spending department and the first spending minister to believe in spending cuts, refusing to believe that the quality of education is affected by the amount of money spent on it. He did advocate the use of education vouchers with which parents could buy the education they wanted from the school of their choice, while schools would have to compete for the goodwill of voucher-holding parents. To Joseph this seemed like the ideal way to introduce market forces into education.

The Department of Education and Science (DES) fought off vouchers over two years of argument. They claimed that schools could not be run as a business, since teachers have no expertise of budgetary control and so the issue of vouchers was shelved for the time being while a new round of reforms was designed to create schools that could handle their own budgets. To increase the influence of market forces in education:

1. The government eased out local government from its control of education spending.
2. The Schools Council was replaced by government-appointed quangos so that curricular changes such as the GCSE and the national curriculum would not be teacher-dominated.
3. The Youth Training Scheme (YTS) and the technical and vocational initiative (TVEI) were handed over to the Manpower Services Commission (MSC) rather than the DES.

When Kenneth Baker took over the DES in 1986, therefore, he inherited a demoralised teaching force. In preparing for what became known as the GERBIL (great educational reform bill) Baker laid down certain priorities in that technical education must be improved, there should be a National Curriculum which would be tested regularly, and there should be local management of schools with open enrolment and formula funding, opted out of local authority control. Typical of the suggested new schools were the City Technical Colleges (CTCs) which were government-funded (but business-sponsored) independent schools run by educational trusts rather than LEAs. They defined the new market-led education system desired by the Conservative Party:

- Directly funded by government on a per capita basis.
- Controlling their own budgets.
- With a centrally determined curriculum.

This laid down the pattern by which schools could opt out of local control to become grant-maintained schools, receiving more money from central government than LEAs were given to run those schools still in their control. Similar moves away from local control to market economy funding were instituted for colleges of further education and those polytechnics which became full universities in their own right. All in all, 415 powers were taken away from LEAs into the hands of the centre, while yet more powers were devolved to parents, governors and the schools themselves.

Baker's plans did not go smoothly:

- The wide-ranging national curriculum of ten compulsory subjects introduced by Baker was repeatedly simplified and the scope of testing reduced because the scheme as originally proposed just did not work.
- Instead of the original 20 CTCs proposed, only 15 were set up in the first round, at a cost three times that estimated. Business firms proved very reluctant to provide the sponsorship money expected.
- Despite huge financial incentives, very few schools voted to opt out and after five years only 1000 schools, or 5 per cent of the total, had chosen to become grant-maintained.

Failures in educational reform alienated Conservative supporters and it has been said that the GERBIL was 'forced through by a parliamentary majority against the wishes of unions, teachers, educationalists, organised parent groups and most LEA politicians' (Johnson, 1991).

Measures put forward in the government's reforms were meant to promote parental choice, competition between schools, freedom from local authority control and a national curriculum dedicated to raising standards. Yet there were anomalies in the reforms which seemed counterproductive: allowing parental choice in open enrolment informed by published examination results and league tables of performance, allied to formula, per capita funding with generous state funding for opted-out schools while local government spending was restricted – all these have helped to overturn any advances made in the education system since 1945.

1. In theory competition in schools is supposed to raise standards overall but parents, children and money will be directed towards successful schools, improving those that are already good but depriving the less successful of resources and making the bad worse.
2. Successful schools will be able to choose their intake on the grounds of ability, possibly through an entrance examination, thereby recreating all the perceived problems of the 11-plus divide. Indeed, before the 1997 election Conservative policy as formulated by John Major and Gillian Shepherd was to restore selection with the expressed aim of once more seeing 'a grammar school in every town'.
3. Although the reforms were introduced to assist the independence of parents and the ability of a school to manage its own affairs, the national curriculum and the introduction of direct-grant funding mean that there is now a strong centralised control of education, at the expense of local autonomy whether for school, councils or parents.

When Tony Blair decided to send his son to a selective school, shortly followed by Harriet Harman making the same decision, it became obvious that New Labour's education policy would not undo the Conservative reforms, suggesting that there has been a permanent move of education into a market economy. It would seem that the principal issue as far as education is concerned has now shifted to the question of how a free market education can be delivered so that all schools improve their standards without those in poor and deprived areas descending to become what Ted Wragg called, 'cheap, cheerless, third-class schools run by clapped-out and impoverished authorities' (*The Observer*, 17 May 1992).

Education assumed a primary role in the 1997 general election campaign. As Martin Jacques said in an article on élitism (*The Observer*, 20 April 1997, p. 27), 'In an extraordinary display of unanimity all the parties agree that education has replaced the economy as the central priority facing the nation'. Despite this general agreement that the priorities for the 1990s were, as Blair said, 'education, education and education', it was only the Liberal

Democrats who seemed ready to promise the necessary funding for education, with a repetition of their 1992 pledge to put a penny on the standard rate of income tax in order to pay for improvements in the education service. New Labour made many promises for the future but were only prepared to make two costed proposals – a programme of retraining for unemployed youth financed by the windfall tax on public utilities, and an intention to reduce class sizes in primary schools, paid for by phasing out the assisted places scheme introduced by the Conservatives.

School standards remain a major issue, particularly standards of English, maths and science teaching, and all political parties seem to be in favour of more changes to the national curriculum – the provision of 'hit-squads' of remedial teachers who would be sent in to rescue failing schools; new training bodies for head teachers; and a Teaching Council which would act for the teaching profession in the same way as the British Medical Association acts for doctors, or the Law Society for lawyers.

One factor in the equation of education as a political issue is the status of teachers, who are accustomed to being vilified by the previous government and sections of the press. Several years of being blamed for most of the faults in educational standards have resulted in a teaching profession which has low morale and poor self-esteem. This is an important issue to be considered in any plans to improve standards in schools since this low morale is leading increasing numbers of experienced teachers to seek early retirement, while the profession is failing to attract new recruits. Plans for secondary education are severely hampered by a shortage of qualified teachers in secondary schools, a shortage that is becoming critical in subjects such as mathematics, science and foreign languages.

The last Conservative government seemed to tackle this problem merely with plans to sack those they considered to be incompetent teachers, and in the immediate post-election period the new Labour government seemed ready to follow that lead by confirming their full confidence in the appointment of Chris Woodhead as head of OFSTED, with his well-known views about failing teachers and the need to be able to sack them. No political party seemed ready to discuss the possibility of paying teachers more money.

As New Labour attempted to move away from the Conservative imperatives of opted-out maintained schools and increased grammar school selectivity, the question of funding and control of schools reasserted itself as an issue. Even before the election New Labour was easing its position on grant-maintained schools, the retention of those grammar schools which exist, and funding partnerships with private industry. The problem for New Labour is their wish to return education to the control of local authorities when the position of local councils has been weakened by a decade of Tory legislation and the incoming Labour governments pre-election pledge that councils would not be allowed to exceed spending programmes agreed by the outgoing Conservative government, even though most needed reforms require spending in excess of that already accounted for. In his first budget, Gordon Brown made £1 billion of extra spending available to schools from the contingency reserve in order to reduce class sizes and purchase resources, as well as £1.3 billion from the windfall tax for capital projects such as the refurbishment of old school property. Even so, two LEAs, Somerset and Oxfordshire, were warned by the Labour government to peg their spending on education to levels fixed by the Conservatives or be rate-capped.

All this activity in recent years ensures that government will continue to involve itself with educational reforms. This immediately produces a new issue which education has in common with the health service and other aspects of social provision. Education has been involved in revolutionary change for over ten years, until teachers are spending more time and effort in managing change than they are in actually teaching. The issue which remains to be tackled therefore is whether the education system needs more change, or whether they might not be better employed in merely consolidating what has already been done?

There does seem to be one area where Labour appears to have turned its back completely on its traditional commitment to free education. Since 1976 there has been a huge increase in students enrolling for university or college education, the number of students in higher education more than doubling to 1.6 million. Yet the government funding per student has been cut by more than 40 per cent in the same period of time and Sir Ron Dearing, in his report published in July 1997, found that another extra £2 billion at today's prices would have to be spent over the next 20 years, just to keep things as they are (*The Guardian*, 24 July 1997). In the light of this funding crisis Dearing had no option but to recommend that universities should charge tuition fees; sums in the region of £1000 a year being mentioned. The new Labour government accepted his proposals in principle and set about producing its own plan, subject to legislation in 1998, whereby tuition fees would be introduced and the old maintenance grants system abolished, to be replaced by a means-tested government maintenance loan which the student would repay once in employment and earning more than a certain sum, such as £10 000 a year. The means-testing would seek to ensure than poorer students did not suffer, but the acceptance of the proposals by a Labour government shows how far the Beveridge ideal of free universal provision has been sacrificed to the sanctity of market forces.

The National Health Service

Of all Beveridge's proposals, the creation of a national health service was possibly the most controversial but it was also the one which most caught the public's imagination and which thereby became the linchpin and focal point of the welfare state.

Prior to 1948 most medicine had to be paid for, except for the poorest members of society. There were a certain number of voluntary hospitals in which consultants worked without charge in a service that was paid for out of the consultant's fees in private practice. The problem was that if the hospital was located where there were insufficient private patients, then there was a shortage of consultants and operations had to be carried out by general practitioners. Other hospitals were municipal hospitals run by the local authority providing a free means-tested service. The municipal hospitals were often the successors to workhouse sick-wards, frequently housed in the old workhouse buildings and for that reason feared by those older patients who remembered the workhouse. For general medical purposes, 43 per cent of the population had a 'panel' doctor under national insurance, while children and the poor qualified for free (though means-tested) treatment. Many people wanting medical treatment had to attend the casualty departments of the voluntary hospitals.

Even without Beveridge, a national health service free to the user at the point of delivery was inevitable and the British Medical Association (BMA) had worked out most of the details between 1940 and 1942. When Aneurin Bevan came to introduce the NHS after 1945 he had very little difficulty with the organisation and administration of the service. The one major problem was a bitter argument with the doctors as to how far they should become paid employees of the state and to what extent they would be allowed to retain their private patients. Bevan was very keen to have the doctors on his side and to assure them that he did not want to turn them into civil servants. He had to pay a price for peace with the doctors by allowing general practitioners to retain private patients and by permitting consultants to have 'pay-beds' in NHS hospitals for their private practices.

Just as the retention of public schools prevented the 1944 Education Act from being a true reform of the system, so the retention of private medicine left the National Health Service flawed. For many years it would be a source of dissatisfaction that patients with the ability to pay might be able to obtain priority over those who were receiving free treatment. It was a Trojan horse within the NHS waiting for the market economy to emerge in the 1970s. This also contributed to a feeling of distrust created by the Conservatives who voted against the NHS on both the second and third reading in the House of Commons. From then on the Labour Party always rather suspected that the Tories were just waiting their chance to destroy and dismantle the NHS.

The Problem of Cost

There was a financial problem surrounding the NHS from its start. Just as the founders of the welfare state believed that social security would be paid for by full employment, so the founders of the NHS actually believed that the service would become cheaper as it cured ever greater numbers of people and, in effect, put itself out of business. It took 30 years for social security to discover that full employment was a mirage, it took the NHS less than 18 months to discover that their estimates were wildly inaccurate. As patients who had not sought treatment for many years, because of the cost, now flocked to doctors, dentists and hospitals, the NHS discovered by late 1949 that it could not afford the treatments demanded.

From that point on it became clear that the one big political issue that never goes away is the problem any government has in funding the NHS. As one prominent Health Minister put it, 'The unnerving discovery any Minister of Health makes, at or near the outset of his term of office, is that the only subject he is ever destined to discuss with the medical profession is money' (Enoch Powell, 1976, p. 14).

Before they left office in 1951 the Labour government had already had to sacrifice the principle of free health care by introducing charges for false teeth. As soon as they took office in 1951 the Conservatives were forced to take even more action to stem the spiralling costs of the NHS. One shilling (5p) prescription charges were introduced, as well as charges for dental treatment and spectacles.

There were many in the Conservative Party who claimed that NHS spending was out of control but an independent enquiry in 1955 showed that costs might be rising in absolute terms but, as a proportion of GNP, real costs were falling. By 1961, however, Enoch Powell had to double prescription charges and transfer many of the costs of the health service from taxation to national insurance contributions. The building of new hospitals was frozen temporarily and exploration began into ways of providing care in the community rather than in institutions. That was a lengthy process and indeed, as far as the mentally ill were concerned, for example, it was 1986 before care in the community finally became available.

The Labour government of 1964 tried to revert to the original principle of the NHS by abolishing prescription charges. But shortly afterwards the NHS was threatened by a virtual revolt on the part of general practitioners who were quitting the NHS at the rate of 600 or more each year in protest at the differentially favourable treatment given to hospital doctors and consultants. The GPs were bought off by a massive salary increase, improved fees for special services and large financial incentives to group practices. In 1968 this had to be paid for by the reintroduction of prescription charges and by requiring dental patients to bear half the cost of treatment. On the other hand, the settlement with the GPs was a pivotal moment in the development of the NHS. In the 1940s doctors had been the main opponents of Bevan's plans for a health service, but from the late 1960s onwards doctors became the most ardent and enthusiastic supporters of the NHS against government depredations.

The costs of the NHS, already substantial at its creation, have continued to rise inexorably. This has given rise to a major anomaly which clouds all discussion about the NHS. All governments, but particularly Conservative governments, have been accused of severely cutting health services, to the extent of coming near to dismantling the NHS. Governments have replied that far from starving the NHS of funds they have actually been increasing its funding in real terms, year after year. Since this is indubitably true statistically, it has been hard to reconcile the reality of increased funding with the public's perception of empty beds in the empty wards of hospitals that have been closed down, and which has created in turn the picture of a service in permanent crisis.

Which is to overlook the most important point affecting the issue of a National Health Service. In comparison to the original idea that the NHS would become cheaper as it improved the health of the nation, the truth has proved to be the exact reverse. The more successful the NHS is in preserving life and in perfecting new medical techniques, the more expensive it is, with costs rising well beyond the rate of inflation:

- Over 90 per cent of all drugs in use by the 1990s were unknown 50 years ago. The more advanced and sophisticated the drug, the greater the research cost and the greater the cost in absolute terms.
- Many thousands of people who would have died before they reached retirement are now living to an advanced old age. The cost of geriatric care and the cost of drugs required to sustain that life are a continuous and increasing drain on health service funds.
- New medical and surgical techniques such as transplant surgery are great advances in medicine and a triumph of the health service, but they are very expensive to develop and provide.

It is estimated that the NHS budget needs to increase by at least 3 per cent a year merely to cover the cost of caring for the old, together with the cost of technological advances. As against that 3 per cent, recent estimates of government spending on the NHS show that the Labour government of 1974–9 increased health spending by 2.2 per cent a year, while the Conservatives between 1979 and 1990 increased their spending by the not dissimilar figure of 2.1 per cent each year (Moran, 1995, p. 176). It can therefore be seen that although successive governments have poured steadily increasing funds into the NHS, there has always been a small but significant shortfall in comparison with the sort of sums that are needed merely to maintain the NHS at a constant level of provision.

When Keith Joseph was Health Secretary in the Heath government of 1970–4 he began to explore ways to save the NHS money and to investigate alternative sources of funding. What were known as 'hotel charges' of as much as £15 a bed were talked of for NHS hospitals where only the treatment would be free. There was also talk of making it compulsory for everyone to have private health insurance in the same way that car drivers are required to insure themselves, transferring the costs of providing a health service to an insurance-funded private sector. The idea was not pursued because of the exemptions that would have to be granted to the young, old and the poor. The financial contributions made by those few eligible to pay would be insignificant. Yet the idea persisted and it was interesting to see something similar proposed in 1997, although it was ironic to find a Labour minister making the suggestion.

For a time it was hoped that the organisation of the NHS into regional, district and family health authorities, which followed the reorganisation of local government in 1973, might help with the overall cost of the NHS by a rationalisation into a unified and integrated service. Unfortunately the most significant change brought about by reorganisation was a 30 per cent rise in administrative and clerical staff.

Towards Market Forces in Health

The aim of the Conservative government elected in 1979, and its successors, was to transform the NHS through a mixture of competition, privatisation and the introduction of market forces. Like many changes introduced by the Thatcher administrations the serious movement in this direction only began in 1987. By that time the NHS was, technically speaking, bankrupt. Many health authorities did not have sufficient money to last them a full financial year unless they closed hospitals, or parts of hospitals, between January and April. In some cases, with a total of 4000 hospital beds closed, this meant that even emergency wards and intensive care units were closed.

The answer was the creation of an internal health market. General practitioners were made fundholders and given a budget out of which they could purchase services from hospitals; any balance remaining being available for spending within the practice. Hospitals were encouraged to become self-governing as NHS trust hospitals, the equivalent of opted-out schools. Elected representatives were removed from health authorities and replaced by appointed quangos so that local health authorities became purchasers of care services rather than providers. The changes were resisted by the

BMA representing most doctors, but they were imposed by Kenneth Clarke as Minister of Health.

Under Margaret Thatcher and John Major prescription charges rose from 20p in 1979 to £5.65 by 1997, an increase more than 40 times the rate of inflation, although 80 per cent of prescriptions were free to children of school age, pensioners and those receiving social security. The responsibility for looking after the old in residential care was shifted from the geriatric units of hospitals into the community as represented by private residential homes, funded for the most part by the social security rather than the health budget. These private places were also means-tested and there was considerable resentment that old people who had carefully saved for a secure old age were now refused assistance because of their savings, while others had to sell the homes they had hoped to pass on to their children in order to pay for their own care. All this means-tested discrimination served to alienate the middle classes in whose name the reform of the NHS was being carried out, and meant that a contraction in tax-funded health care was taking place at a time when support for such a health service, among the middle classes in particular, was growing rather than decreasing (Taylor-Gooby, 1991).

Such alienation from the so-called 'care in the community' programme was boosted by several well-publicised instances of mental care patients, schizophrenics, who were released into the community without adequate supervision and who committed particularly horrific murders because they had failed to take medication. There was a suspicion at large that the community was being put at risk and mental patients were being abandoned, all for the sake of saving a minimal amount of money.

The fears of many were that the market reforms in the NHS would lead either to the privatisation of the NHS or the formation of a two-tier service, with those patients registered with a fundholding GP receiving preferential, fast-tracked treatment in comparison with the rest. As Timmins has said, the NHS reforms 'might make future privatisation easier but none of them need automatically produce that result' (Timmins, 1995, p. 478). As the reforms continued and even Labour recognised that some changes were irreversible, the most logical outcome seemed to be that the NHS would become a publicly-funded but privately-provided service.

One aspect of this new attitude towards provision of health care began to emerge in the 1990s with talk of rationing, or 'priority setting' as the Tory government preferred to call it. Under this process local health authorities drew up lists of medical conditions for which they would not provide unlimited treatment, and fund-holding doctors had to decide in terms of priorities whether some treatments did not take too great a share from their budgets. Some rationed treatments were for non-critical operations such as those on varicose veins or wisdom teeth, others concerned screenings or other preventative measures; but the most controversial have been those which involve life or death decisions. In the summer of 1995 there was a public furore over the decision by a local health authority not to fund any further treatment for a child terminally ill with cancer. The case opened up a major issue for the new budget-conscious NHS in posing the question as to whether doctors should strive to keep alive the very old or the terminally ill if the cost of doing so seems excessive to the budget-holders.

The Labour Party was always considered as the defender of the National Health Service which a Labour government had created. Through all the 18 years of opposition after 1979 the Labour Party represented itself as the champion of the NHS against what it claimed were the Conservative government's plans to privatise the health service, even including clinical care. Yet, examination of the 1997 manifesto and the limited statements about health included in the first Queen's Speech of the new government, showed that New Labour's approach was not so different from that of the Tories, and indeed could not be, given that Labour was committed to remaining within Tory spending plans. After their election the issues on health were very much the same for New Labour as they had been under the Conservatives. This tended to cause consternation among the followers of Old Labour for whom any dilution of the universal health service was a betrayal of basic principles. Hence the upset when Frank Dobson, the Secretary of State for Health, announced that every possible alternative scheme for funding had to be considered, even consideration of paying for doctors' visits, 'hotel charges' for patients in hospital, or transferring some costs to private insurance.

A report by the King's Fund, an independent health think tank, commissioned by *The Guardian* and published in that newspaper on 18 April 1997, concluded that it was probably impossible for the NHS to continue in its existing form and that for reform to take place it would be necessary to redefine the clinical function of the NHS, disposing of all the non life-threatening or peripheral services that have become part of NHS provision but which are arguably not necessary for the better health of the nation:

> Is it the job of the NHS to provide fertility treatment, physiother-apy for sports injuries, long-term nursing care, gender re-assign-ment, adult dentistry and cosmetic surgery? Or should these services be provided by local authorities, voluntary agencies or commercially by the private sector? The question does not rely on clinical judgment. It is an issue about the boundary of a public institution's responsibilities.

It was made abundantly clear in the aftermath of the 1997 election that, for all Labour's continuing commitment to the National Health Service, New Labour would remain critical of too great an increase in public spending. The days of universal free provision are probably over in health, as they are in education, but Labour will seek to retain its reputation for compassion as was witnessed in Gordon Browns first budget when, despite renewing his commit-ment to the spending limits of the Major government, he still found £1.2 billion in the contingency reserves to be spent on reducing hospital waiting lists.

Housing

Of all the areas covered by the Beveridge Report it was housing which represented the greatest and most immediate problem when the time came in 1945 to implement the Report. During the war a quarter of all British housing stock had either been damaged or had deteriorated through the effects of the war, with half a million houses either destroyed or made uninhabitable. There was also a shortage of building materials and most building workers were in the forces. Not only had no new houses been built for more than five years, but no repairs had been carried out on prewar housing. Add to these problems the massive number of wartime marriages and a rapidly rising birth rate, and it is understandable that Michael Foot could say that 'the housing problem caused more anguish and frustration than any other of the nation's manifold problems' (Michael Foot, 1973, p. 62).

During the 1950s and 1960s massive house-building projects were promoted and completed, leading to a general availability of council or 'social' housing for the postwar generations. There were controversies over the cost of council housing and building standards, and of course a long dispute over the merits and demerits of high-rise accommodation. These boom years brought about another social revolution in the housing market as increasing numbers of people were able to buy their own homes. The ratio of home-owners to house-renters changed, until owner-occupiers became the majority and a shrinking proportion of the population continued to rent. Public attitudes to council housing changed as the need for cheap social housing shrank to concern only the poorest sections of society. The great social revolution of the 1950s and 1960s was the creation of what the Conservatives called a property-owning democracy.

The Thatcher Years

A major change in the issue of social housing came after Mrs Thatcher took power in 1979. With her joint aims of reducing local government influence and spreading even wider the idea of a property-owning democracy, the Thatcher administration began the sale of council houses, at first voluntarily and then by obliging councils to sell houses to anyone who wanted to buy. It was a very popular policy and 500 000 houses had been sold by 1983, while sales had topped 1.5 million by 1990. The policy did, however, produce a long list of problems:

- The houses sold were all the better quality council houses, in good repair. Those left in council hands for renting were the houses no one really wanted so that the less-advantaged members of society were forced into deteriorating housing: a new version of the poverty trap.
- Since councils were not allowed to spend the money they had gained from council house sales, any new building of council property declined until there were virtually no council houses at all being built in the 1990s. New council house starts fell from 65 300 in 1979 to 2600 in 1992 (McKie, 1994, p. 117). Without their own houses, councils found it very difficult to meet their statutory requirements to house the homeless, having to use private housing associations or bed-and-breakfast accommodation; both of the solutions, ironically, being more expensive than actually building houses. According to a National Audit Office

report of 1991 the cost of providing bed-and-breakfast accommodation in an inner-city hotel would pay for two new houses to
be built.

- In a process that transferred housing costs to the social security
budget, state aid for tenants was switched from housing subsidies
paid to councils to housing benefit paid to individuals. Unfortunately, housing benefit provides a poor return on all but the
cheapest housing and this is another factor in the creation of 'sink
estates.

- In 1987 the government set up Housing Action Trusts which
would take over rundown council housing, renovate it and then
transfer ownership to anyone other than the council from which it
had been acquired. This meant that many council tenants were
transferred to private landlords, with a subsequent rise in rents.

- The voluntary housing associations which took over from the
councils as the main providers of social housing were welcomed at
first by government, and were well-endowed with government
money in the same way as the government welcomed hospital
trusts and opted-out schools. When Kenneth Clarke became
Chancellor, however, the government proceeded to reduce the
money given to housing associations despite the fact that they had
become the main agent of government housing policy.

Homelessness

The problem of homelessness has become the major housing issue in
the 1990s. At the time of the 1992 election the number of households
who were officially listed as homeless was said to be 143 000. But
this did not include the swelling numbers of the single and young
homeless living on the streets of Britain's cities, created by the
withdrawal of many social security benefits in the 1980s. The
Conservatives withdrew relief when they believed that people had
deliberately engineered their own eligibility for council housing; as
with unmarried girls who, it was claimed, deliberately got pregnant
to get a home.

A major factor in the growth of homelessness has been the slump
in the home ownership market during the recession of the late 1980s
and the consequent rise in the number of repossessions of homes
from people who have found themselves unable to keep up mortgage
repayments. Particularly badly hit were those who had bought their

council house at the height of the council-house sale boom, tempted by the generous discounts and favourable mortgages offered as inducements by government at the time, but who were no longer able to maintain their mortgage payments.

There is now a desperate shortage of affordable rented accommodation, which currently represents less than 8 per cent of the housing stock. Large numbers of the homeless who left home because of marital or family conflict are not entitled to housing benefit and therefore cannot afford even the poorest of council housing, while they certainly cannot afford property owned by the housing associations now that the government has cut their funding. Even the statutory requirement of local authorities to provide accommodation for the homeless was affected by the action of Sir George Young as housing minister when he tightened the rules defining homelessness to exclude anyone who left their homes voluntarily, were evicted by family or friends, or had any form of temporary housing available however unsatisfactory.

Despite its importance in 1945, an importance that has not diminished since then, it is striking how little attention is paid to housing which is seldom an election issue as health or education are, and which seems to be an area largely ignored by the political parties. Even in their 1997 manifesto promises for the homeless, New Labour had little to say on the subject except to promise that funds from the sale of council houses, to the tune of about £5 billion, would be released to pay for the building of new council accommodation aided by a relaxation in the rules governing council borrowing.

Summary

In the social field just as much as in the economic there has been a total change of attitude in recent years that has created a new consensus over social provision, as a radical move away from free and universal provision by the state to one that relates more to a selective, safety-net form of provision. The welfare state as it was initiated in the aftermath of Beveridge may not be dead but it has certainly changed. And the policy reviews instituted by the Blair government have set about the creation of a New Welfare State to go with New Labour. And the most important innovation will be the way in which that welfare programme will be funded.

7

Law and Order

In the distant past, when government was little more than a meeting of tribal elders, the maintenance of law and order was not only a major concern of government, it was the only concern of government and its reason for existing. It therefore cannot be surprising that it has been seen as important throughout history that a government should make good laws, should preserve order and should do so in ways which satisfied the people's sense of justice and guaranteed their security.

Perceptions of law and order are divided between two basic views of humankind:

- Those who believe that humankind is naturally selfish and inclined to be violent or disruptive in the pursuit of self-interest. Viewed from this perspective, society can only be held together by a strong law enforcement arm with the ability to control firmly all anti-social tendencies among members of that society. This perspective also sees the judicial and penal systems as having a duty to be firm and harsh in order to punish offenders suitably and, through example, to deter others from offending.
- Those who believe that humankind is naturally law-abiding and cooperative but is led astray, or even forced, into criminality by adverse social conditions. Viewed from this perspective the important element in law and order is the prevention of a crime before it can be committed. According to these values, the purpose of the judicial and penal systems should be to reform and rehabilitate the criminal rather than to punish.

These two perspectives have led to two different ideological stances on the issue of law and order.

1. A belief that there is the equivalent of a war against crime. Rising crime figures can be countered only by a stronger police presence, a more severe sentencing policy in the courts and a harsher regime of custodial prison sentences. This is the view traditionally adopted by large sections of the Conservative Party who believe that 'crime is the result of inborn psychological factors such as envy, greed, malice and hatred' (Coxall and Robins, 1995, p.453). Margaret Thatcher most famously refused to believe that social factors caused crime when she declared, during an interview with *Womans Own* magazine on 11 October 1987, that 'There is no such thing as Society. There are individual men and women, and there are families'. The view of the Thatcher government was that any criminal act was the purely selfish act of an individual and any failure of control lay in the failure or rejection of family values.

2. A belief that crime is the product of social factors like poverty, unemployment, bad housing and racist attitudes. This is an ideology which looks to social policies to remedy these evils and to remove the causes of crime. This viewpoint sees the penal system as being primarily for the rehabilitation of the criminal and, in that light, punishment should be non-custodial as far as possible. This is the view traditionally espoused by parties of the left and centre-left such as New Labour or the Liberal Democrats. There have also been 'one-nation' Conservatives who felt like this. Douglas Hurd when he was Home Secretary in 1991 had said that 'prison is an expensive way of making bad people worse'. It was making statements like that which made it inevitable that liberal-minded home secretaries would receive a hostile reception from the reactionaries of the Conservative party conference. To the right wing of the Conservative Party it was this 'soft on crime' attitude, which Mrs Thatcher and others claimed arose from the 'permissive society' of the 1960s when Labour was in power, that was mainly responsible for the alarming rise in crime statistics during the 1970s.

Fear of Crime

A perception that crime is increasing rapidly and is out of the control of those in authority, together with an amplification of that perception through the more alarmist crime stories printed by the tabloid press, has led to an atmosphere of fear among large sections of the population. The 1996 *British Crime Survey* showed that one in 10 women and one in 20 men never go out of the house after dark, while 47 per cent of women feel unsafe alone on the streets at night. Despite government statistics showing that crime decreased between 1993 and 1995, the BCS showed that only 4 per cent of the public actually believed that the figures really were decreasing. Ironically, the official crime statistics published by the Home Office on the same day as the BCS showed that reported crime figures for 1995–6 had risen by 0.4 per cent, an insignificant rise in itself but bringing an abrupt end to the steady reduction of the previous three years. More serious than that minor reversal in the overall figures was the fact that violent crime had increased by 10 per cent year-on-year, and it is obviously violent crime which inspires most fear among the public.

Another disturbing factor leading to public unease about crime, as revealed by the BCS, was that there is an increasing number of crimes that do not appear in the police figures. According to the *Survey*, four times more crimes are committed than are reported to the police, either because the public do not think the crimes worth reporting or because they feel that it is not worth the bother because the police cannot do anything about it. The *British Crime Survey* is published biennially and is considered more accurate than official police statistics because it is based on 16 000 direct interviews with members of the public.

Because of this fear and unease, the general public tend to favour the political party which proposes strong measures against the criminal. This populist feeling has always been reflected in the rank and file of the Conservative Party: the party conference being known for years as the arena within which calls were made for the return of capital and corporal punishment and where liberally-minded home secretaries like William Whitelaw have always been given a rough ride by the body of the conference. Ever a populist in her thinking, and supported by such populist voices in the press as the *Sun* and *Daily Mail*, Margaret Thatcher always advocated a tough line on law and order, private members' bills to reintroduce hanging being presented to the Commons on several occasions during her premiership.

Traditionally, therefore, law and order is an issue that has favoured the Conservative Party in electoral terms; Labour having been weighed and found wanting by the electorate through their being 'far too soft' on the criminal. In the past, whenever opinion polls have asked voters which party they thought was best equipped to deal with the issue of law and order, those questioned almost invariably chose the Conservatives. In 1994, however, the mood changed quite spectacularly and increasingly opinion polls began to show a regular lead for Labour over the Conservatives on the issue.

This change came about largely as a result of the way recorded crime statistics had shown a steady increase over those years since 1979 that the Conservatives had been in office. In a written answer given by the Home Office to Douglas French, Tory MP for Gloucester, on 7 May 1993 (McKie, 1993, p. 156) the comparative figures were shown as being:

- 4833 crimes reported for every 100 000 people in the population in 1979; and
- 10 614 crimes reported for every 100 000 people in the population in 1992.

This means that 2.2 times the number of crimes were reported in 1992 as had been reported 13 years previously and represents an increase of 127 per cent. An even more ominous indicator was that over the same period clear-up rates (the percentage of crimes solved) fell from 41 per cent to 26 per cent. According to one political commentator in 1994, these statistics,

> reflected the failure of a Conservative government to deliver on its promises after 15 years in office. They had promised rough action and a fall in the crime rate: yet crime had grown faster than ever and was spreading now from familiar urban locations to rural Britain. (McKie, 1994, p. 139)

In the final period of the Tory government Michael Howard made great play with statistics showing a steady decrease in official crime statistics after 1993, claiming that he was responsible for the greatest reduction in crime figures in history. This was later strikingly put into context by a report, *Criminal Victimisation in Eleven Industrialised Countries*, prepared for the EU conference of 14 May 1997 held at Noordwijk in the Netherlands, which showed that the reduction in official figures for recorded crime between 1993 and 1996 merely stabilised the figures after unprecedented rises in the period 1988 to 1993.

This survey showed that, while crime figures for England and Wales did show a drop between 1993 and 1996, that drop was only in line with similar reductions in all the other ten countries studied. Between 1979 and 1991 crime in England and Wales had more than doubled so that, of the 11 countries studied, including the United States, Canada and France, people in England and Wales were most at risk of being the victims of crime, particularly burglary or car crime. The risk of suffering 'contact' crime – robbery, assault or sexual attack – is at least as great in England and Wales as it is in the United States. England and Wales also came out on top of the tables when people were asked if they had been victims of crime in the previous 12 months – England and Wales (31 per cent), Netherlands (31 per cent), Scotland (26 per cent), USA (24 per cent), Austria (19 per cent) and Northern Ireland (17 per cent).

As early as 1995, disillusioned by the Conservatives' failures, the electorate turned to see what the Labour Party might propose. And here Tony Blair, shadow home secretary under John Smith's leadership, managed to sustain a delicate balancing act over Labour's law and order policies, maintaining Labour's belief in social justice while not appearing to be soft on the criminals. Labour's policy, said Blair, would be 'Tough on crime and tough on the causes of crime.' It was one of those defining terms that catch the public imagination and which enabled the public to believe that Labour might have an answer to rising crime statistics where the Conservatives had manifestly failed. It was also a phrase that did Blair's reputation as an effective politician no harm when it came to the Labour leadership election of 21 July 1994.

When Jack Straw replaced Tony Blair as shadow home secretary he continued with the populist approach to law and order. In one infamous speech he attacked the aggressive beggars on London streets, categorising them as 'winos, addicts and squeegee merchants', whose behaviour intimidated the elderly in particular and contributed to the general fear of crime on the part of the public. For critics on the left of the Labour Party Jack Straw came to represent a typical example of the New Labour desire not to rock the boat in his careful avoidance of public utterances that might make Labour look any less tough on crime than the Tory Party. By 1997 Jack Straw, not without reason, was being lampooned as a Michael Howard clone. Interviewed shortly after the 1997 election he himself was philosophical about this, claiming that in the face of reality home secretaries cannot afford to be too liberal in their policies, whatever their personal inclination:

> I don't adorn my approach to these matters with the adjective 'liberal', but I certainly hope to adorn it with the adjective 'effective'. Some of my critics are trapped in a past that doesn't take account of today's realities. (*New Statesman*, 23 May 1997, p. 16)

When Howard tried to use his 1996 Police Bill to deregulate the guidelines on the use of phone taps and electronic surveillance, removing the need for a judges approval, Straw supported Howard and Labour abstained on that part of the bill. It was only a rearguard action by the Liberal Democrats, backed by members of the judiciary, that defeated the measure in the Lords. It was especially their approach to law and order that led critics of New Labour to claim that they could see no substantive difference between the manifesto promises made by New Labour and the policies of the Major government.

'Prison Works'

The Conservative answer to the problems of law and order has always been to show themselves as more determined than anyone else to crack down hard on the criminals. Yet despite their efforts in this direction the situation in 1993 was that they had failed on three major points:

1. A two and a half fold rise in crime since 1979, the biggest increase in recent history.
2. Prisons with an overflowing population of more than 52 000 – one of the largest prison populations in Europe.
3. Increasing numbers of suicides, attempted escapes and disturbances in prisons. (Puddephatt, 1995, pp. 59–62)

Their answer to the growing reputation of the Labour Party in this field was the Criminal Justice Bill, introduced in December 1993, which promised no fewer than 27 'get tough' measures, including:

- removal of the right to silence;
- six new prisons to be built (to be privately run);
- doubling maximum sentences for young offenders;
- heavy restrictions on granting bail;
- powers to act against 'new age' travellers, those holding 'rave' parties and those protesting over animal rights; and
- new powers allowing the police to stop and search anyone they think fit.

Other measures introduced by Michael Howard as Home Secretary included,

- changes in the caution given by police to suspects;
- granting the right for police to be armed (including the carrying of guns);
- automatic life sentences for certain crimes such as rape; and
- a reduction in the amount of money available to compensate the victims of crime.

The Home Secretary's plans were very popular with the Conservative Party Conference and his 27 tough measures were greeted by tumultuous applause, as any advocacy of a hard policy has always received at these conferences, and made Michael Howard into that rarest of creatures – the Conservative Home Secretary who is popular with the rank and file of the party. Away from party enthusiasts, however, the reception of his measures was rather less than rapturous.

- Civil rights groups disliked changes to the 'right to silence', a move seen as removing a basic human right: a right which is, after all, enshrined in the American constitution and other Bills of Rights elsewhere in the democratic world.
- Civil rights groups also disliked the measures taken against new age travellers, rave parties and protest groups. These were seen as attempts to criminalise events simply because they might possibly cause disruption.
- Judges and magistrates did not like to see the right to fix sentences taken away from them. The insistence of the Home Secretary that those found guilty of murder or rape should receive mandatory life sentences, and that all custodial sentences should be made more severe, reduced the freedom judges have always had in

allowing for extenuating circumstances or for help given to the police in fixing the length and nature of the sentence. The judiciary were also concerned at what they saw as even more pressure being placed on an already overcrowded prison system.
- The police were not happy at being given extra work without any real increase in numbers. They were also subjected to new guidelines they did not like and required to carry weapons when the majority of police officers did not want to be armed.

In 1996 Howard stepped up the pressure with policies on sentencing that would produce mandatory minimum sentences and automatic life sentences for repeat offenders. All his many critics, including the Lord Chief Justice, Lord Taylor, who called Howard's plans 'a denial of justice', united in telling the Home Secretary that it is not severe sentences that will deter criminals but the risk of being caught. The concentration should be on helping the police with clear-up rates. Lord Woolf, who had investigated the riots at Strangeways and who questioned the effectiveness of custodial sentences as a result, described the new policies of the Home Secretary as 'short sighted and irresponsible' (*The Observer*, 29 May 1994). In the same newspaper article he was backed up by seven senior judges, all of whom told the Home Secretary that prison sentences were not the cure for rising crime.

Nevertheless, the Conservative government, with Michael Howard as Home Secretary, continued to place its faith in prison as a deterrent. By September 1996 the estimated prison population had risen to 57 000, despite cuts in government spending which required a reduction of 13 per cent in the money available to the prison service. Measures introduced to meet the situation included not only an expanded prison-building programme, but such stopgap measures as hiring a prison-ship from the United States. Official estimates in 1997 predicted a prison population of 74 500 by the year 2005.

The combination of rising crime figures and a universal condemnation of government policy by influential figures has helped alter the electorate's perception of New Labour's policies on law and order. In line with Labour's longstanding belief that increased crime is closely related to social conditions such as unemployment, poverty, bad housing and poor education, New Labour's approach has been to argue that the problems of law and order cannot be solved just by harsher penalties intended merely to punish and deter. Alongside a tough policy in the courts there should be:

- Increased police presence on the beat and in the community to prevent crime happening in the first place.
- A social policy to such problems as poverty and badly planned housing estates which contribute to the extent of criminal activity.

It is measures like this that Tony Blair meant by 'being tough on the causes of crime'. There was a time when the electorate would have felt that such a policy was impossibly weak, but by reiterating that Labour would be tough on crime as well as tough on the causes Blair managed to weaken the 'soft and flabby' image of Labour policy. Since the Conservatives had been seen to fail singularly to curb the rise in crime and had been reprimanded by prominent members of the police and judiciary, the electorate seemed more ready to try an alternative approach to the issue.

New Labour strategies on law and order tended to concentrate on youth crime. This was partly because official statistics seemed to suggest very strongly that high crime rates are concentrated within the 14–25 age group. The Audit Commission report of November 1996 estimated that the under-18s are responsible for 28 million offences a year, while one-fifth of the prison population (including remand prisoners) is in the 15–20 age group. The main reason for concentrating on the young offender, however, is the nature of the crimes committed by the young, particularly young men and teenage boys. They are associated with mugging, anti-social public behaviour, vandalism and criminal damage, car crime, racially-motivated violence and drink-related crime – all of which are particularly disturbing to other people, especially the elderly, and contribute to a general fear of crime and the possibility of becoming a victim of crime.

The outgoing Conservative government had responded to youth crime by various repressive initiatives, including the possibility of electronic tagging and the New York practice of 'zero tolerance' towards petty crime. New Labour, and particularly Jack Straw as shadow home secretary, conceded the attractions of zero tolerance for a party wanting to appear to be 'tough on crime'. However, there was also a recognition that zero tolerance is essentially short-term with immediate effects being felt, but that in the long term more attention needs to be paid to judicial procedures rather than policing methods. As home secretary, Straw stressed the streamlining of judicial procedures to create a fast track for dealing with teenage offenders, thereby reducing the time lapse between offending and punishment; other early proposals were for a review of the working methods of the Crown Prosecution Service, a reduction of the age of criminal responsibility from 14 to 10, for parents to be made more accountable for their children's actions, and, as far as possible, for custodial sentences where young offenders learn about crime through association to be replaced by alternatives such as reparation orders under which the young offender must work to pay back the debt to the crime victim.

An issue of increasing importance in the field of law and order is the extent to which the community itself can become involved in coping with crime. Encouraged by the success of many neighbour-hood watch schemes, reformers are looking to neighbourhood partnerships against crime in which members of the local commu-nity work with and alongside the police, probation service, local government, social services, housing associations and so on. This may well be the path chosen in future to combat those forms of crime that can be seen as anti-social and hostile to the community.

For all that, the slogan repeatedly used by Michael Howard – 'Prison works' – proved harder to shake off than would have seemed likely under the terms of reference set by New Labour. Only ten days after the election Straw was forced to concede that the prison population was growing faster than could be catered for by the money made available for prison-building under government spend-ing plans. The Labour government conceded the continuing need for prisons to be built and run by private security firms, despite the many criticisms they had levelled at the practice while in opposition. A week later, on 19 May 1997, Jack Straw had to concede another point which he had disputed with Michael Howard. He confirmed that the new government would accept and apply Tory legislation on mandatory sentencing. Before the end of July the Home Secre-tary's ability to impose a sentencing tariff was confirmed through the clarification that in the case of two prominent women prisoners, Myra Hindley and Rosemary West, life would mean life.

The Police

There is an ideological divide concerning the role of the police. Despite the democratic position, stated by Sir Robert Mark, former Commissioner of the Metropolitan Police, that the police are neutral guardians of social order who 'act on behalf of the people as a whole' (Jones, 1994, p. 516), the fact is that the police have traditionally been seen as upholders of middle-class values such as the right to own property. In that respect they have always been seen as the civil arm of the political establishment, to be used in maintaining the status quo. Therefore, by inference, the functions and values of the police are inimical to those radical groups who wish to change society. The police have always been supported by the right wing in politics. But, beyond the actual right wing the police have always found favour within the consensual model of British politics, the naturally conservative British middle classes and respectable working class clinging to the friendly stereotype of the helpful 'bobby on the beat', typified and ultimately parodied by television series like *Dixon of Dock Green*.

In contrast, the left-wing in politics has always been suspicious of the police, whom they regard as tools of the property-owning classes. Police officers have been stigmatised, backed by a certain body of evidence, as being sexist, racist, venial and guilty of loutish behaviour. This jaundiced view of the police has seemed to become more widespread in society in recent years, partly because of the decline of social deference but largely because of some major developments of the 1980s:

- The riots in Brixton, Toxteth and elsewhere during the early 1980s, which showed the extent to which relations had broken down between the police and the black community.
- The use of the police as an instrument of social control to suppress protests and strikes, most notably their use during the Miners' strike of 1984–5.
- Repeated examples of malpractice in the police handling of evidence and the interrogation of suspects which led to some sensational reversals of judgments and sentences in criminal cases.
- Many accusations of corruption among police forces, particularly in the Metropolitan Police.

In the agenda led by the left, the real issues concerning the police are:

- Who is in charge of the police and how far might the police be subjected to democratic control?
- In the light of revelations about the extent of police malpractice, who investigates complaints against the police?

Control

Back in the nineteenth century the public was afraid of a national police force controlled by the government, such as the gendarmeries of so many European countries, since it was thought that it might be used by an authoritarian government to suppress the people. For that reason the only police force that is directly controlled by the Home Secretary is the Metropolitan Police in London. Elsewhere in the country, until very recently, the police have been largely funded and run by local government through what was once called the Watch Committee and is now usually known as the Police Committee or Police Authority.

Many critics have always believed that there are those who would like to see the police having a greater control over society. During the Miners' strike of 1984–5 these critics pointed to the cooperation which developed between various police forces and a national incident room set up to deal with information fed through a centralised computer system. Civil liberties groups claimed that this was intended to be the beginning of a national police force with secret records of all British citizens, and these groups re-emphasised the need for control of the police to be retained at local level.

Under the dispensation existing until 1994, the Police Authority has been responsible for all policy decisions related to the policing of their area, while the Chief Constable and his or her officers retained the responsibility for all police operational matters. This meant, however, that police authorities were always complaining about Chief Constables who made policy decisions without consulting their democratically-elected authorities, while at the same time Chief Constables were complaining about police authority politicians who interfered in operational matters without knowing anything about how the police work.

This control of the police by politicians in local government has led to regular conflict because of the division of responsibilities between policy and operational decisions. There is a basic paradox in the reasons behind the way these responsibilities are divided. The reason given for this division of functions was that the inability of the police authorities to control operational matters prevented the police from coming under the control of corrupt councillors or local government officials. In other words, the police were removed from democratic control in order to preserve democracy!

In 1993 a Home Office report into greater police efficiency recommended that:

- there should be fewer police authorities;
- that the heads of those authorities should be appointed by the Home Secretary; and that
- police matters would be removed from local government control.

There were protests at what were seen as further moves towards the centralisation of the police but the reform was part of the continuing process by which central government was reducing and replacing the roles and functions of local government. In the Police and Magistrates Courts Act (PMCA) of 1994 it was proposed that police authorities should become free-standing corporate bodies which would still be largely staffed by local councillors but where the chief constable would have a stronger managerial position. The PMCA also gave new and important powers to the Home Secretary who 'would be empowered to set the broad strategic framework for policing, including key national policing objectives, and to appoint a significant number of members (including the chairpersons) of the new police authorities' (Cope, Starie and Leishman, 1996, pp. 19–22).

Other powers given to the Home Secretary by the PMCA include the ability to demand the merger of police forces, to call for performance reports from police authorities and to cap their expenditure, not to mention the greater powers of patronage in the appointment of police authority members. These changes are all part of the ideological shift that has taken place in the 1980s with the marginalisation of local government and the introduction of market forces. The police have not proved immune to the growth of privatisation and there are proposals for measures that could be regarded as such, including:

- Hiving off, or load-shedding, by which certain duties such as policing special events or some traffic work might be ceded to commercial providers like private security firms.
- Contracting out certain police functions through competitive tendering. Already private firms like Group 4 have bid for and taken over prisoner escort duties. Other similar tasks, such as escorting heavy loads on motorways, are in line for private provision.

- Charging for police services. This has always been possible, as with private functions which hire a police presence for security or organisation. But the money-making potential may well be expanded further.

Malpractice and Complaints Procedure

A major issue is the problem of complaints against the police and allegations of wrong or corrupt practices. There have been many examples of bad practice in recent years, from widespread corruption in the Metropolitan Police to allegations of rigged and faulty evidence made against the West Midlands Crime Squad. However, the policy is that complaints against the police are investigated by the police themselves. This leads to suspicion in the minds of the public as to how far the reports of enquiries into the police can be trusted and how far there have been cover-ups to shield the guilty.

The demand is for an independent investigator, like the Ombudsman, who can look at all accusations against the police without being biased in any way. After the Brixton riots of 1981 the Scarman Report stated that one of the critical factors in the breakdown of trust between the police and an urban and largely black community like Brixton was the absence of an independent complaints procedure. Partly as a result of the Scarman Report the Police and Criminal Evidence Act of 1984 replaced the Police Complaints Board with the Police Complaints Authority (PCA) on which an independent observer would have a watching brief over police investigators in the case of a serious complaint.

It is very doubtful that the PCA in itself will do much to alleviate the public's suspicions of the police's ability to 'look after their own' and to cover up any potentially embarrassing matters. In the PCA Annual Report of 1987 it was stated that the authority had received 15 865 complaints during 1986 but no disciplinary action was taken in 12 505 of those cases. Charges against police officers were only brought in 48 instances (Kingdom, 1991, p. 558). In July 1997 the Director of Public Prosecutions (DPP), Dame Barbara Mills, had to admit that her office was guilty of failing to prosecute police officers involved in the deaths of men in police custody. As a result of her admission the DPP lost the right to a final say as to whether police or prison staff should be prosecuted over deaths in custody.

Reforming the Police – the Sheehy Report

If the political left has always been critical of the police, the right has always appeared to be supportive. This certainly seemed to be true of the Thatcher administration after the election victory of 1979. While other areas of public spending were starved of funds and facing steady cuts in their budgets the police had money lavished upon them. Between 1979 and 1993 spending on the police rose by 88 per cent (representing £5.4 billion each year) while police pay had risen by 70 per cent in real terms (Jones, 1994, p. 518).

Towards the end of the 1980s the right had suffered a change of heart. The whole thrust of the market forces economy advocated by the Conservative government was that enterprises, whether public or private, should give value for money. And it was manifestly obvious that the police were not giving value for money. The crime figures for 1993 have already been given in this chapter and it can be seen that this lavish provision of money for the police produced a two and a half fold increase in crimes reported and a 15 per cent reduction in the clear-up rate. Even the most vocal of the grassroots supporters at party conference were demanding that the police should be called to account for their failure in the marketplace.

The result was the Inquiry into Police Responsibilities and Rewards (known as the Sheehy Inquiry), set up in May 1992 under the leadership of a prominent businessman. The intention of the committee of inquiry was to look critically at the pay and career structure of the police service in terms of greater efficiency. When the Sheehy Report was published a year later, in June 1993, it found that the structure of the force was top-heavy with too many officers of senior rank; a fact which increased the management pay bill of the police by 60 per cent. The committee also found that promotion was largely determined on length of service rather than ability or merit. There were a number of very contentious proposals:

- Three senior ranks – chief inspector, chief superintendent and deputy chief constable – should be abolished, with the possible loss of 5000 positions.
- There should be lower starting salaries, determined at local level.
- There should be performance-related pay.
- Police officers should be offered fixed-term appointments (FTAs) of possibly ten years rather than the 'jobs for life' currently on offer.

The report enraged the police. Together with the Police and Magistrates Courts Act scheduled for 1994 and the Criminal Justice and Public Order Act also expected in 1994, there suddenly seemed to be so much legislation that was less than friendly to police interests. The staff associations which act as the equivalent of trade unions for the police – the Police Federation, the Police Super-intendents' Association and the Association of Chief Police Officers – began an orchestrated campaign against Sheehy. Forbidden by law to take strike action, the police associations managed to organise a protest rally at Wembley attended by over 20 000 officers. The Police Federation even pleaded its case with a newspaper advertisement in which Lord Callaghan, the former prime minister and Police Federation representative in the Commons when he was a backbench MP, said, 'The Sheehy Report is a series of dogmatic conclusions backed by very little argument and based upon an inaccurate analysis of the problem' (Jones, 1994, p. 520).

Faced with such opposition the Home Secretary Michael Howard was forced to climb down. In October 1993 he announced that although some senior posts would be lost, it would not be in the numbers envisaged by Sheehy. Also abandoned, to the great relief of the police, were the proposals for performance-related pay and fixed-term contracts. The government climb-down was humiliating enough and a serious blot on Howard's already tarnished career, but the political influence wielded by the police associations was such that it is hard to see how any worthwhile reform of the police has any chance of success.

8

Foreign Relations and Defence

The point about both foreign affairs and defence is that one was never really an issue with the British electorate, and the other while once of major election-winning importance has now shrunk to something approaching disinterest as far as the general public is concerned. We are therefore talking about issues that are not seen as vital in the eyes of the ordinary voter. There are basically two points to bear in mind concerning the public's political perceptions of foreign affairs:

1. The electorate may well divide along partisan lines when dealing with taxation or education, however, just as families argue among themselves but unite against any threat from outside the family circle, so does the British people tend to unite against any threat from abroad. Public opinion is therefore not as divided over foreign policy as it is over domestic policy, and the capacity of foreign affairs to represent a political issue is thereby diminished. There was widespread and vocal dissent in the UK about British participation in both the Falklands War of 1982 and the Gulf War of 1990, but the vast majority of the British people, from all parties, supported the action and there was never a point where either conflict became a contentious issue in party terms.

2. There is also the point that much of our relationships with other countries is kept secret for reasons of security and average members of the public, being largely uninformed, have to take on trust whatever the politicians choose to tell them about foreign affairs. It was this aspect that made the Scott Inquiry so significant: none of the government's actions over arms for Iraq

was known to parliament, let alone to the public. The obscurity in which foreign affairs are clouded is aided by the attitude of the popular and tabloid press which prints very little in the way of international news, partly because most British journalists are vaguely xenophobic, but more because of the fact well-known to all editors that 'foreign news does not sell newspapers'.

It must be remembered, however, that although foreign policy might leave the electorate unmoved it still retains a great and significant importance for politicians. As Hugo Young has said, 'The earliest discovery which new prime ministers make is the extent to which foreign affairs dominate their lives' (Young, 1989, p. 168). There are two main reasons for this:

- Unlike economic and domestic policy which is pro-active and can be initiated by, guided by and remain under the control of the British political parties, foreign policy is reactive to often unforeseen events in the world outside Britain and its formulation and execution is at the mercy of circumstances beyond the control of politicians at home.
- Foreign policy might not excite the British electorate but voters do like their leaders to be seen as figures of importance on the international scene. It does the prime minister or leader of the opposition no harm at election time to be seen visiting Washington or Moscow for talks with the American president or Russian leader. Every politician knows that the ultimate in political achievement is to be hailed as a 'world statesman'. Even more potent with the electorate, moreover, is the image of prime minister as war leader, as witness the benefit gained by Mrs Thatcher from her role in the Falklands conflict.

Foreign Relations

There was a time when the conduct of relations with foreign countries was one of the most important duties carried out by the government, with the foreign secretary second only to the prime minister as holder of one of the three great offices of state. As recently as 1949, the then leader of the Conservative Party and war-time prime minister, Winston Churchill, could claim that Britain still held a unique position in the western world at the start of the Cold

War. In a speech of 28 November 1949, Churchill expressed the opinion that there were, at that time, three very important groupings in the non-Soviet world, forming what he called 'three majestic circles':

1. Britain's special relationship with the USA within the Atlantic alliance (NATO).
2. Britain's relationship with a potentially united Western Europe.
3. the British Empire and Commonwealth.

Within those interlocking circles, Britain had a crucial role as the only nation with a foot in all three camps (Gilbert, 1988, p. 496).

At the time Churchill was speaking there seemed to be some truth in what he was saying. Despite the economic damage to Britain caused by the war and despite the beginning of the end of empire represented by the independence granted to India and Pakistan:

*   Britain still had a permanent place on the United Nations Security Council as one of the five victorious allies in the Second World War.
*   Britain still headed a large and prosperous empire.
*   With the acquisition of its own nuclear bomb in 1952, Britain became a key member of the western alliance.

Since that time the international role and significance of Britain has declined considerably. There have been four main strands in that changing significance:

1. De-colonisation and the loss of empire.
2. Decline of the British economy and the rise of new economic powers.
3. The subordination of Britain to the United States in the special relationship and the western alliance.
4. The loss of Britain's independent international status as a result of membership of the European Union.

De-colonisation

Britain ended the Second World War still believing that the British Empire was as powerful and important as ever. In fact the ties were loosening and a Britain impoverished by the war no longer had the economic ability to maintain the military presence and worldwide communications needed to uphold all the old imperial connections. Before the war the government had decided that India would become a self-governing dominion along the lines of Australia or Canada, despite the opposition of Winston Churchill who famously said in a speech given at the Lord Mayor's Banquet of 10 November 1942 that 'I have not become the king's first minister in order to preside over the liquidation of the British Empire'. However, the events of the war and the activities of the Indian Congress Party under Gandhi rendered a solution to the governance of the Indian sub-continent far beyond what could be solved by mere dominion status, and led to demands for full independence. The Labour government elected in 1945, struggling with problems at home and anti-imperialist at heart, felt unable to deny the sub-continent its independence, for either practical or ideological reasons. In 1947 India was granted independence, albeit partitioned into India and Pakistan, and the other imperial possessions in the sub-continent, Ceylon (Sri Lanka) and Burma, followed in 1948. Most significantly, except for Burma, these countries remained in what now became known as the British Commonwealth of Nations but as republics, recognising the British monarch as Head of the Commonwealth but not as their own monarch.

For some time after the independence of India, Britain tried to hold on to its colonial possessions partly for the sake of trade and partly as part of Cold War strategy against the Soviet bloc. During the late 1940s and early 1950s Britain found itself in conflict with independence movements in a wide range of colonies, protectorates and mandated territories. There were 'police actions' against Zionist fighters in Palestine and minor colonial wars in Cyprus, Kenya, Malaya and Aden among other troublespots. Most of these places gained their independence sooner or later but a fundamental shift in British policy was forced by the Suez incident of 1956.

Colonel Nasser, who had emerged as leader from the group of young officers who overthrew King Farouk in 1952 and who had became a formidable nationalist president of Egypt, made strenuous efforts to rid Egypt of the British presence. In 1956 he nationalised the Suez Canal then jointly owned and run by Britain and France, the two countries being outraged at this seizure of their assets. Wishing to retaliate without being directly involved, the British and French governments connived in an Israeli invasion of Egypt, after which the two countries intervened invading Egypt in order, so they said, to protect the canal from being caught up in the fighting. It was a disaster both militarily and diplomatically. The rest of the world, including the United States, condemned Britain and France in the United Nations and forced them to withdraw without any of their objectives being achieved. Even more significantly, the Suez crisis caused a major fall in the value of sterling and a run on the pound.

It was a great blow to Britain's prestige and it forced the government to realise that in a world divided between two superpowers and with the American dollar supreme, Britain could no longer pretend to have either the money or the ability to sustain its role as a major imperial power.

Without the economic ability to sustain the empire and with the pressure of world opinion totally opposed to colonialism, Britain calmly accepted the reality of the new order, especially in Africa. In 1960 the British prime minister, Harold Macmillan, speaking in Cape Town on 3 February during a visit to South Africa, acknowledged the new climate of opinion by saying, 'The wind of change is blowing through this continent and, whether we like it or not, this growth of national consciousness is a political fact'. White South Africa itself refused to recognise the 'wind of change' and, with the Boer Nationalist Party in power and imposing its racist policy of apartheid, was forced to leave the Commonwealth and fight world opinion for nearly thirty years, joined for a time in the 1970s by the breakaway British colony of Southern Rhodesia (now Zimbabwe). Elsewhere in Africa, in Asia and the West Indies, Britain quietly disposed of what was left of the empire, granting independence to colony after colony, with ceremony, help and approval.

In 1968 the Labour government recognised the economic reality of Britain's place in the world and withdrew all British forces and military commitments 'east of Suez'. It was not widely recognised as to what part Britain would play in world affairs when the colonial empire was finally dispersed. As the American statesman, Dean Acheson, said in the aftermath of Suez, during a speech to the Military Academy at West Point on 5 December 1962, 'Great Britain has lost an empire and has not yet found a role'.

Virtually all former British colonies remained as members of what was known originally as the British Commonwealth but which is now known simply as 'The Commonwealth'. In a post-colonial world the Commonwealth heads of government meet at regular intervals to discuss world affairs, the Commonwealth having its own headquarters, secretary-general and secretariat like any other international organisation. All countries within the Commonwealth are regarded as being equal, including Britain, although the Queen is thought of, in purely symbolic terms, as Head of the Commonwealth, despite there now being some member countries such as Mozambique that were never part of the British Empire. Apart from a few small islands that are largely not viable independently, there were no British colonies left after the return of Hong Kong to China in 1997. But long-standing colonial responsibilities can remain, as with the dispute with Spain over Gibraltar and the case of the Falkland Islands and the war with Argentina in 1982, while former colonial links with Kuwait involved Britain in the Gulf War with Iraq in 1990.

The principal result of de-colonisation is that Britain no longer has the unquestioning support of the empire for its actions. Britain might hope for the support of the Commonwealth but that support is not automatic and has to be earned in the same way as support from the United Nations or Europe. In the international community Britain has changed from being a major world power to being no more than a small group of islands off the coast of Europe. Comparatively speaking Britain is still a reasonably wealthy country with a strong military capability. But it is a regional power base rather than one of world stature, and any external support for Britain on the world stage has to come not from a subordinate colonial empire but from alliances with states of similar strengths.

The Special Relationship and the Cold War

Several events of the late 1940s, including the Russian blockade of West Berlin, the Communist takeover of China, the detonation of a Russian nuclear bomb in 1949 and the outbreak of the Korean War in 1950, all led to the division of the world into two opposing power groups – the Western Alliance led by the USA and the Eastern Communist bloc led by the Soviet Union, a division that became known as the Cold War. In 1949, largely at the instigation of the British Foreign Secretary, Ernest Bevin, who persuaded the Americans to commit themselves to the defence of Europe, the North Atlantic Treaty Organisation (NATO) was formed. Britain took a leading role in the foundation of NATO and, after the development of Britain's own nuclear weapons (the A-bomb in 1952 and the H-bomb in 1957) placed Britain alongside the United States and the Soviet Union as a nuclear power, Britain seemed to be resuming its place as a leading world power.

The Suez crisis brought that dream to an end. The United States refused to support either Britain or France; it became clear that Britain was no longer strong enough militarily or economically to support the role of world 'policeman' and the slow loss of empire reduced Britain's world commitment. Beginning in 1957, Britain started to withdraw the number of troops committed to Europe in Germany and this slow reduction in British foreign commitments continued in parallel with de-colonisation until the 1967 withdrawal from east of Suez.

Although Britain maintained its own nuclear weapons it could no longer afford to provide the means of delivering those weapons and, from the early 1960s to their replacement by Trident in the mid-1990s, British nuclear warheads were fitted to US-built Polaris missiles. It was Harold Macmillan, having established a good understanding with President John F. Kennedy, who rebuilt Anglo-American relations after Suez, and the Bermuda agreement between the two in 1962 allowed for the use of American missiles in the delivery of the British nuclear deterrent. What Macmillan and Kennedy claimed they were doing was re-establishing the 'special relationship' between the UK and USA that had been built up by Churchill and Rooseveldt during the Second World War. The historical links of a common language, culture and heritage made the relationship between America and Britain closer than any relationship between the United States and countries that were not part of the Anglo-Saxon tradition. This special relationship formed a central factor in the western alliance throughout the Cold War period.

The special relationship was strained on several occasions after Suez, particularly during the 1970s when Britain's withdrawal from Asia meant that no support could be given to the American involvement in Vietnam. The feeling in America that Britain was withdrawing from the closeness of the relationship was aggravated by Britain's increasing involvement with membership of the European Community. The relationship was, however, renewed more strongly than ever before when Ronald Reagan became president of the United States and found a soul-mate in Margaret Thatcher. 'The Reagan–Thatcher axis was the most enduring personal alliance in the Western world throughout the 1980s. From Moscow to Pretoria, from Tripoli to Buenos Aires, no theatre of global conflict failed to feel its effects' (Young, 1989, p. 249).

The special relationship with Ronald Reagan bore fruit in the United States' support for Britain during the Falklands War, but the relationship grew so close that there were those who claimed that Britain had abandoned any foreign policy of its own in order to follow blindly whatever was decided by the Reagan administration, with a consequent complacent belief on the part of the United States that they could do what they wished on the international scene without consulting Britain and would still receive British support. This was clearly seen on at least two occasions:

- In 1983 the United States invaded the West Indian island of Grenada to overthrow a Marxist government sympathetic to Cuban communism. This invasion of a member of the British Commonwealth was carried out without telling the British government or even Grenada's head of state, the Queen.
- In 1986 Reagan asked to be allowed to use British bases for bombing raids on Libya in a form of anti-terrorist action that Mrs Thatcher had previously described as a breach of international law. Despite her misgivings and previous remarks, and despite the opposition of many of her cabinet colleagues, the Prime Minister not only gave her permission but vigorously defended the American action.

For most of the postwar period, therefore, the American alliance has dominated and directed British foreign policy. After the end of both the Reagan administration and Margaret Thatcher's premiership, however, it seemed as though the special relationship had cooled. This was partly because there was never the friendship between Clinton and Major that there had been between Reagan and Thatcher, a coolness made even icier by British Conservative support for Bush's campaign for re-election against Clinton. But the change in the relationship had more to do with the end of the cold war and a subsequent waning of US interest in Europe. As a prominent Liberal Democrat spokesman on foreign policy, William Wallace, said, 'Europe is no longer the US's first and foremost foreign policy commitment and Britain is no more important than Germany or France among America's European allies' (*The Observer*, 15 August 1993).

Nevertheless, Clinton's first visit to Europe after the British election of 1997 seemed to suggest that a new Blair–Clinton special relationship might be building that was every bit as mutually supportive as the Reagan–Thatcher partnership. On 29 May 1997, when Clinton addressed the British Cabinet and conducted a joint press conference with Tony Blair, the two leaders stressed repeatedly the strength of their mutual admiration and Tony Blair seemed to reinstate the special relationship when he declared, 'I hope this does usher in a new time of understanding and co-operation between our two countries, which have such strong bonds of history and heritage'.

Britain's Future Role

In the 1990s the truth of Acheson's comment about Britain seeking a new world role is ever more true. At one time it was felt that Britain would assume a leading role in the development of the European Union but two factors seem to prevent that from becoming the ideal answer and both are linked to a lingering fear and suspicion in Britain about the role and intentions of a reunified Germany:

- Because of relative economic strengths, Britain has to face the domination of the EU by Germany and specifically the domination of the Bundesbank and the deutschmark.
- The strong Eurosceptic tendency in the Conservative Party has withheld support from an institution in which Germany has a major say on foreign and defence matters.

Even after the Labour victory of 1997 this slightly Eurosceptical view of the EU's role in foreign affairs continued to influence the Labour government, as Tony Blair and Robin Cook rapidly made clear. For all New Labour's change of approach towards Europe there was still an unwillingness to see Brussels play a major role in foreign policy and defence, while the UK, as an island state, insisted that the national government should have full jurisdiction over external frontiers.

It is for these reasons that London clings both to the 'special relationship' and to its 'world role' even though the Soviet threat which nurtured them both has now disappeared and Britain has, for a very long time indeed, lacked the economic strength to sustain either of them. (Dunleavy *et al.*, 1993, pp. 303–4)

Nevertheless, the British government tends to rely on a belief that only Britain can act as a true link between the European Union and the Atlantic Alliance and it is in that intermediary role that Britain feels it still has a major part to play on the world stage. Tony Blair reinforced this message within four weeks of winning the election when he played an important mediating role in the meeting between the leaders of the NATO alliance and President Yeltsin of Russia on 27 May 1997. At that meeting the Founding Act on Mutual Relations, Co-operation and Security between NATO and the Russian Federation was signed, allowing for a Euro-Atlantic security system. As a result of this Founding Act, NATO gained the right to expand its membership eastward towards former Soviet bloc members like Poland or Hungary. In this new world order Britain could well have a pivotal role at the hinge between the United States and Europe.

Even before the end of the Cold War reduced the need for collective security alliances, the emphasis in foreign relations had long since shifted from the diplomatic power game to being a matter of trade and economics. Most foreign contacts now – including state visits by the Queen abroad, or by foreign heads of state to this country – are for the purposes of promoting trade with foreign countries and the commercial section is often the most important part of British Embassies abroad.

Trade and economic imperatives also affect Britain's post-colonial role in the countries of the former empire. Britain gives a lot of aid to Third World countries and the government includes a Minister for Overseas Development. But that aid often takes the form of helping to pay for British firms to undertake development work in the countries concerned. Allied to that trade-aid link is something that has become an important issue in recent years. This is the extent to which trade and overseas aid has become associated with the arms industry and the extent therefore to which ethical values should determine the nature of foreign relations. The Scott Report revealed the extent to which Britain had been selling arms to Iraq despite a trade embargo, a trade which was even kept secret from parliament.

In January 1994 it was revealed that government aid of £234 million had been paid to Malaysia to help in the building of the

Pergau Dam project, the overseas aid payment only being made in return for arms sales orders from Malaysia worth £1.3 billion. Since the dam is largely unnecessary and Malaysia is becoming prosperous enough in its own right as a member of the flourishing Pacific Rim, there is a suspicion that the overseas aid budget is being used to conceal support being given to British armaments manufacturers in a bid to gain market share with the lucrative South-east Asian 'tiger' economies. More recently there has been a row about fighter aircraft being sold to Indonesia supposedly for defence purposes, whereas the fighters are being used by the Indonesian government against their own people and in their occupation of East Timor. In the light of the Scott Report and these other examples, New Labour was keen in opposition to depict itself as morally and ethically sound in these areas. One of the first acts of the new government within a week of the 1997 general election was to outlaw the sale of anti-personnel land-mines, alongside a promise to work for an international ban. Therefore the possibility exists that Britain's role in world affairs at the turn of the century is to take on an ethical role in a watchdog capacity.

Soon after his appointment as Foreign Secretary, Robin Cook re-stated the basic freedoms of the UN Declaration of Human Rights. 'These are rights we claim for ourselves', he said, 'and which we therefore have a duty to demand for those who do not enjoy them' (quoted in Lloyd, 25 July 1997, pp. 28–9). There is therefore evidence that Cook and the new Labour government would like to see Britain's role in the world as a sort of ethical watchdog. Unfortunately, the British government works under constraints that make this option difficult:

1. If Britain were to take the lead in banning arms sales to authoritarian and repressive regimes the effect at home could be devastating. Since open and democratic governments tend not to buy arms in anything like the quantities that authoritarian regimes do, a ban on these arms sales would cost Britain's arms manufacturers most of their export market, representing something like £5 billion in lost sales as well as thousands of jobs. And the buying countries would still get their arms from less scrupulous vendors such as Russia.

2. Rich western countries like Britain itself, the United States, Australia, Canada and Europe tend to have a good record on human rights. The oppressive regimes tend to belong to Asia,

Africa and the Third World. Any intervention by the first group of countries in the affairs of the second could be dismissed as neo-colonialism and an unwarranted interference in the independence of sovereign states. Any involvement in this area needs to be conducted tactfully and diplomatically by contact and influence rather than through outright confrontation. For example, even though Nigeria was suspended from the Commonwealth over human rights abuses, Cook did not want to see the country expelled, as others in his party demanded, because he felt it was important to keep lines of negotiation open.

One human rights issue where the new Labour government did show itself willing to be confrontational over was the question of war criminals in former Yugoslavia. On 10 July 1997 British troops in Bosnia arrested one Bosnian Serb wanted for war crimes, and shot another. At much the same time, Cook pledged £1 million of British money to the International Court at The Hague where the International Criminal Tribunal is pursuing war criminals from the former Yugoslavia. It could well be that Britain sees its future role in foreign affairs as being that of an international police force in support of international agencies like the United Nations.

Another ethical future path for Britain is in financial aid for developing countries, currently running at around £2 billion but which Clare Short as Secretary of State for International Development would like to see increased by 150 per cent in line with UN policy. As she said shortly after her appointment, 'We want to see a global moral community where economic endeavour goes hand in hand with accountable government'. One of the paths being taken by Short is to bypass governments as recipients of aid when the democratic credentials of those governments are in doubt; as with Indonesia where British aid was channelled directly to civil rights groups and trade unions. This is another example of the issue of the 1990s – how the government can adopt an ethical and moral line in foreign relations without offending the niceties of diplomacy and foreign trade.

Defence

Defence has always been an important political issue since there have always been pacifists and conscientious objectors who dislike war and who therefore find the defence capability of a country controversial. There are also many electors who resent the vast sums of money spent on aeroplanes and warships when that money could be spent on social areas such as the NHS. However, these are minor matters and hardly qualify as issues important enough to influence election results since the vast majority of the people have always agreed on the need and duty of a country to defend itself against real or potential aggressors. What was meant for many years by the defence issue, however, was really the possession by Britain of nuclear weapons and the protest movement created in response to those weapons; a protest movement closely allied to the Labour Party.

After the start of the Cold War in the 1940s, Britain's defence concentrated on the alliance with America and membership of NATO. NATO policy centred on the deployment of nuclear weapons and, while it was hoped that Britain could depend on the American alliance, it was still very important for successive governments that Britain should maintain its own independent nuclear deterrent. And, as has been pointed out earlier in this chapter, Britain acquired its atomic and hydrogen bombs during the 1950s.

Possession of nuclear weapons formed part of deterrence theory, which stated that no country would use nuclear weapons while there was the threatened possibility of retaliation from the other side. In the nineteenth century world politics were dominated by the so-called balance of power under which no country was likely to start a war because no one country was stronger than another. The nuclear deterrent worked in much the same way because any country contemplating a first strike with their nuclear weapons knew that they would be wiped out in their turn by a nuclear counter-strike. The 'balance of power' had become the 'balance of terror', as they said, but supporters of deterrence theory claimed that this balance prevented world war for over 30 years. It has to be admitted, even by those opposed to nuclear weapons, that it is indeed true that there has been no direct shooting war between the major powers since 1945, except for the minor, proxy – and non-nuclear – war in Korea.

There were many people in Britain who did not want the nuclear arms race in which countries competed with each other to see how many nuclear weapons they could make and possess, not to mention the competition to build the biggest and most powerful bomb.

Pressure groups like the Campaign for Nuclear Disarmament (CND) tried hard to persuade all countries to give up their nuclear weapons but they particularly wanted Britain to give up its independent nuclear weapons as an example to other countries. This one-sided surrender of nuclear weapons, known as unilateral disarmament, was much favoured by the Labour Party, and was official party policy at times in the 1980s. Many senior Labour politicians, like Neil Kinnock, had been or were members of CND and even Tony Blair fought his first general election in 1983 under the disarmament banner. However, given the tradition of anti-nuclear protest in the Labour Party it is ironic that the Cold War began under a Labour government; it was that same Labour government that began development work on Britain's nuclear weapons, and it was a left-wing Labour politician Aneurin Bevan in a speech to the 1957 Labour Conference (*Daily Herald*, 4 October 1957) who said that to get rid of nuclear weapons would 'send Britain's Foreign Secretary naked into the conference chamber'.

Unilateral disarmament was not popular with the electorate, and during election campaigns the Conservative Party would make a great deal of fuss about how the Labour Party would throw away the country's weapons and leave Britain defenceless. The defence issue was one of the main reasons for Labour's poor performance in the elections of 1983 and 1987, when former CND members Michael Foot and Neil Kinnock respectively were party leaders. The lukewarm nature of Labour's stance was particularly noticeable when contrasted with Mrs Thatcher's claims to be in favour of strong defences and in the light of her performance during the Falklands War. Recognising the suspicion with which the majority of the electorate viewed the link between Labour and unilateral nuclear disarmament, the Conservatives became increasingly jingoistic during the 1980s 'wrapping themselves in the flag' as was said of the election campaigns and party political broadcasts which featured the waving of Union flags and the sound of 'Land of Hope and Glory'.

Defence is no longer so important an issue, as it was even as recently as the 1987 general election, seeming to have lost its importance and become a non-issue overnight. Changes in Russia during 1989–90 brought the end of communism, the break-up of the Soviet Union, the fall of the Berlin Wall, the re-unification of Germany and the ending of the Cold War between East and West. The lessening of the risk of war with the Soviet Union brought what was known as the 'peace dividend', which was a way of saying that money which had once been spent on defence could now be spent on other things. Normal defence with conventional non-nuclear weapons was still important, as was seen in the Gulf War of 1990. But nuclear defence was the issue which concerned the electorate and, without the threat from the Soviet bloc, the British electorate rapidly lost interest in the importance of unilateral disarmament and CND seemed to vanish from view.

The swing in opinion between 1987 and 1992 can be seen in figures produced by the Gallup post-election surveys of those years. Asked to name the issue which had most influenced their voting intentions, 35 per cent named defence in 1987, as against a mere 3 per cent in 1992. In the earlier election defence was second only to unemployment as an issue of concern, while in 1992 the issue had slipped to a very poor eighth in order of importance. Moreover, since the Conservatives had had a 63 per cent lead over Labour on defence in 1987, the change in the electorate's perception of defence as an issue was important for the electoral recovery of the Labour Party (Crewe, 1992, pp. 2–11).

In 1997 the issue of defence played even less of a role in electoral policy. The issue has now been reduced to two questions:

1. Who is the enemy now that the Soviet bloc has dispersed?
2. With whom is Britain likely to fight a major confrontational war, especially one in which nuclear weapons have a role to play?

In the light of the end of the Cold War and the fragmentation of the Warsaw Pact it has to be said that there is no chance whatsoever of a major conflict breaking out in Europe. It also has to be said that there is little likelihood of any other enemy emerging for the West in the immediate future. Two possibilities – and they are no more than possibilities – in the longer term are:

1. A pan-Arab alliance of militant Islam, engaged in a *jihad* with the West. Since wars usually have an economic basis and are fought about market dominance, it is worth pointing out that some of the most militant Islamic countries are themselves, or are neighbours of, the world's major oil producers. Oil exists therefore as an economic flashpoint.

2. China is a developing world power with huge potential where a distinctive ideological perspective could well lead to confrontation, particularly if China seeks to dominate the emergent Asian economies of the Pacific Rim.

It has to be said that, even if Britain were to become involved in major conflict, it is doubtful as to whether Britain has the resources to sustain such a conflict. In 1982 it was touch and go as to whether Britain had the equipment and organisation to fight the Falklands War against Argentina. Since then Britain has seized on the 'peace dividend' afforded by the end of the Cold War in order to trim the size and overall equipment of the armed forces, until it is now thought unlikely that the Falklands War could have been fought, let alone won, ten years later. Here, too, the new Labour government of May 1997 has sought to influence matters with an urgent defence review under George Robertson aimed at reducing government spending on arms and the armed forces. Yet again, however, as with the trade element of foreign relations, any cut in spending on defence would be extremely expensive in terms of jobs in the defence supply industry.

Summary

Both in foreign affairs and defence the Labour government seems to be moving towards an ethical dimension that includes a respect for human rights and international law. It could be that Britain is looking to a future role in what is sometimes called 'the Canadian option', under which highly trained fighting units are available to assist international agencies like the United Nations in police actions or as part of a peace-keeping force, such as have been used in the former Yugoslavia, Cyprus or Somalia. The issue here is the dilemma posed by the role of Britain's arms manufacturers in the economy. The sale of high-value armaments such as fighter aircraft or tanks makes a large contribution to Britain's balance of payments, while their manufacture provides much needed employment. But international peace-keeping missions do not need high-tech jet fighters or nuclear-powered submarines. Some future defence review considering the options open to the armed forces might well decide that the high-tech weaponry is not a prime necessity. But the cost to the country in lost employment is likely to make governments think twice about their intentions. As John Lloyd said (*New Statesman*, 25 July 1997, p. 28), 'morality abroad is cruelty at home'. That dilemma remains the issue in British foreign and defence policy but, given the relative importance of home and foreign affairs when the electorate has to decide between the parties, it is not difficult to see how it is likely to be resolved.

9

Britain and Europe

The original issue represented by what was then generally called the Common Market and subsequently the European Economic Community (EEC), the European Community or Communities (EC), and eventually the European Union (EU) concerned the simple question as to whether or not Britain should be a member. By the 1990s, after 20 years' membership and despite a recent hardening of attitudes among the more vehement of opponents, the important issue for most people has become not so much whether Britain should be a member of the European Union as such, but more a disagreement over the form the European Union should take, and over the nature of British membership.

Contrary to public perceptions, the debate over Europe in recent years has not been primarily about membership, but about what the politicians of the component states hope to gain from membership. Over the years there have been at least two perspectives governing attitudes towards what is involved in European cooperation and these two, often diametrically opposed, perspectives lay constraints upon the functioning of European institutions and determine the degree of British commitment to the European ideal.

It must be stressed that the position on Europe adopted by individuals, parties or even entire countries does not follow a consistent pattern but tends to move according to the political climate or economic realities of the time. This movement tends to be between the extremes of federalism and pragmatism and between the perspectives of supranationalism and inter-governmentalism.

Federalists are those who ultimately aim at full political and economic union of Europe, with considerable powers in the hands of a federal government. On the whole they believe that the national interests of component states should be subordinated to the general good of the European Union as a whole. Opponents of federalism often use the term 'Euro-centrism' to describe this viewpoint, implying that it means authoritarian centralisation in Brussels.

Pragmatists are those who are members of the Union for what they can get out of it. As far as they are concerned, the institutions of the Union only exist to satisfy the individual needs of member states. Pragmatists are unwilling to surrender any aspect of national sovereignty but believe instead in the supremacy of the centralised nation state. Pragmatists adhere to the EU for the pragmatic reason that it is more effective to cooperate than to face cut-throat competition in the modern industrial and commercial global market. The reverse view is that pragmatists ignore the general good in favour of self-interested nationalism.

Supranational institutions are the bodies favoured by the federalists since the policies they advocate are in the interests of all and take precedence over national positions. The Commission, Court and Parliament of the EU are supranational institutions.

Intergovernmental institutions, on the other hand, are institutions where members discuss and negotiate as representatives of their national governments, retaining their national loyalties and defending their national interests against the encroachment of federalist ideas. The Council of Ministers and, even more so, the European Council of heads of government, are intergovernmental bodies.

Subsidiarity is a concept which attempts to reconcile the federalist and pragmatic positions and was evolved, largely at the behest of John Major, in the immediate aftermath of Maastricht to show that pragmatists can adhere to the European ideal without embracing federalist beliefs. Subsidiarity agrees that community policy decisions should be made at the centre but that the way in which those policies are implemented should be decided as close to the people as possible. In other words the Union-wide policy is decided in Brussels but each individual national government can interpret that policy in the way which best suits the individual state's interests. Ironically, since subsidiarity was evoked to challenge federalism, that definition of subsidiarity is what many people understand is meant by a federal system.

This argument of perspectives between federalists and pragmatists has had most effect in making Europe and membership of the European Union the great divisive issue affecting British political parties. Both Labour and the Conservatives have split over the question of Europe, the Conservative Party losing first a leader and then the 1997 election over the issue. In the development of British political parties the argument over Europe and European integration has assumed the same importance as the Repeal of the Corn Laws or Home Rule for Ireland did in the nineteenth century – a contentious issue that has dominated the political agenda and re-drawn the political map.

Historically, the anti-Europe party was Labour, especially during the leftward drift of the party in the early 1980s. In the run-up to the 1983 general election the Labour Party advocated an alternative economic strategy which included,

> a programme of socialist economic expansion which would include domestic reflation and the use of import controls. An essential prerequisite was full economic sovereignty. In other words, a potential Labour government would need to have full control of the British economy. This was not deemed to be possible with continued membership of the EC. (Rosamond, 1994, p. 21)

And therefore the Labour Party fought the 1983 election on the policy of complete withdrawal from Community membership. It was the most extreme and hostile position to be adopted by Labour in opposition to Europe and it seemed at the time to be so deep-rooted that nothing was likely to change. Little more than a decade ago two of our more distinguished political commentators could confidently write, 'It is quite possible that a future Labour government will want to take Britain out of the EEC, or demand such fundamental structural changes as the price of staying in, that withdrawal becomes inevitable' (Jones and Kavanagh, 1983).

Change came very quickly. The policy review initiated by Neil Kinnock after the 1987 election accepted as desirable the social policies advocated by Jacques Delors as President of the Commission, policies which later became the Social Chapter of the Maastricht Treaty. To Labour, Europe seemed a logical way by which the social policies desired by Labour could be introduced into Britain, despite the Conservative government. A pro-European stance was adopted successively by Neil Kinnock and John Smith, while the modernising tendency in the party associated with the rise of Tony Blair was most definitely pro-European. The final irony in the Labour Party was to see Neil Kinnock, who had campaigned against Europe in 1983, accept the post of European Commissioner in 1994, to go to Brussels where his wife was already a prominent MEP and where a member of the British Labour Party was leader of the socialist group, the biggest supranational party grouping in the European Parliament.

The same decade which saw the Labour Party move to a pro-European position found the Conservatives moving in the opposite direction, to a situation where leading members of the party can now openly advocate withdrawal from the Union. Whereas the common market aspect of Europe was the thing which Labour originally found most objectionable, for many Conservatives that remained the sole justifiable reason for membership. Once the Single Market was established, the European Community had served its purpose in their eyes and senior Conservative politicians became determined not to let the movement towards European integration proceed any further.

The movement of opinion in the Conservative Party began with Margaret Thatcher. The impression created by Lady Thatcher has always been one of single-minded dedication and undeviating steadfastness of purpose. In reality her views were a mixture of two contradictory nineteenth-century ideologies – nationalistic conservatism and economic liberalism. The economic liberal could take pride in the creation of the Single Market but the nationalist in her reacted against the consequences of that act, mainly against the imposition of a single currency and a European Central Bank and at the whole social dimension which formed part of the Delors Plan.

> Mrs Thatcher seems to believe that the Community will introduce socialism by the back door. She has been particularly vitriolic in her attacks on the 'social dimension' of the Community, whether in the form of the social charter or the social chapter discussed at Maastricht. At her 1988 speech in Bruges Mrs Thatcher argued that she would not allow the frontiers of the state to be rolled forward by the EC when she had spent nine years rolling them back in the UK. (Wincott, 1992, p. 12)

The Bruges speech led to the formation of the Bruges Group, a faction within the Conservative Party opposed to any suggestion of European federalism, political or monetary union or indeed any measure which might lead to a further diminution of British sovereignty.

The attitude towards Europe adopted by Mrs Thatcher was ultimately one of the major factors in her downfall and resignation. Such was her hostility to Europe that once out of office and freed from the restrictions of her position, Lady Thatcher, as she had become, became the leading voice and propagandist of the Euro-sceptical tendency. And that tendency was rapidly assuming the characteristics of a party within a party. In parliament there were a number of Conservatives of ministerial rank who were unable to criticise Europe too openly because of the constraints of office, but a sizeable group of backbenchers grew up dedicated to opposing any hint of movement towards European integration. As their obvious strength grew, even prominent and ministerial figures within the party openly adopted an anti-European stance in public (Pilkington, 1995).

Contrasting Party Views

In March 1994, Martin Kettle wrote an article (*The Guardian*, 19 March 1994) bemoaning the fact that the common terminology employed by the media tended to divide opinion on the issue of Europe into just two groups, the Euro-enthusiasts and the Euro-sceptics, whereas he claimed that he could distinguish at least four different attitudes:

- Euro-enthusiasts are those who welcome membership of the Community and the moves towards integration. In their way they are somewhat uncritical of European measures and are typified by the Liberal Democrats or Ted Heath and his supporters.
- Europhobes is the more accurate term for those generally known as Eurosceptics, such as Bill Cash, John Redwood or Teresa Gorman, who are rather more than merely sceptical, being in fact against anything European and who would welcome a British withdrawal from Europe.
- Eurosceptics, in the true sense of the term, are what Kettle describes as people 'who doubt the wisdom of the European project but who are prepared to go cautiously along with it'. They accept that in a few areas such as the Single Market the European Union has its uses but are highly sceptical about any European involvement in areas like social policy, defence or

internal security. This was largely the position taken by the Major government in its latter years, before the Europhobic tendency gained the upper hand.

- Euro-progressives or Euro-positives. This is the group no one mentions but who, according to Kettle, probably form the majority not only in Britain but throughout the Community. They are people who 'are basically in favour of the Euro-project but who don't want to endorse change indiscriminately'. These are the people who voted two to one to remain in the Common Market in the 1975 referendum and who would probably vote in the same proportions today. And they roughly represent the majority position in the Labour government.

The point Kettle was making in his article was that John Major, at the time he took over from Lady Thatcher, was a Euro-positive, eager to put Britain 'at the heart of Europe' and able to say at the European Council in Edinburgh, 'the majority of people in this country want us to make a success of our membership'. The conflicts of the debate over Maastricht and the need to protect his dwindling majority against party divisions dragged Major out of the Euro-progressive camp into the Eurosceptical. In order to accommodate the Europhobes in the party the prime minister had to adopt a highly critical attitude in European circles, blocking measures that appeared to be integrationist not for the sake of Britain or Europe but in order to keep the favour of his party at home; tactics which reached their peak in the British blanket veto during the BSE crisis of 1996.

The move by the leadership of the party from a positive to a sceptical perspective did not seem to appease the Europhobes in the party. Rather, they became more and more openly phobic as Major changed his position. Very much a backbench movement at the time of the Maastricht debate the phobes increasingly attracted government ministers and even members of the Cabinet to the cause. Prominent cabinet ministers, including Michael Portillo, Peter Lilley, Michael Howard and John Redwood, not only spoke out openly in a critical manner about aspects of the Community, but used the increasingly phobic reactions of the Tory grassroots to form a power-base for their own ambitions and career prospects. Major recognised this fifth-column in the Cabinet and was overheard to refer to them as 'bastards'. In 1995 John Redwood challenged John Major for the party leadership largely on an anti-Europe platform and with the support of eight Tory MPs who had lost the party whip for voting against the government over Europe.

European Issues and Party Attitudes

Monetary Union

The Treaty of Maastricht agreed to unite the economies of member countries, with a common currency and a European Central Bank. Eurosceptics are bitterly opposed to any form of monetary union which they believe would represent the final surrender of British sovereignty since the existence of a central bank would mean that a British Chancellor could no longer control British tax and interest rates. Also in their use of patriotism to argue their cause they are opposed to '*giving up the pound*' in favour of some EU currency such as the 'euro'. In the Maastricht Treaty John Major won an opt-out for Britain which meant that this country could choose whether or not to join the monetary union if and when it happens. From 1995 and through to the election of 1997, this question of whether Britain would or would not choose to join the monetary union came to dominate the argument in the Conservative Party with an increasingly vocal and influential minority wanting the party leadership to rule out British membership at any time, now or in the future.

Government policy at that time, most strongly represented by the Chancellor, Kenneth Clarke, was that the opt-out granted to Britain meant that Britain was in the fortunate position of being able to wait and see what was on offer before deciding about membership of monetary union. According to Clarke it would be the height of foolishness to close off possible options in advance of knowing what the options might be. Increasingly isolated by Eurosceptical adherents, Clarke managed to retain prime ministerial support but whenever Europe was mentioned it was as though members of the government were forever looking over their shoulders to see what the backbenchers had to say. By the time of the leadership election within the Tory Party, when Clarke was a candidate, the issue of monetary union had become the defining factor in choosing a leader. The eventual winner, William Hague, had even gone so far as to say that he would not appoint senior colleagues to his shadow cabinet unless they were prepared to rule out the prospect of Britain joining a single currency within the next ten years.

A Referendum on Europe

The anti-Europe section within the Conservative Party produced the demand for a referendum to be held before any further move was made towards European integration. Such was their success in appealing to a certain section of the electorate in gaining the uncritical support of the tabloid press that the Eurosceptics came to believe that public opinion was overwhelmingly on their side and that a referendum would go very much in their favour. This position was reinforced by the formation of an explicitly anti-European party, the Referendum Party, by the wealthy, ex-patriate business-man the late Sir James Goldsmith. According to Goldsmith in a speech to the Federation of Small Businesses in Newcastle-upon-Tyne on 27 June 1996, '. . .if we want our government to respond to our national requirements, the right to govern must first of all be returned to these shores.'

The irony of the situation was that the size of the Labour majority in 1997 meant that the position adopted by the Conservatives over Europe was completely irrelevant. A reduced Tory Party was unable to influence government actions and all the crucial decisions on Europe, including monetary union, will have been taken well before the earliest possible date at which the Conservatives could regain power.

The Social Chapter

The Maastricht Treaty included many social policies based on the socialist principles formulated in the Delors Plan, like a minimum wage, equal rights for women workers and safeguards for part-time workers. The Conservative government claimed that the cost to employers in increased wages and redundancy payments, for exam-ple, would make British firms uncompetitive, and John Major got a British opt-out on social policies as well. The Labour Party, how-ever, counter-claimed that Britain was the 'sweat shop of Europe' thanks to the very low wages paid simply so that British manufac-turers could undercut competitors. Labour were very much in favour of the social chapter, and it was the social policies of the EU that turned the Labour Party under Neil Kinnock into becom-ing pro-European instead of anti-European. The first action of the Labour government in its relationship with Europe was to sign up to the Social Chapter.

The National Veto

Normally the decisions made by the Council of Ministers have to be unanimous, with all member states agreeing. Just one country can block any decisions approved by the other 14 members. In the early days of the Common Market the French bias evident in the Common Agricultural Policy was created by the French President, Charles De Gaulle, who refused to agree with anything that did not suit French farmers; he used the veto to the extent of becoming known as 'Monsieur Non'. There are those in the EU who want to replace this national veto with a form of majority voting, seen as fairer and much more democratic. The Eurosceptics disagree because they believe that the right of a British minister to block the wishes of the other member countries is the last defence of British rights. In 1996 the British government used its veto to block any decision-making in Europe as part of its strategy to force Europe to abandon its ban on British beef.

Over issues like BSE, the British attitude towards Europe, particularly as represented in the tabloid press, became rabidly jingoistic and xenophobic in tone. The argument was presented as though war had been declared and the president of the CBI, Sir Bryan Nicholson, was spurred into saying, on 21 May 1996, 'I sometimes wonder if there are some among us who have failed to notice that the war with Germany has ended'. The one thing that was clear in the summer of 1996 was that Britain's European partners were weary not just of the way in which Britain was repeatedly out of step with all the other member countries but at the extent to which the Conservative government seemed willing to play with the smooth working of the Communities simply for the sake of some advantage in the internal party battles of the Conservative Party.

Common Security

In what is known as the 'Schengen Agreement', the EU wants to do away with border checks between member states. Visitors from countries outside the EU would have their papers checked once, when they arrived in the first European country, but the papers would not be checked again as the tourist moved between member countries. Eurosceptics in Britain object very strongly because they think that removing passport and customs checks at the border will encourage the activities of terrorists, drug smugglers and illegal immigrants. Moreover, passportless travel would argue the need for compulsory identity papers, together with the right of police to carry out checks on identity at any time and in any place: infringements of what the sceptics see as traditional British freedoms. This, alongside the issue of defence and external security, was the principal area in which Labour upheld the position of the previous Tory government. At the Amsterdam summit of June 1997 the United Kingdom together with the Republic of Ireland won the right to uphold its external borders because of its particular situation as an island nation, together with the ever-present problem of nationalism.

The Cost of Europe

When Mrs Thatcher became prime minister in 1979 she was upset by the amount that Britain paid into Europe. Britain was a net contributor, paying as much to the European Community as Germany but getting far less back than many other countries. The amount of Britain's overpayment was calculated as £1000 million a year. Mrs Thatcher accused her European partners of '*stealing Britain's money*' and demanded that '*we want our money back*'. Originally raised in 1980, the problem of Britain's missing money dominated discussions for five years. According to Lord Jenkins (1989), who was President of the Commission at the time, the argument over money was referred to as the BBQ the British Budgetary Question – but which according to Jenkins was generally taken to be 'the Bloody British Question'. The matter was finally resolved at the Fontainebleau European Council of June 1984 when it was agreed that Britain should receive an annual rebate to cancel out any overpayment.

These arguments over the cost of European membership had been the main basis of the Eurosceptics' arguments and led some Conservatives, like John Redwood, to demand British withdrawal from the EU. No one appeared to doubt the truth of press reports concerning the vast expense of membership for Britain. Then, during the Madrid European Council of December 1995 figures were released by the German government which showed that however serious the problem may once have been, this belief in Britain's unfair treatment is no longer true. Two reasons for this change have been, firstly, the rebate agreed by Mrs Thatcher, which was as much as £1.5 billion in 1994; and secondly, and far more significantly, the reform of the Common Agricultural Policy which is now a very much smaller part of the EU budget than it was ten years ago, and which is likely to get smaller still with the reforms necessary prior to the entry of Eastern European countries like Poland. The reforms of 1992 meant that the subsidies paid to farmers by the CAP are much smaller but the money is paid for every hectare of land under production and there are even large subsidies for not planting land that might otherwise produce a surplus. It was estimated in 1996 that the average farm in eastern England could get £100 000 a year in subsidies alone before they actually sold any of their produce (*The Guardian*, 13 April 1996).

Equally as important as these reforms in funding are changes produced by Britain's economic decline:

- Two-fifths of all those Europeans who live in areas in need of re-development live in the United Kingdom, and qualify for regional aid.
- Three UK regions – Northern Ireland, the Scottish Highlands and Merseyside – have a standard of living less than 75 per cent that of the EU average, and as a result qualify for major sums of money from what is known as Objective One funding.

As a result, the UK can receive as much as £3.5 billion in aid from various EU spending programmes.

The 'Democratic Deficit'

Most criticism of Europe has concentrated on the issues of sover-eignty and cost, as has been discussed, with less attention paid to accusations that the EU is essentially undemocratic. The expression 'democratic deficit' normally refers to the unelected powers of the European Commission, to the fact that the unaccountable Council of Ministers is the EU's main decision-making body, and the impotence of a European Parliament (EP) which has no control over legislation and no ability to curb the Commission or Council.

In 1972, by signing the Treaty of Accession, the British govern-ment tacitly accepted as part of British law some 43 volumes of European legislation, made up of more than 2900 regulations and 410 directives; the sum total of legislation agreed by the Community over the 20 years since its formation. Admittedly much of this legislation was trivial: most regulations or directives from Brussels dealing with small points of detail such as intervention prices for commodities within the Common Agricultural Policy. Nevertheless there were some major issues involved and, in any case, the triviality of certain details is unimportant compared to the basic principle that a solid body of law became binding upon the peoples of the United Kingdom, despite never having been scrutinised or debated by the British parliament.

Eurosceptics, in their criticism of Europe often use the terms 'unelected' and 'undemocratic' in talking about the institutions of the Community. Britain needs to defend its parliamentary sovereignty, they suggest, and go on to say that at least the British parliament can claim to speak for the British people who elected it. For whom can the European Commission claim to speak when its members are appointed rather than elected and to whom is the Commission accountable?

There is, however, an anomaly in the situation when national parliamentarians criticise the Community for its lack of democratic institutions; the so-called 'democratic deficit'. There are three simple solutions to accusations of non-accountability and they are:

1. strengthen the powers of the European Parliament;
2. make more European institutions and their officials answerable to the EP; and
3. open up even more European legislation to scrutiny by MEPs.

The anomalous situation, however, arises because proposals to democratise the Community through strengthening the European Parliament are bitterly opposed by national governments.

● To increase the democratic nature of the EP would be to legitimise its activities, whereas now its actions can be contemptuously dismissed as being 'unrepresentative' allowing national governments to ignore it.
● To legitimise the EP is to strengthen it in relation to national parliaments, to the extent that it is not impossible that national parliaments could become irrelevant in time.

So we end with the ironic paradox that the very ministers who can criticise the Community for being 'undemocratic' are the same people who, as members of the Council of Ministers, refuse to legislate for democracy within the Community.

The House of Commons seeks to exercise some scrutiny of European legislation by insisting that when a proposal goes from the Commission to the Council the British minister concerned will not approve the measure until it has been seen by the relevant parliamentary committee. This is backed up by a series of resolutions by the House, most recently in a Resolution of 24 October 1990 (Public Information Office of the House of Commons, 1991):

> In the opinion of this House, no Minister of the Crown should give agreement in the Council of Ministers to any proposal for European Community legislation which is still subject to scrutiny (that is, on which the Select Committee on European Legislation has not completed its scrutiny); or which is awaiting consideration by the House.

It has to be said that the scrutiny process can do nothing to prevent the implementation of Community legislation; the committees involved only being allowed to concern themselves with prospective legislation. Parliament can advise ministers on the line to take in future negotiations but it cannot amend or revise legislation that has already been through the European legislative procedure. However, despite these limitations parliament obviously believes in the need for national scrutiny of European legislation, and Select Committees for both Houses of Parliament to investigate the scrutiny process were set up even before the UK formally became a member of the EC.

Stay or Go?

During all the debates on federalism versus pragmatism, on the cost of British membership and the iniquities of the CAP, there was one constant. Even the most Eurosceptical of critics seemed to accept that Britain had to remain a member. There were reasons for this:

- With the Single Market in operation British trade and industry was part of a large internal market. Very few members of Britain's commercial and industrial community were ready to retreat from that, with the possible threat of European tariff barriers being raised against British goods and services.

- Britain has received a great deal of inward investment from the United States, Japan and the Far East by firms who wished to set up a manufacturing base within the Community so as to avoid the external trade tariff. Withdrawal from the Community would mean the loss of these companies, with a consequent loss of investment, tax revenue and jobs.
- If Britain rejected her trading partners in Europe it is hard to see who would replace them. The old Commonwealth countries such as Australia and New Zealand have found new markets, especially in the Pacific Rim countries. And the United States has made it clear that their interest in Britain is solely as a link with Europe, and that if they were offered a choice between Europe and Britain alone they would choose Europe.

Yet, as the sceptics continued their arguments over the nature of British membership there were those among them who followed the logic of their argument and began to talk openly about withdrawal. At first this attitude was an emotional one among those who did not understand the pragmatic reasons for continued membership stated above, and whose thinking was largely guided by the more jingoistic tabloid press. However, the scepticism (or more properly the phobia) evident in the Conservative Party had not gone away after the debate over the Maastricht Treaty, and the most sceptical deepened their distrust of Europe and their total opposition to a federal solution. They would like to reduce the EC to little more than a free trade area but, if continued membership meant more than this then Britain should contemplate withdrawal as the best way to protect British interests.

The first leading politician to put this idea into words was the former Chancellor, Norman Lamont, speaking about resisting federalism to the Selsdon Group of the Conservative Party in Bournemouth on 11 October 1994 during the Party Conference. If federalism were not rejected, he said, 'it would continue to dominate our politics and poison the Conservative Party for many years to come'. There were various alternatives to federalism but, if all these failed, the British government should not be afraid to accept the alternative. 'One day it may mean contemplating withdrawal. It has recently been said that the option of leaving the Community was "unthinkable". I believe this attitude is rather simplistic.'

The Conservatives and Europe Before the 1997 Election

The issue of European Union membership came to dominate the 1997 general election to the detriment of most other issues, and not necessarily to the benefit of those members of the Conservative Party who insisted in bringing the matter to the fore. The subject of debate and controversy was the question of European Monetary Union (EMU) and the acceptance of a common currency but, for many of those involved, arguments over EMU were just a coded way of opposing European unity and advocating British withdrawal from the EU.

The Maastricht Treaty had laid down a timetable for monetary union, with the first wave of members to join on 1 January 1999, as well as establishing the convergence criteria which are the measures of unemployment, inflation, national debt and other economic indicators which member countries have to satisfy before being allowed to join the common currency. At the time of Maastricht the UK won an opt-out clause in the treaty which meant that Britain did not have to join if it did not want to. Since at the time the opt-out was granted the economic recession in Britain suggested that the UK would never satisfy the convergence criteria, no one worried overmuch about an issue like EMU which it seemed would not be relevant to British interests. As the UK economy improved, however, and it looked as though Britain might easily satisfy those criteria, there were those – even in the Tory government – who began to contemplate the possibility of the UK joining EMU in the first wave. The mere prospect made the Eurosceptical wing of the Conservative Party ever more strident in their opposition and in their demands that government and party must rule out membership of EMU at any time and under any conditions.

Even beyond the Conservatives there was a growing opposition to Europe in the country. This was manifested in 1996 by the formation of the Referendum Party by the millionaire, the late Sir James Goldsmith. The new party was aimed at the failure of the Conservative government to allow a referendum on constitutional matters such as any deepening of the European Union. To put pressure on the Tories to adopt a more sceptical approach, Goldsmith claimed in his election material that his party would fight 'every seat where the leading candidate has failed to defend your right to vote on the future of this nation'. Outwardly the Referendum Party was not anti-European – after all, Goldsmith was half-

French by birth, retained French nationality, lived for part of the year in France and was an MEP for a French constituency – but it claimed to want no more than to permit the British people a say through a referendum that had been denied them by the traditional parties.

Unfortunately for Sir James' logic there were certain anomalies in the Referendum Party's position:

- There was a clear difference between the party's stated intentions and its real purpose. Goldsmith claimed that 'we are not politicians and our only aim is to secure a Referendum'. Yet all its election literature was openly opposed to the European Union, with statements such as 'unelected Brussels bureaucrats will soon be handed almost total control of our lives'. The explicit aim of the party was the referendum but its implicit purpose, hardly hidden and understood by the electorate, was to achieve Britain's withdrawal from Europe.

- Although the stated reason for the Referendum Party's existence was that no other party would allow a referendum, this was quite clearly untrue as even the most perfunctory reading of the relevant party manifestos would show. In speaking of entry into EMU the Conservatives stated that 'no such decision would be implemented unless the British people gave their express approval in a referendum'; Labour said, 'the people would have to say "Yes" in a referendum'; while the Liberal Democrats had always held the opinion that 'the British people must give their consent through a referendum'.

- The Referendum Party was essentially a single-issue group, with nothing to say about all the other issues which concern the electorate at election time. The British electorate has always shown itself ready to support single-issue pressure groups over matters that concern them, but they have equally always demanded a full programme of government from their political parties.

It is hard to see what the Referendum Party hoped to gain from participation in the general election. The only possible explanation of their strategy was that the Conservative Party would adopt a far more Eurosceptical position in order to avoid opposition from a Referendum Party candidate who would split the right-wing vote.

The official position of the Conservative Party, as advocated by the Chancellor, Kenneth Clarke, was to say that it was extremely doubtful that Britain would join EMU on the first wave in 1999, but it was nevertheless foolish to rule out the possibility while there was a chance of playing some part in the negotiating process by keeping Britain's options open. A policy of 'wait-and-see' was therefore adopted and maintained by John Major and the cabinet. A similar wait-and-see approach was also taken up by the Labour Party. Only the Liberal Democrats were willing to accept unqualified membership of EMU from the first.

Opposition to the official Conservative position came from the Referendum Party, the UK Independence Party and many Tory backbenchers. Even before the election campaign began, the arch-Europhobic Tory MP, Sir George Gardiner, was deselected by his Reigate constituency for making disloyal statements and ultimately fought the election as a Referendum Party candidate – losing his deposit by so doing. A multi-millionaire right-wing businessman, Paul Sykes, offered up to £2500 in election expenses to any Tory candidate who was willing to campaign against the introduction of a single currency.

As many as 232 candidates accepted Paul Sykes' offer and included opposition to Europe in the personal election messages to their constituents. This was significant enough when only backbenchers were involved, but towards the end of the campaign even government ministers like John Horam and Angela Rumbold were breaking collective responsibility by campaigning against EMU membership. Kenneth Clarke, as the only Europhile of any substance in the government, was increasingly isolated as other ministers remained strangely silent on the subject or made studiously equivocal statements with one eye on future contests for the Tory Party leadership, even left-of-centre Tories like Stephen Dorrell moving to a Eurosceptic approach, 'Dorrelling away pretending to hold views that they don't' as one senior Tory was quoted as saying (*The Guardian*, 21 April 1997).

Europe therefore became a major issue in the 1997 general election but not in the way that anyone might have expected:

- The final three weeks of the election campaign were dominated by Europe to the exclusion of virtually every other issue.
- Discussions were almost exclusively about whether the candidates would rule out British entry into the single currency, and other

matters like fish quotas and beef bans, which were of some concern to the electorate, were largely ignored.

- There is no evidence that the British people are as Europhobic as the right wing of the Conservative Party think they are. The British are sceptical in the true meaning of the term; they dislike foreigners, particularly the Germans; they do not like the idea of 'losing the pound' and they can get very annoyed with the more futile bureaucratic measures from Brussels. However, abstract arguments over concepts such as national sovereignty come a very poor second to bread and butter issues like taxation or education.
- The arguments over Europe were very clearly not about Europe itself but far more about internal arguments and divisions within the Conservative Party. As one prominent Tory politician, Lord Whitelaw, said, 'The reason they got into trouble was over Europe. If they can't work together they won't achieve anything'.

New Labour and Europe After the Election

The re-establishment of Britain's position in Europe was one of the first priorities of the Blair government after the 1997 victory. Within days of becoming foreign secretary Robin Cook had committed the British government to signing the Social Chapter and agreed to extensions of majority voting. Doug Henderson was appointed as the first specifically European minister at the Foreign Office and it was made clear that in future intergovernmental talks Britain would be represented by Henderson as a minister, rather than by a civil servant as had been the case under the Conservatives: thus bringing the UK's procedures into line with other member states. Within a month Robin Cook had gone even further than any British minister had gone before. Alongside the MP who was appointed as Cook's parliamentary private secretary within the House of Commons, Cook had appointed an MEP to be his European parliamentary private secretary (EPPS) to handle liaison with the European Parliament. Other ministers also looked likely to appoint EPPSs.

These instant concessions, together with a new willingness to negotiate and accept compromises rather than seek confrontation, sent out new messages to Europe and hinted that Britain would henceforth be far less obstructionist than had been the case in recent years. Any change in relations between Britain and the EU was more a change of style and attitude rather than one of substance but it proved very acceptable to the other member states, and Tony Blair's first European Council meeting in Noordwijk seemed bathed in goodwill.

The new mood of give and take meant that other member states were more ready to accommodate British positions on contentious issues. Final solutions were only possible through intense negotiation but answers were promised to such difficult questions as the quota-hopping dispute and the Common Fisheries Policy. On thorny issues such as Britain's position on internal frontiers, immigration and common defence, there seemed to be a prospect of replacing the 'opt-out' special treatment extracted by John Major at Maastricht by a looser 'opt-in' kind of arrangement.

The EMU and common currency remained as potential problems but the economic and electoral problems of France and Germany seemed to make the postponement of EMU's starting date ever more likely, thus making British concerns about early membership far less relevant. In any case the overwhelming electoral victory for a wait-and-see approach meant that, at least as far as the British electorate is concerned, European issues have become far less relevant to anything except for the internal divisions of the Tory Party.

Summary

The problems which face the European Union as the new millennium approaches have much to do with the question of enlargement; an increase from the present 15 to 20 or 21 members being envisaged by the year 2002, with a further increase to between 30 and 40 members by the year 2020. The New Labour approach, followed partially by the French, is to say that the EU must forget its obsession with institutions and procedures and concentrate more on:

- effective action on employment throughout the Union;
- greater economic growth to increase the general prosperity of the Union; and
- a concern for social justice and a better quality of life for the people of the Union.

The response of the Europhiles in Britain and elsewhere is to say that these are laudable aims but can only be realised, especially within an enlarged EU, if the institutional procedures are reformed, especially in respect of an increased sharing of sovereignty and a relaxation of the national veto. A fairly sceptical view of New Labour's stance was taken by John Palmer, who was the first newspaper correspondent ever assigned to Europe full time, writing in what was virtually his last despatch before retiring,

> For all the refreshing change of style in Britain's European policy introduced by the Blair government, its stance on some of these cornerstone issues remains ambiguous . . . [and] . . . the new government has adopted some Tory shibboleths which will make it difficult, if not impossible, for the EU to build a community of 'freedom, justice and security'. (*The Guardian*, 9 June 1997)

10

Constitutional Reform

There are various concerns about the British political system that have come to the surface in recent years and which can be grouped together as constitutional issues. These issues surfaced because it was felt that the British political system, as it has existed for so long, is no longer right for the democratic needs of today. In 1988 a pressure group known as Charter 88 was formed to campaign for a number of reforms to the British constitution and political system, such as:

- a written constitution;
- a Bill of Rights and Freedom of Information;
- reform of the House of Lords; and
- modernisation of the Monarchy.

Before all these, however, and crucially central to all proposed changes, Charter 88 would like to see a complete reform of the electoral system used in Britain.

Electoral Reform

Arguments over electoral reform can become very heated about the relative merits of majority and proportional electoral systems because, as has been said, 'electoral systems are not mere details but key causal factors in determining outcomes' (Reeve and Ware, 1992). Any argument over systems, however, is very seldom resolved because the protagonists in the debate seldom argue from the same position. The fact is that elections meet a variety of different purposes and no one electoral system is effective in fulfilling all of them. By choosing to emphasise one purpose of an election rather than another, an individual will also have indicated a preference for the type of electoral system to be used:

1. Those wanting clear results and strong government will favour a majority system.
2. Those concerned with fairness and equity will favour a proportional system.

Third parties like the Liberal Democrats have always protested that the British electoral system of first-past-the-post is unfair to them in that they can gain a large number of votes without winning many seats in parliament. For example, the Tory government which was first elected in 1979 won its victory on no more than about 40 per cent of the vote, which meant that Britain was governed for 18 years by a party that was unwanted by as much as 60 per cent of the people.

Under the first-past-the-post system only two parties have any real hope of forming a government. This sharp division of politics into two main parties opposed to each other produces a divided parliament and a confrontational style of politics. As a result, many people want to change the electoral system. In 1990 when Neil Kinnock embarked on Labour's policy review he set up a committee of enquiry under the guidance of Professor Raymond Plant into the question of the electoral system to be used for the proposed Scottish Assembly. It was also felt that it might find a system that could be used by a future Labour government in local, European and Westminster elections (Coxall and Robins, 1995, p. 274). The criteria that such systems would have to satisfy were clearly defined:

- Proportionality was an important criterion, but there were others.
- There ought to be fair representation for women, ethnic minorities and the regions.
- The power to create a government should lie in the hands of the people voting in the election, and not in the hands of party 'fixers' making deals, often in secret.
- Elections should produce effective governments.
- Any proposal for electoral reform must have the support of a majority of MPs.

First Past the Post

The electoral system used in Great Britain is a simple majority system in that a candidate merely needs one more vote than another candidate to win: hence the term 'first-past-the-post'. For parliamentary elections the country is divided into constituencies of between 60 000 and 70 000 electors each, and each constituency elects one MP. This is true also for Northern Ireland when Westminster elections are involved; although different rules apply to local and European elections where the delicate politico-religious differences require a degree of proportionality. Peculiarities used to exist in the British system, such as extra votes for university graduates and owners of businesses, but the university seats and the business vote were abolished in 1949, as were the surviving 12 multi-member constituencies.

The British system is remarkably easy to understand: the voter places a cross against one name on the ballot paper and, a little later, a straightforward count results in a clear winner for the constituency or ward. There is, therefore, also a clear link between the constituency or ward and the elected member. In most general elections the results also provide a party with a good governing majority in the House of Commons. However, the first-past-the-post system only really works within a two-party system. As soon as any serious third candidate or party intervenes, the chances are that the winner in an election will have gained the most votes but not a majority of the votes. Within a constituency this can mean an MP being elected with only 30 to 40 per cent of the vote. Take, for example, the constituency of Brecon and Radnor in the 1992 election which the Conservatives won on 36.1 per cent of the vote, as against the 35.8 per cent gained by the Liberal Democrats, 26.3 per cent by Labour and 0.9 per cent by the Nationalists. The result was that Brecon was represented by an MP who had been rejected by 64 per cent of those voting. At national level this same factor has meant that no government since 1935 has been elected on a majority of the popular vote. Even the massive Labour landslide of 1997 was won on only a 44 per cent share of the vote. Prior to that, in the February 1974 election, there was an even more striking anomaly when Labour became the largest party in the Commons despite only having 37.2 per cent of the vote, as against the Conservatives' 38.2 per cent.

In recent years, with third parties becoming stronger, the argument of effectiveness has become less easy to sustain, particularly in local government. An increasing number of councils, particularly in England, have come under no overall control and many counties and districts have administrations run through cooperation between either Conservative or Labour councillors and the Liberal Democrats, in exactly the type of coalition that was once thought of as peculiar to a system of proportional representation and which the first-past-the-post system was supposed to make unlikely if not impossible.

The arguments against the current system put forward by those in favour of electoral reform are largely based on the criteria of fairness and value:

- The system produces too many wasted votes. In safe party seats, which form something like three-quarters of the total, large numbers of votes cast for unsuccessful candidates are wasted, as are equally large numbers of surplus votes for winning candidates.
- Third parties are adversely affected when their support is spread thinly and widely. This was most obviously seen in 1983, when Labour won 209 seats with 27.6 per cent of the vote, while the Liberal/SDP Alliance won only 23 seats with 25.4 per cent of the vote.
- Voters are disenfranchised because their views are never taken into consideration. It is significant that the Thatcher governments between 1979 and 1990 were able to introduce the most radical legislation despite being opposed by more than 55 per cent of those voting. It must also be remembered, when percentages of voting figures are quoted, that only 70 to 80 per cent of the electorate actually vote in general elections. 50 per cent of those voting can mean no more than 40 per cent of those able to vote. What is more, the failure of the Tories to win a single seat in Scotland and Wales in 1997 left a sizeable number of Conservative voters effectively disenfranchised.
- The system leads to confrontational politics and the adoption by parties of extreme positions, largely because there is no need for the consensus view required in the formation of coalition administrations.

The Case for Reform

The argument that the first-past-the-post system should be replaced with a more proportional system is quite old. Early in the present century there was agitation that the fledgling Labour Party would never get off the ground while the electoral system was so weighted against small third parties, and in 1917 legislation was drawn up to introduce a fairer system of voting which failed as a result of disagreements as to the best system to be used. After Labour overtook the Liberals as the main opposition to the Conservatives in the 1920s it was the turn of the Liberals to advocate electoral reform, and MacDonald's Labour government of 1929 introduced the question once more, although this move also failed. Obviously, small parties have always been the ones who would benefit most from proportional representation just as the two larger parties benefit most from the existing system.

During the peak years of the two-party system, after 1945, when the third-party share of the vote remained below 10 per cent as it did for the Liberals until 1974, the public was not greatly concerned. However, when the Liberal vote grew from 7.5 per cent in 1970 to 19.3 per cent in 1974, but the number of seats gained by the Liberals only increased from six (1 per cent) to 14 (2 per cent), it became rather too great a discrepancy to be overlooked. Nine years later, in 1983, the Liberal/SDP share of the vote grew to 25.4 per cent, but that only represented 23 parliamentary seats. The distortion created by the system was now too glaringly unfair to be overlooked and an increasing proportion of the population began to realise that something might be wrong.

The Labour Party began to take an interest in 1987 after they had lost their third successive election to the Conservatives and it began to look as though Labour would never be able to unseat the Conservatives unaided. In 1990 the Plant Committee was set up, as has already been stated. In 1992 Neil Kinnock actually introduced the topic of electoral reform into the election campaign as a sort of sweetener for the Liberal Democrats in case the parliament resulting from the 1992 election should be hung.

The Plant Committee reported in 1993 and the Labour Party became committed to some reform of the electoral system in the elections for the devolved assemblies promised for Scotland and Wales. An EU ruling already exists stating that a Europe-wide proportional system has to be in place before the European elections of 1999 and this point was conceded by the Labour government in July 1997. It was also proposed that a form of proportional representation might be best for any elected second chamber chosen by New Labour to replace the House of Lords. On Westminster elections, however, Tony Blair has always expressed himself as sceptical, or agnostic at best, and this attitude was not likely to be changed when the size of landslide achieved by Labour in 1997 (by means of first-past-the-post) is taken into consideration. In looking back at the 1997 election results Blair was not likely to be reconciled to electoral reform by the thought that proportional representation would have denied him an overall majority. Nevertheless, as far as Westminster elections are concerned Tony Blair had reached agreement with the Liberal Democrats before the 1997 election that there should be a referendum in which the electorate is allowed the choice between first-past-the-post and a specified proportional system; the actual system to be chosen later. What was not known is the position Blair himself would take in any campaign associated with that referendum.

Although the Conservative Party appeared to remain totally hostile to any talk of electoral reform, there is the chance that even they might think again when they consider the size of the task facing them in overturning the 1997 result. This is because the Conservatives as much as any party can suffer from the distortions of first-past-the-post if they find themselves in a third-party situation. A spectacular example of this came in the 1995 elections for metropolitan district councils when the Tories polled 20 per cent of the votes cast for a mere 6 per cent of councillors elected, while Labour gained 81 per cent of the seats for 57 per cent of the vote (*The Observer*, 21 April 1996). After the 1997 election the Conservatives also face the fact that they are totally unrepresented in Scotland and Wales, despite quite large Conservative votes in both countries. Indeed, there is the irony that the Conservatives took more votes in Scotland than the Liberal Democrats but captured no seats, whereas the Liberal Democrats with 11 constituencies was now the second largest party to represent Scotland in parliament.

Alternative Electoral Systems

Absolute or overall majority systems are designed to modify the 'winner-takes-all' aspect of the first-past-the-post system to give a greater degree of proportionality and reduce the number of wasted votes; this is achieved by some device whereby the least successful candidates are eliminated and the second preference votes of their supporters are transferred to the more successful, either through a second ballot or by listing preferences on the first ballot, until one candidate emerges with more than 50 per cent support.

These overall majority systems satisfy the same criteria as first-past-the-post (FPTP) in that they maintain close constituency links, produce clear-cut results and are relatively easy to understand. The system does eliminate the wasted vote factor in that, even if a voter's first preference has no effect on the result, their second preference might be crucial. Second ballot voting or the redistribution of second preferences is also marginally more proportional in that it would tend to favour third parties which regularly take second place in FPTP contests. Take, for example, Michael Howard's constituency of Folkestone and Hythe in the 1997 election, which Howard won with 20 313 votes against the Liberal Democrats' 13 981, with Labour in third place on 12 939. If an alternative system had been in operation and the Labour candidate had been eliminated, it would seem likely that virtually all of Labour's second preference votes would have gone to the Liberal Democrats and thus ensured the defeat of Michael Howard and the Conservatives.

The main charge levelled against proportional systems in general, and list systems in particular, is that the proliferation of parties that they promote leads inevitably to coalition governments formed from two or more parties. Criticism of proportional representation therefore amounts to criticism of the undemocratic nature of coalitions:

1. Coalition governments are inherently unstable. The list system has notoriously produced so many ineffectual governments in Italy that moves have been made in recent years to introduce some elements of majority voting.
2. Small parties who should be the junior partners in a coalition have a disproportionate share of power. In Germany the Liberal Free Democrat Party has always been a poor third in terms of popular support, but they have always been able to dictate their own terms for entry into a coalition with either the Social Democrats or the Christian Democrats.
3. It is hard to assess the performance of a party when it is not known which party in a government is responsible for which policy: a coalition government can thus never be truly accountable to the electorate and the electorate can never know exactly for what it is voting.

4. The junior partner in a coalition can change their allegiance to the larger party at any time, thus changing the government without reference to the electorate.
5. Proportional representation can also encourage the growth of small extremist parties, whether of the fascist right or communist left.

In public debate the argument over electoral systems and the possibility of electoral reform for Britain has all too often been reduced to arguments over fairness on the one side and an effective choice of government on the other. Yet the question involves much more than that and, in a way, the argument is not capable of resolution while those involved in the argument disagree over what they see as their priority purpose in holding an election. Nor is there likely to be any change when the two major parties both feel secure in their ability to win an election on their own and unaided; with the desire for reform restricted to the minor parties who lack the power to do anything about it.

However, electoral systems are more than mere technicalities because, as David Butler has said, they 'lie at the heart of a nation's arrangements' (David Butler, in Jowell and Oliver, 1985). And, as repeated by Cowley and Dowding (1994, p. 21):

> Any change in the electoral system will change the system of representation. Our prior decision really needs to be: what sort of representation do we want? We should then create our electoral system in terms of the answer to that question.

A Bill of Rights

All Britons are proud of the rights they have as British citizens but in fact there is nothing to guarantee them those rights. The Law is full of rules telling them what they cannot do, but there is nothing to tell them what they can do. If the law is vague about this then it is often left to a judge to decide whether someone has acted 'within their rights' or not.

This liberal or *laissez-faire* approach to rights, which says that you can do whatever you like if there is no law against it, is very attractive and was held up for a long time as evidence of the superiority of 'England's ancient liberties'. Events of the 1970s and 1980s, particularly the suspension of civil rights in anti-terrorist legislation, forced people to realise that a negative definition of individual freedom alone meant that there was nothing to stop the government from issuing whatever legislation they liked to curtail that freedom.

> The liberal approach stresses in particular the inability of existing structures to protect the rights of the individual from encroachment by agencies of the state. . . Political power has been centralised in Downing Street and Cabinet, with neither House of Parliament able to stand up effectively to the wishes of the executive. Control of a party majority in the House of Commons is all that is needed to ride roughshod over the rights of the individual. (Norton, 1994, pp. 6–11)

It is recognition of this flaw in the existing political system that has led increasing numbers of individuals and groups to call for a Bill of Rights:

- If civil rights were clearly stated and existed in written form it would help individuals to understand exactly what they are and are not entitled to do. A codified Bill of Rights taught in school would mean that everyone could grow up as an informed citizen.
- Someone whose rights were abused would have the backing of the courts to give redress. Officials might be less likely to abuse peoples' rights if they felt they might be taken to court as a result.
- Any legislation passed by parliament would have to observe the Bill of Rights and any proposed laws that infringed it would be rendered invalid.
- A Bill of Rights would protect the interests of vulnerable minorities such as travellers, gays, certain religious sects and other minorities, groups whose elected representatives might fear to champion them for fear of majority opinion.

Those opposed to a Bill of Rights argue that there is no such thing as an absolute right: the rights of one individual have to be measured against the effects those rights would have on the rights of others. This view was very evident after the Dunblane massacre in 1996: a majority of caring people claimed that the right to life and happiness of the dead children had been destroyed by the ability of their killer to carry arms. Yet there was still a minority who believed in the right of individuals to own a gun if they wanted to do so.

In one respect Britain already has access to a Bill of Rights. In 1950 Britain, as a member of the Council of Europe, was a signatory of the European Convention of Human Rights which, modelled on the United Nations 'Declaration of Human Rights', set out to define those civil and natural freedoms which should belong by right to the citizens of Europe. Britain ratified the Convention in 1951 and has continued to ratify it each year ever since, but the Convention has never been incorporated into British law. A civil rights issue cannot be tried in a British court but a British citizen can appeal to the Commission of the Convention and have their case heard in the European Court of Human Rights in Strasbourg.

Some 800 complaints from British subjects come before the Commission each year. Only a few of these are judged suitable for hearing by the Court but almost a quarter of all cases heard come from Britain and only the Italian government has a higher record of adverse judgments than the British. In cases against the British government the Court has:

- found that the IRA members shot in Gibraltar by the SAS (the 'Death on the Rock' incident) were 'killed unlawfully';
- condemned the use of corporal punishment in schools; and
- upheld the rights of workers not to join a closed shop.

It would have been very easy for Britain to acquire a 'ready-made' Bill of Rights at any time since 1951 simply by accepting the European Convention and incorporating it into British law. However, until the election of 1997 all governments showed themselves to be hostile to such a move. Indeed, decisions by the Strasbourg court, especially the Gibraltar shootings case, so angered the Tory government as to generate talk of a British withdrawal from the Convention, while Michael Howard during his time as Home Secretary seemed to have a particular grievance against the Court of Human Rights. The constitutional lawyer Anthony Lester, contributing to a symposium on Michael Howard in *The Observer* newspaper (19 May 1996, p. 7) listed at least four occasions on which Howard thwarted attempts to make the European Convention applicable to member governments.

The attitude shown by Howard is part of the dichotomy in British government thinking which, on the one hand, says it wants to allow freedom of choice and independent action to the citizen while, on the other, centralising all power into own hands. The first sign that this was about to change came with New Labour's declared intention to incorporate the European Convention into British law. This would still not give Britain its own Bill of Rights, nor would it give the British citizen any rights that were not there before. What it would mean is open access to the civil rights of the European Convention through a normal British court of law, without any need for the time-consuming delays of going to Strasbourg for judgment.

Freedom of Information

Alongside the need to know our rights there is a need to know what is happening and what is being done in our name by government, local authorities, the courts, the police and so on. Enquiries like the Scott Report have shown how much of government is carried on in secret and, as a result, people generally feel that a lot of things they need to know are deliberately being kept from them; often simply so that the government should not be embarrassed. There is a feeling that government should be open, with everything clearly explained except in cases where making information available would endanger national security or breach personal privacy.

Recent governments have resisted a freedom of information act on the American model, most recently in 1988 when the government imposed a three-line whip to kill off a private member's bill introduced by the Conservative MP, Richard Shepherd, to repeal section 2 of the Official Secrets Act. The Act was originally introduced in the interests of state security before the First World War, but section 2 actually made it a criminal offence for any public servant to disclose any information whatsoever which they had learned in doing their job and this section was never repealed, even after the wartime emergency was over. There are obviously times when such secrecy is important but section 2 was such a catch-all clause that it was said to mean that 'a civil servant could be imprisoned for disclosing the number of biscuits consumed by a permanent secretary' (Kingdom, 1991, p. 364).

Section 2 of the Official Secrets Act was finally abandoned but there is still a lot of information that is kept secret from the public. Some legislation has been passed to prevent government bodies holding secret files about individuals. Any records that might be kept – such as the medical records made by doctors, or academic records kept by schools – may be confidential, but the person about whom the records are kept has a right to see what has been written about them. One of the first bills promised by the new Labour government in 1997 was a data protection bill intended to extend an individual's access to personal files held by governmental agencies or private institutions. On the other hand there was a movement towards secrecy rather than openness in moves to restrict the ability of the media to intrude upon an individual's privacy.

The Blair government had included the institution of a Freedom of Information Act in its election manifesto but it was a little slower in committing itself over introducing the relevant legislation. It seems to be a fact of political life that freedom of information is very popular with political parties in opposition but is a commitment they seem to forget once they have come into power.

The Monarchy

Like that other hereditary body, the House of Lords, the Monarchy is the subject of much earnest discussion at the close of the twentieth century as commentators try to evolve a *raison d'être* for what are often seen as anachronisms in this period of our history. In both cases the choice is not, as it once was, simply between retention and abolition. It is also possible to retain a reformed institution by stripping it of some of its more traditional trappings in order to make it relevant to the age. This is particularly the case as it concerns the present members of the royal family, where criticisms of the constitutional role of the heir to the throne and his brothers have become confused with personal criticisms of the behaviour and marital misfortunes of those same people.

There is a belief that the monarchy is out-of-date and has no place in a modern democracy. Along with the House of Lords, the monarchy represents the rigid class structure of Britain and all the unfairness and snobbishness of any system based on heredity. The problem with royalty is like the hereditary peers' ability to hold up the workings of parliament – it is 'power without responsibility' and the ability to influence political decisions without having to answer to the public for their actions.

Even among people who believe in the monarchy there are those who believe that the present royal family has gone too far:

- Becoming too involved with scandal in the tabloid press, while too many members of the family have had marital problems which ended in divorce.
- Few people criticise the Queen but there are seen to be too many hangers-on, more distant relations who are paid an allowance from public money for doing very little.
- Television and the tabloid newspaper gossip columns have destroyed the air of remote mystery that used to surround royalty, turning them into soap opera stars.

However, it is not the underpinning of élitism nor the behaviour of the House of Windsor that is the most anti-democratic feature of the monarchy. Far more important is the Royal Prerogative, which represents powers formerly belonging to the monarch but now possessed by the prime minister and government, including:

- the appointment of ministers, bishops, judges and military chiefs;
- patronage in the granting of honours and appointments to quangos and other bodies;
- the summoning and dissolution of parliament and thereby the choice of election date; and
- the declaration of war and the signing of treaties.

These powers are exercised by the government in the name of the monarch but without having to consult or inform parliament before so exercising them! Through the use of the royal prerogative the monarch becomes a symbol behind which a government can hide when overriding the wishes of the people's representatives.

In 1867, the constitutionalist Walter Bagehot divided the constitution into what he called its 'efficient' and 'dignified' elements; the former covering the work done by prime minister, government and parliament in actually running the country, the latter referring to institutions like the monarchy which lend legitimacy to the efficient elements by gratifying the need of the masses for an element of pomp and circumstance to act as a focus for their loyalty. As part of the dignified constitution the monarch has two roles:

- To act as a symbol of the nation representing the personification of that country in the eyes of the nation's own citizens, and also personifying an image of the nation which can be presented to other countries. The monarch is almost an abstract construction

like the flag or national anthem, and is necessarily divorced and remote from political partisanship.
• To carry out, or legitimise, certain largely ceremonial functions to symbolise the British definition of government as being by 'the Crown in Parliament'. The State Opening of Parliament is a prime example of the purely symbolic nature of this ceremonial, typified by the Queen's Speech delivered on that occasion which is presented as though it were the monarch addressing her parliament but which is in fact a declaration of intent from the government, and written by the prime minister and the prime minister's advisers.

Criticism of the institution of monarchy in a democracy is centred on the non-elected and hereditary nature of that institution. As the critics say, democracy chooses MPs and councillors as its own representatives, but whom does the monarch represent except the abstract idea of the monarchy itself? If the monarch is given any power, can it be right that that power is exercised by someone who was chosen not on merit but by an accident of birth. Beyond these criticisms the monarch is also said to be undemocratic in a social sense, in that the royal family can hardly represent the people of this country when their wealth and their way of life is so very different from the social norm.

As Lord Plant has said, there is something to be said for the hereditary principle in producing a head of state who is above politics. Unfortunately, as he goes on to say, 'the point about hereditary monarchy is that you have to put up with what the accidents of birth produce. . . and there is absolutely no guarantee that the hereditary principle will produce a monarch who is capable of symbolising the nation and its values' (*The Guardian*, April 1996). The importance of the tabloid debate about the behaviour of the young royals and their marital problems is that this behaviour debases the standards we should expect from people who are supposed to symbolise all that is good about the British way of life.

Criticisms of the royal family only have an importance if royalty's behaviour has a political content. For example, the fact that the heir to the throne is about to divorce his wife is largely irrelevant in political terms. Prince Charles' great-great-grandfather, Edward VII, was notorious for his love affairs without this noticeably bringing the monarchy into disrepute. Indeed, the king's affairs seemed to contribute to his popularity with the people. Of Edward

VII's popularity despite his infidelities we may say the same as Anthony Barnett says of George III's popularity despite his madness, 'Being mad didn't matter. It just showed that he was human – the more human, the more lovable' (Barnett, 1995, pp. 2–4).

The point being made by Barnett in his article – a point reinforced by a conference on the future of the monarchy, jointly organised by Charter 88 and *The Times* on 22 May 1993 with three leading contributors: Charles Moore for retention, Shirley Williams for reform, and Sue Townsend for abolition – is that the time of Edward VII was still one where the royal prerogative could be seen as a safeguard against the abuse of power and political office; just as had been described by Victorian constitutionalists like Dicey and Bagehot. By the end of the twentieth century, on the other hand, the royal prerogative is seen as a way by which over-powerful governments can legitimise their actions and cloak them in secrecy. As Shirley Williams said at the conference, 'The executive in Britain has something very close to absolute power. It hides behind the crown as a way of hiding from us the extent of that power'.

There are still those who argue that a hereditary monarchy with its traditions and ceremonial can serve a useful purpose as a figurehead symbol of the state, even if it is merely in its contribution to the tourist trade. For this to work, however, there has to be reform of the institution as part of a wider constitutional reform, which will give a new and different legitimacy to the monarchy. Without a set of written constitutional obligations or democratic legitimacy, the royal family has to rely on its unimpeachable behaviour for its continuing legitimacy – and this is beyond the capacity of any human family to guarantee (Hutton, 1995, p. 323).

Possible reforms might be:

- Remove the royal prerogative. If the royal prerogative were taken away the government would have to consult parliament before doing anything and would no longer be able to hide non-democratic decisions behind the symbol of the monarchy.
- Disestablish the Church by giving up the royal title of Head of the Church of England, which is no longer a realistic position to hold in the modern multicultural world.
- Maintain the present monarch and the immediate royal family but end public payments to cousins and more distant relations. There have already been cuts in the Civil List (money granted by parliament to support the royal family), and the Queen is now

paying income tax. But some people feel that this could go much further. The matter is one of those under discussion by the Way Ahead Group, a sort of royal think tank which meets twice a year under the direction of the Queen. This group would like to see the Civil List abolished and the very valuable Crown Lands restored so that a slimmed-down royal household could be self-supporting and free of dependence on government money.

- Remove the automatic right of the Prince of Wales to succeed to the throne. If it is felt that the troubles of the prince's marriage should rule him out from ever becoming king, then it should be possible to bypass him in favour of one of his sons. The Way-Ahead Group would also like to see the rule of male primogeniture abolished, so that older daughters would inherit before a second or third born son.

As is fairly obvious, the abolition of the monarchy would demand a written constitution in order to define the duties and function of an elected president. What is perhaps less obvious is that reform of the monarchy would not only demand a written constitution but would in fact be an inevitable by-product of the writing of a constitution. This is particularly true for the two areas of the royal prerogative where the monarchy could be said still to have a political role in the governance of the country:

1. As a protector of the country's liberties, so as to safeguard us against dictatorship or absolutist government. Although there is a statute limiting the life of a parliament to five years, there is nothing constitutionally to prevent a government from passing an act of parliament to prolong its own life. Because of two world wars this has happened twice in this century, the parliament elected in 1910 surviving until 1918, and that of 1936 lasting until 1945. The only safeguard against this happening for a less democratic reason is that the monarch has the right to dissolve parliament and invalidate the acts of that parliament, with the ability to call on the army and police to support the monarch's actions. Some parliamentary device would have to be found to maintain that safeguard.

2. As the person who appoints the prime minister and government ministers. Mostly this is settled by convention and the leader of the party which has the largest number of parliamentary seats

after a general election is asked to form a government. The possibility does exist, however, that a situation could arise where there is no obvious candidate and the monarch would actually have to choose who should become prime minister. With the growth of electoral volatility in the mid-1980s, there was a great deal of speculation as to what would happen if a general election resulted in a hung parliament, with no clear majority party. This would mean that the queen would have had the equivalent of a casting vote in deciding which of the various party leaders should be asked to form a government, which would represent a constitutional crisis as the monarch made a political decision. Again, some statutory device would have to be developed to cover this eventuality.

The House of Lords

Very few countries – New Zealand and Israel are rare examples – have only one house of parliament; most are made up of two houses in what is known as a bicameral parliament. So, why two houses?

1. The upper house acts as a check on government by looking closely at any legislation passed by the lower house.
2. A second chamber can represent minority interests.
3. A second chamber can take some of the work-load on behalf of the lower house.

The same arguments centre on the House of Lords as surround the monarchy, but with an added importance in that the Lords is part of the efficient element of the constitution, as well as the dignified. As with the monarchy there are three perceived responses to the House of Lords – it could be retained as it is, abolished completely, or reformed.

Criticisms of the House of Lords are based on its undemocratic nature. Prior to the 1997 election the situation was that:

1. Out of a total 1200 accredited peers, 775 were hereditary peers. Only 15 of these were peers of first creation, which means that they themselves were awarded the title on merit; the remaining 760 had all inherited their titles.

2. There were only 79 women in the Lords and, since succession in Britain is based on male primogeniture, 62 of these were life peers.
3. The Lords remained an overwhelmingly Conservative body, with 480 accepting the Tory whip as against 116 for Labour and 58 for the Liberal Democrats. Many of the 278 peers who claim no party allegiance but sit on the cross-benches are conservatively inclined even if not actual Conservatives.
4. Only a minority of peers were active in the House of Lords. About 300 attend on a daily basis but no more than 800 attend at least once a year (Shell and Beamish, 1993).

It has to be said that, whatever the criticism of the Lords, there would seem to be overwhelming arguments for the retention of a second chamber of some kind:

- The Lords has an important function as a revising chamber since it has the time to look at the detail rather than the principle of proposed legislation. The Lords is particularly good at picking up and amending errors that have crept into government bills through faulty drafting: in the 1992–93 parliamentary session the House of Lords passed a total of 1674 amendments to 28 government bills (Shell, 1995, pp. 21–4).
- The Lords is able to ease the strain on the parliamentary work-load by taking the lion's share of routine and non-controversial bills from the Commons. This is particularly true of the largely technical and formalised private bills.
- Since life peerages in particular are awarded for achievements in fields other than politics, there is an authority based on wide experience in the Lords. The scientists, academics, industrialists and so on. who are given life peerages all contribute what David McKie has called 'influence based on expertise' (*The Guardian*, 18 March 1996, p. 13).
- That same expertise lends considerable authority to the growing number of select committees which the Lords has created in recent years. This is particularly true of the scrutiny of matters relating to Europe, where the Lords has five sub-committees but the Commons only two.
- In parliaments where the Commons is dominated by a heavily whipped party system, the Lords manages to retain sufficient independence to represent a serious agent for the scrutiny of

government legislation. As Philip Norton points out in *Politics UK*, 'In the period from 1979 to 1991, the government suffered no less than 173 defeats at the hands of their Lordships' (Jones, 1994, p. 352).

Despite these very strong arguments in favour of the status quo there remains the problem of accountability and non-representation which leaves the argument divided between retention, abolition and reform.

Retention

Until recently only a very few die-hard traditionalists still wished to keep the House of Lords as it is and they were either High Tories or rigid parliamentarians in the mould of Enoch Powell. They argue that the nature of the Lords ensures that it can take decisions without fear or favour and without being subject to the demands of party or special interest group. During the premiership of John Major the Conservative Party seemed to regress and adopted a policy of full-blooded defence of a hereditary House of Lords, part of a general reaction against proposed constitutional changes put forward by New Labour.

Abolition

This was once the position adopted by the Labour Party, as exemplified by Michael Foot, and was official party policy after 1977. The Labour abolitionist argument was expressed by Lord Wedderburn (quoted by Norton, 1994, pp. 6–11): 'Either the second chamber is less democratic than the Commons, in which case it should not be able to delay legislation, or it is just as democratic, when there is no point in having two chambers'. However, as part of Neil Kinnock's policy review, the party shed its abolitionist stance in recognising the value of a second chamber.

Reform

Most politicians from all parties, including the Tories at one time, seem to be in favour of the principle of reform. Unfortunately no one can agree on the nature of that reform. Most people would recognise the case for phasing-out the hereditary element in the

Upper House, and a move to replace the hereditary lords has been on the table since it was adopted as Liberal Party policy in 1891. The last serious attempt to reform the Lords was made by the Wilson government of 1969, by which hereditary peers would have remained solely as non-voting members, with only an enlarged number of life peers having the right to vote on legislation. That move was defeated by the unlikely alliance of Enoch Powell and Michael Foot, since reform was neither the retention nor the abolition they respectively wanted. Between 1977 and 1979, in response to Labour's abolitionist stance, the Conservatives proposed that hereditary peers should be removed and replaced by a second chamber that was one-third appointed and two-thirds elected. The plan did not survive the Tory victory of 1979.

New Labour came into power in 1997 with the expressed intention of removing voting rights from hereditary peers. This would then move to appointment as the only way to introduce new members, with ultimately the intention of electing members to the second chamber. The problem with reform, however, remains an inability to decide between the rival merits of appointment or election as a means of choosing members for the second chamber.

1. Appointment would enable the Lords to continue possessing the virtues of experience and expertise since appointments would be on the grounds of merit and judgment of the contribution they could make to the work of parliament. The suggestion has been made that a second chamber should be representative of interest groups, enabling trade unions, environmental groups and the professions among others to have a direct input into the political process. On the other hand, appointment is not much more democratic than heredity, it would increase the prime ministerial power of patronage and would open up the prospect of purely political appointments.

2. Election of members would certainly be more democratic. But, if a reformed Lords were merely elected on the same lines as the Commons, even if at different times, the risk is that the two chambers would either be carbon copies of one another or they would be in perpetual conflict. One possible suggestion has been that if plans for devolution go ahead an elected second chamber could represent Scotland, Wales, Northern Ireland and the English regions, in the same way as the Senate represents States' rights in the American Congress. Another suggestion is that a

second chamber elected by proportional representation could act as a useful check and balance for the heavily-whipped majorities produced in the House of Commons by a first-past-the-post system.

Although he seemed a little slow in making clear his intentions towards the Lords, Tony Blair did state from the start that something would be done. Very early in his government he made it clear that the days of using honours as a means of paying off favours to party activists was over. His first honours list showed that no party members would be elevated to the peerage merely to look decorative but would go there to work in the party interest. That first list nominated no fewer than 31 working Labour peers in an attempt to redress the deficit in comparison with the Conservatives.

Conclusion – a Written Constitution

Many, if not all, of these reforms would make it virtually obligatory that Britain should have a written constitution.

- A Bill of Rights would certainly require a written constitution – in fact it would form the major part of a written constitution, as is the case in the United States.
- If the monarchy were reformed by withdrawing the royal prerogative, or the House of Lords were abolished or reformed, there would have to be a written set of rules to replace what is currently done on a traditional basis.

Yet it is not only constitutional reforms like a Bill of Rights or reform of the monarchy which demand a root-and-branch review of the British political system because, as Will Hutton has pointed out, shortcomings in Britain's constitutional position undermine the whole of the country's political and economic culture:

The British constitution is at the root of the problem. The first-past-the-post system of voting means that whole regions can have few or even no elected members of the governing party and so have negligible leverage over political decision-making. And the doctrine of parliamentary sovereignty means that the machinery of government ends up serving the governing party rather than any conception of the public interest. (Hutton, 1997, p. 78)

The important thing to remember about constitutional reform is that something as complicated as the British Constitution cannot just be toyed with. Change in one area affects change in another. Charter 88 did not draw up its list as a series of alternatives, they want all the reforms mentioned – as an all-in package, clarified by being written down. The Blair government of 1997 was elected on the most comprehensive programme of constitutional reform that has been seen for many years, and it is all a product of the interrelatedness of reform – electoral reform, a bill of rights and reconstruction of the House of Lords all stemming from the proposals for devolution. The whole package was evolved and stated by the Joint Consultative Committee on Constitutional Reform created in interparty agreements by New Labour and the Liberal Democrats. In the report of the committee published in March 1997, the interrelatedness of constitutional reforms is stressed even when the reforms are described individually, 'The proposals set out are presented as distinct measures, yet they are closely related. Through them runs the common thread of empowering the people' (Barnett, 1997, p. 34).

The importance of constitutional reform to New Labour was stated early in 1997 when Gordon Brown gave the Crosland Lecture:

Political reform is central to this . . . It must enable people to participate in decisions that affect them. . . we should see our constitutional proposals – which range from abolishing the hereditary principle in the Lords to devolution of power – as part of a programme that makes sense of people's aspirations by redistributing power from the state.

11

Accountability and Sleaze

An issue of increasing importance in recent years has been the damage done to the political process by the public's growing disillusionment with, and alienation from, politicians. A Gallup poll carried out at the end of 1994, and reported to the Nolan Committee by Professor Ivor Crewe, Vice-Chancellor of Essex University in January 1995, showed the extent of the damage:

> Some 77 per cent of people polled reckoned that MPs cared more about special interests than about ordinary people, 87 per cent believed that MPs will tell lies if the truth would harm them politically and a full 64 per cent asserted that most MPs make a lot of money by using public office improperly.

For many people there is a suspicion that MPs and councillors are working, not in the interests of their constituents, but in the interests of various outside bodies who are paying them very well for the privilege. In the final analysis, the people's representatives are not working in the interests of constituency, country or party but largely for their own personal benefit, financial and otherwise. It is because of this distrust that during the first week or so of the 1997 election campaign, the Conservative Party could not escape from the issue of sleaze despite their attempts to drag the focus back onto more positive matters.

The general issue of sleaze and scandal among individual councillors and MPs can be subdivided into either personal scandals usually sexual in nature that lay representatives open to charges of hypocrisy or double-standards, or to the acceptance of financial rewards for representing outside interests. Of these the tabloid press makes the most of the private lives and personal behaviour of MPs or ministers, which usually means their sexual peccadillos.

Ironically, it is very seldom that MPs or ministers feel driven to take any action as a result of their sexual practices being revealed. Sexual misbehaviour in itself is not thought to be such a serious political issue that it would require resignation from office, some other issue usually forces that. For example, the number of adulterous love affairs indulged in by David Lloyd George, including keeping a mistress in 10 Downing Street while he was prime minister, was an open secret in the 1920s but it did not lead to his resignation. 'His colleagues . . . protected him from public criticism because of his value to the party in attracting votes' (Doig, November 1994, pp. 2–6). Normally such behaviour goes largely unnoticed, it needs some other factor to bring it to the public's attention.

It is worth noting that the greatest incidence of sex scandals in recent history – in 1963 and 1994 – both took place at a similar point in long-serving Conservative administrations. A governing party that has gone on too long appears to become jaded, careless and somewhat accident-prone, alienating the electorate in the process. As even a newspaper friendly to the Conservatives said, 'We've had it all: sex romps with actresses, researchers, men friends and a satsuma. . . At this rate even abolishing income tax and doubling pensions wouldn't persuade most people to vote for this lot again' (editorial in the *Sun*, October 1994).

Possibly more important than the sex itself as far as the electorate is concerned is the hypocrisy and hint of double standards that can be found in governments which say one thing and do another:

> It is interesting to note that, although Labour ministers are not immune in this sphere, the Conservatives seem to make a speciality of the sex scandal . . . this can be ascribed to the Conservative Party's penchant for describing itself as the 'party of the family'. . . Those who seek to seize the moral high ground are vulnerable when their own personal failings are exposed. (Pyper, 1994, pp. 12–16)

The Major government announced a 'Back to Basics' campaign in October 1993, intended to restore a sense of family values and reestablish the importance of public morality. Well to the fore in the campaign, making a number of speeches critical of unmarried mothers and single-parent families, was a government environment minister, Tim Yeo. In January 1994, within a few months of making these speeches, Yeo was forced to admit to having recently fathered the illegitimate child of a Tory councillor from Hackney. At first Yeo resisted calls for his resignation, but a week later further revelations in the press forced Yeo to confess that he had also fathered an illegitimate child while at university and at that point he did resign.

During the first half of 1994 a whole series of sex scandals was extensively reported in the tabloid press, helping to reinforce what was increasingly being called the 'sleaze factor' surrounding the government, the upshot of which was the setting up of the Nolan Committee. The sordid details of these affairs lent an air of seediness to the Conservative administration and projected a general impression that the government had grown careless and run-down through having gone on for too long. Over the course of just a few weeks a junior minister, Lord Caithness, resigned after his wife committed suicide over his infidelities; the MP Stephen Milligan was found dead after indulging in auto-eroticism; a Tory MP was accused of a homosexual affair; and at least three others were revealed as having had heterosexual adulterous affairs.

There is a tendency to dismiss personal scandals as unimportant; matters which refer only to the politician's private life over which the public need not be concerned. On the other hand, the hypocrisy and duplicity involved in most of these affairs do have their importance for the public: 'What causes a scandal, how it unfolds and how it is or is not resolved, reveals much about how the political world works, its set of values and its priorities' (Doig, 1994). Most importantly, the aura of immorality and sleaze which surrounds cases such as those mentioned above tars all members of parliament with the same brush and helps contribute to the low esteem in which an alienated public is coming to regard all politicians.

The Representation and Misrepresentation of Interests

More invidious than sexual malpractice, however, is the risk of being involved in corrupt practices because of the opportunities open to MPs for the receipt of quite substantial payments in return for making their expertise, experience, political knowledge and useful contacts available to outside interests. There is nothing illegal in an MP receiving payment for acting as a consultant or adviser, as long as he or she is open about it and declares the interest. However, it is a grey area, particularly if an MP is known to be closely involved with a professional lobbyist.

The growth of professional lobbying on the American model, by which a 'parliamentary consultant' offers clients the benefits of high-level political contacts in return for a substantial fee, is a fairly recent phenomenon. The lobbying organisation will offer their clients the services of MPs willing to do various things such as host public relations dinners in exclusive parliamentary surroundings; give advice on the correct avenues through which to bring influence to bear; open up contacts with ministers and senior civil servants; or even ask questions in parliament on the client's behalf. Virtually unknown before 1980, commercial lobbying expanded with great rapidity over the Thatcher years. By the mid-1990s there were over 60 such organisations in Britain with a joint turnover of tens of millions of pounds. One of the largest, and most famous (or infamous), was Ian Greer Associates, with an annual turnover of £3 million, of whom the *Guardian* said, 'The company's clients include Coca Cola, Taylor Woodrow, British Airways and Cadbury Schweppes. Mr Greer relies on parliamentary and Civil Service contacts he has built up over 30 years. His friendship with John Major, for example, goes back a quarter of a century' (*The Guardian*, 6 October 1993).

As has been said, much of this work done by MPs on behalf of some special interest is quite legitimate, as long as the interest is declared openly by them beforehand. Traditionally, the attitude of the Commons towards a declaration of interests has not gone very far beyond the vague indication in Erskine May, the authoritative manual of parliamentary procedure, that an MP with a personal interest in a matter under debate should declare that interest before speaking in the debate. However, Erskine May was written before the introduction of professional lobbying made activities other than the debating chamber important in the eyes of outsiders. As Professor David Butler says in an essay for *The Guardian*, 'Every good cause, every business, every citizen has the right to make its voice heard in government. Often guidance is needed on where to shout in Westminster, and it is not wrong to pay for help. But lobbying must be controlled lest it distort decision-making' (*The Guardian*, 22 October 1995, p. 25).

Following doubts about MPs working on behalf of outside bodies, an agreement had been reached on the disclosure of interests and a Register of Members' Interests had existed for some time. It was not, however, very vigorously enforced and continued protests led to an *ad hoc* Select Committee on Members' Interests, which investigated ways in which rules governing the declaration of interests might be tightened up. Reports from the Committee in 1991 made a number of specific requirements:

- There should be a register of recognised professional lobbyists with the right to work in parliament. These companies would need to reveal the names of their clients and to identify the MPs working for them. There should also be a code of conduct preventing the payment of money to MPs and civil servants for influencing legislation.
- Members of parliamentary select committees should be forbidden to have any financial interest in companies tendering for, or in receipt of, government contracts. Chairs of these committees should not be allowed either directorships or consultancies in these companies and, although ordinary members might be allowed to remain as consultants, they should not be allowed to be directors.

Despite these measures it was evident that the self-regulation of MPs was not working, as was made clear during what, in 1997, became quite easily the most famous case of parliamentary sleaze.

In October 1993, *The Guardian* newspaper was contacted by Mohammed Al Fayed, owner of Harrods, who revealed that he had made considerable cash gifts and granted other favours to two junior ministers, Tim Smith and Neil Hamilton, in return for their undertaking parliamentary lobbying on his behalf including the asking of questions. Smith accepted at once that he was guilty of the offence of accepting cash for questions and resigned from his position. Hamilton on the other hand tried to ride out the storm by denying everything; deriding the triviality of declaring interests by announcing on television that he wished to declare having received the gift of a biscuit and a cup of coffee from a school he was visiting. Al Fayed then made further revelations of some thousands of pounds worth of hospitality given to Hamilton at the Paris Ritz Hotel, and the minister was forced grudgingly to resign from his government position.

Hamilton and Greer sued *The Guardian* for libel, Hamilton protesting that his innocence would be proved beyond question. Hamilton even went so far as to have the constitution changed for the sake of his law suit, using a bill going through the House of Lords to pass an amendment giving MPs the right to waive their right to parliamentary privilege under the 1690 Bill of Rights if they wished to use statements they had made in parliament as evidence in a court of law. Then, on 30 September 1996, within days of the court case being heard, Neil Hamilton and Ian Greer pulled out of their legal action claiming that they could not afford to continue the case. The *Guardian* immediately responded on the next day with a front-page photograph of Hamilton under the headline 'A Liar and a Cheat', and many details that had been gathered as evidence by the newspaper were now published.

Later a book was published listing all the dubious practices indulged in not only by Hamilton but also a whole stable of MPs who were working for Ian Greer (Leigh and Vulliamy, 1997). Over the next six months the MP refused to budge from his position and clung on to his seat despite moves to deselect him, and despite Tim Smith being forced to stand down in his constituency. In spite of the evidence John Major and the Conservative leadership refused to condemn Hamilton and he remained as MP and candidate for Tatton until unseated by Martin Bell in the 1997 election.

During the course of 1994, the Conservative Party had been hit by no fewer than 18 different scandals, sexual, personal, financial and concerned with abuse of members' influence, which made the word 'sleaze' the most over-used cliché of the year in the press and contributed to a continued decline in public respect for politicians. The government response was to set up a Standing Committee on Standards in Public Life under the chairmanship of Lord Nolan.

The Nolan Committee

When the Committee was set up in 1994, it was assumed that it would be a short parliamentary inquiry into the current wave of sleaze. However, the Committee had a wider remit, a wider membership and a considerably longer projected life than had been anticipated (Baggott, 1995a, pp. 33–8). The Committee's frame of reference was to:

examine current concerns about standards of conduct of all holders of public office, including arrangements relating to financial and commercial activities, and make recommendations as to any changes in present arrangements which might be required to ensure the highest standards of propriety in public life.

Those at whose activities they would be looking included ministers, MPs, MEPs for the UK, civil servants, policy advisers, local government councillors and officials, senior officers of public bodies (including NHS bodies) and all officers of publicly-funded bodies.

The Committee was appointed for an initial three years but it was made clear that it might well have an indefinite future: this would not be a one-off, one-report committee. Once the matters which led to its institution had been investigated and reported upon, it would turn to other matters in a rolling programme of enquiry that could become a permanent feature of parliamentary life.

Among the subjects given priority by Nolan was the question of MPs' interests and their receipt of payments from outside bodies. According to Hugo Young, when the committee began its work it was an open secret that members of the committee were

> startled to discover how unwilling some MPs were to recognise any accountability in their private business lives, or to obey the resolutions of the Commons. They have been reluctant to disclose interests at all [and] studiously misleading about the interests they have disclosed. (*The Guardian*, 18 July 1995)

In Nolan's first report, published on 11 May 1995, severe judgments were made concerning MPs' behaviour. The Committee agreed that:

1. MPs should only be free to undertake any outside employment if it did not have a direct relation to their parliamentary role.
2. MPs should be prohibited from working for professional lobbying companies.
3. MPs should not be prohibited from working as political consultants but each consultancy should be considered individually on its merits and the size of payments made to MPs for consultancy work should be disclosed.
4. The interests listed in the Register of Members' Interests are given in too vague a fashion, and a much clearer description of

the nature of those interests must be given in future. The Register must be constantly updated and the updated version must be widely available, including access through computer networks.
5. An independent Parliamentary Commissioner for Standards should be appointed, who would administer a code of conduct for MPs, handle complaints against MPs and clarify the legal position as regards the bribery of MPs.

The government accepted most of Nolan's recommendations for the executive, civil service and quangos. But, when the recommendations on parliament were discussed on 18 May 1995 feelings ran very high. In one infamous incident a Conservative MP, Alan Duncan, blocked Lord Nolan's way into the Commons, verbally abusing the judge and claiming that he was attempting the financial ruin of many MPs in the current parliament and stating that no able individual would even consider standing for parliament in the future if the Nolan proposals were accepted. Duncan was an extreme example but there were enough of a like mind on the Tory back-benches to make the government wary of implementing the measures as they stood. Hugo Young reported that the contender for the party leadership, John Redwood, even claimed that Nolan was subverting the idea of parliamentary sovereignty. 'Those who seek to marginalise Parliament, or ignore it, or set it under external control, are out to undermine the very foundations of our settled and unwritten constitution' (*The Guardian*, 18 July 1995). A committee of senior MPs was asked to look again at what Nolan was proposing for the regulation of MPs, and implementation of this part of his report was delayed until the new parliamentary session.

When the issue returned to parliament at the start of the 1995/6 session, the advice from the government's advisory committee was that the Nolan proposals should be accepted in the main. But the government, under pressure from Tory backbenchers, were unwilling to make the disclosure of earnings compulsory. Despite widespread condemnation of the practice it seemed that backbench MPs, almost all of them Conservatives, were ready to make the non-disclosure of their earnings into a major matter of principle. As Hugo Young had said in July, 'A Tory MP demands the right to earn any amount of money from politics, as long as nobody knows what it is'.

Rather than face them, the government backed down and omitted any such requirement to disclose from the legislation endorsing the Nolan proposals. The Labour Party, however, put down an Opposition amendment to reinstate the measure. Despite impassioned pleading from Tory MPs, including the now-hackneyed claim that such a measure could well destroy parliamentary sovereignty, the amendment was passed and accepted by the government. The disclosure of MPs' earnings is now statutory.

The Quangocracy

The recommendations of the Nolan Committee as they concerned MPs suspected of underhand dealings were those which received most attention. Almost overlooked, but possibly of equal importance, was the threat to democratic accountability posed by the quangos set up by successive governments.

The term 'quango', first coined in the 1970s for organisations created by the then Labour government, originally meant quasi-non-governmental, or alternatively quasi-autonomous non-governmental. This is, however, a vague definition and the term has been used to mean a wide variety of different things. The bodies referred to were set up for a variety of reasons – administrative, managerial or political – and this has resulted in a very mixed group, vastly differing in size and nature.

This accounted for the dispute between the Conservative government and its critics as to the actual number of quangos that were in existence; the government claiming that there are far fewer than there were said to be by those opposed to what they call a 'quangocracy'. Closer examination shows that this discrepancy results from the two sides arguing on the basis of two very different definitions of what is meant by a non-governmental body.

The Conservative government in an official publication (HMSO, 1994) defined quangos as non-departmental public bodies (NDPBs) and divided them into three types:

- *Executive NDPBs* – which carry out a range of operational and regulatory functions. Examples are the Arts Council, the Countryside Commission or the Commission for Racial Equality.

- *Advisory NDPBs* – which advise government on the application of policy in certain specific areas. Examples are the Police Advisory Council or the Parliamentary Boundary Commission.
- *Tribunals* – with a judicial or quasi-judicial function, often providing an appeals procedure for the adjudication of public grievances, as with rents tribunals or the supplementary benefits appeals tribunal.

In addition to the above three types of NDPBs, the government also recognises public bodies in the National Health Service – *NHS bodies* – as falling into the same category.

These government-defined quangos all fall within the remit of national government, and government action after 1979 did indeed reduce the number of quangos thus defined from 2167 in 1979 to 1389 in 1994.

The Labour Party while in opposition followed the view presented by Weir and Hall (1994) in a survey carried out for Democratic Audit, which saw an entire 'new wave' of unelected bodies being created, largely as a result of the erosion in local democratic controls over local authorities and the health service.

Since 1987 responsibility for the delivery of a wide range of local services has been given to a number of unelected 'local public spending bodies' as a result of changes in education, training, housing and health fields instituted by the government. (Stott, 1995–6, pp. 122–7)

These diverse bodies were defined by Weir and Hall as extra-governmental organisations (EGOs) and stigmatised by Stewart as a 'new magistracy – a non-elected elite of appointed individuals' (Stewart, 1995, pp. 17–18).

This is hidden government, run by bodies unknown to the public . . . their members may not even live or work locally . . . they may ignore local wishes and there is nothing local people can do about it . . . instead of giving power to individual citizens the government . . . has set up government quasi-markets in which individuals have little or no power. (Jones and Stewart, 1993)

To quote Stott from his article in *Talking Politics* (1995–6), 'the question of quangos and their use has become the subject of a political game in which both Labour and Conservative politicians engage in attacking quangos when in opposition and using them as instruments for carrying out their policies when in government.'

The ability to appoint executives to the quangos opened up a whole new area of political patronage to ministers. In October 1994 the Labour MP, George Howarth, speaking to his constituency party in Knowsley North, highlighted the extent to which Conservative ministers appointed friends of the Tory Party to these positions. Heads of quangos were often Tory councillors, MPs or party workers but even more significant was the failure to appoint known supporters of the Labour or Liberal Democrat Parties. The Conservatives in their turn accused Howarth of hypocrisy, pointing out the numbers of trade unionists and left-wing academics who staffed quangos during the Labour government of 1974–9. However, the prizes to be won were worthwhile indeed. In the Department of Health's first *Public Appointments Annual Report*, published as the result of pressure from the Nolan Committee, it was stated that 3436 individuals serviced the quangos running the National Health Service, at a cost to the taxpayer of £22.5 million in salaries and fees (Belton, 1997, p. 24).

As long ago as 27 January 1994, the Public Accounts Committee of the House of Commons produced a report on the running of the 1400 quangos, agencies and trusts that were then controlling state services. In a damning review, the report stated that standards in running public services had declined significantly over the previous two years and cited more than 20 instances of massive waste, corruption or fraud. From that point on the Labour Party championed the cause of returning services to local and democratic control. As was said by Frank Dobson, the new Health Secretary, in a speech to Unison in June 1997, 'We want boards which ensure the effective stewardship of limited resources. Some will quite rightly still be recruited from local businesses. But the balance must change'.

One effect of the Labour Party's plans for constitutional change will be to reduce the role of quangos in public administration. In Scotland and Wales many of the duties which had been given to quangos would be transferred to the control of the devolved assemblies of those two countries, returning them to democratic control. Similarly, services which had passed to quangos after the dissolution of the GLC would revert to any new elected mayor and authority for the Greater London area. The same is true for any further devolution to English regions or cities that may come in the future.

Decline in Ministerial Responsibility

Over 18 years of Tory government a deliberate programme was followed to diminish the role of government, and government did indeed withdraw from whole areas of administrative activity. Typical of this hiving-off process was the opting out of schools into grant-maintained status; or NHS trusts with self-governing hospitals and budget-holding doctors. Such changes in the bureaucracy of operation have meant that ministers at the departments of Education and Health have very little left to say concerning the day-to-day running of the education and health services. Elsewhere, whole areas of public provision are in the hands of private firms and the Next Steps initiative has led to the autonomy of many civil service agencies. In early 1994 it was estimated that over 30 per cent of all public expenditure was now in the hands of autonomous agencies or quangos over whom the relevant ministers have very little control. As a former Labour minister Gerald Kaufman said, 'We have the biggest government ever, the least accountable government ever, the most expensive government ever, and the most under-occupied government ever' (*The Guardian*, 30 December 1994).

With operational power out of their hands there is little left for ministers to do, apart from make policy. And it becomes questionable as to whether a Social Security Secretary needs six junior ministers to help him make policy decisions. And if ministers only make policy and leave operational matters to other agencies, the question of who is accountable throws considerable doubt on the convention of ministerial responsibility. In the past, during the Attlee administration for example, convention stated that civil servants were anonymous and that a minister, being personally accountable for any act of maladministration, was expected to resign over the matter, even if the error was committed by an official without ministerial approval. Today, with named agencies in charge of operational matters, ministers are far more likely to apportion blame rather than accept it. As Vernon Bogdanor has said, the convention of ministerial responsibility has been stood on its head and 'instead of the minister taking the blame for the misjudgment of his or her officials, his or her officials must now take the blame for the misjudgments of their minister' (*The Guardian*, 14 June 1993).

Following the introduction of the Next Steps programme, important changes were made to the doctrine of ministerial responsibility. Under the old system ministers were called upon to answer questions from MPs about the workings of their departments. Whether the answers to these questions were given in writing, or verbally in the debating chamber during Question Time, both question and answer were recorded in Hansard and were therefore available for public scrutiny. Under the new system, however, chief executives of Next Steps agencies were required to answer operational questions in letters sent direct to the MP asking the question, thus by-passing parliament and the issue of ministerial responsibility, and leaving no public record of the exchange. It was only after a prolonged protest that the situation was amended and it became standard procedure for the letters between chief executives and MPs to be published in a supplement to *Hansard* (Pyper, 1994, pp. 12–16).

Ministerial Responsibility and Resignation

It is a major convention of the unwritten British Constitution that a government minister is responsible for the conduct of his or her department and indeed for the actions or inactions of the civil servants in that department. The minister is accountable for this responsibility to parliament and, in the past, it was always understood that parliament could require the resignation of a minister for failure to meet that responsibility, even if the fault was that of civil servants rather than that of the minister personally. The classical instance of this was the Crichel Down affair in the 1950s, when a Conservative minister resigned because of mistakes made by his civil servants under the previous Labour incumbent. The most recent example of a traditional resignation on a point of principle was that of Lord Carrington as Foreign Secretary after the invasion of the Falkland Islands in 1982.

In fact, despite a few honourable and even anachronistic exceptions like Carrington, the willingness of ministers to resign has all but disappeared in recent years, even in the face of gross errors and manifest incompetence. Andrew Rawnsley has referred to the current attitude among politicians as 'the spirit of this political age, the guiding principle of which is that nobody resigns' (*The Observer*, 8 January 1995). On the other hand, Pyper has pointed out that the willingness of ministers to resign can easily be over-stated, and has never been particularly noticeable. In 1956, S. E. Finer made the point that he could only find evidence for 20 ministerial resignations in the century since 1855. It has always been the case that erring ministers have attempted to sit tight and brazen it out: what has changed is the increased seriousness of the errors which ministers feel can be overlooked. During the Major admin-istration:

- In 1992 the entire economic policy of the government collapsed on Black Wednesday, when billions of pounds were lost in an attempt to prop up a discredited system. Afterwards the prime minister actually wrote a note to his Chancellor affirming that he did not intend to resign and saying that he hoped the Chancellor would not do so either.
- In 1994, thanks to an admission by Alan Clark during the Matrix Churchill trial, it emerged that four ministers were prepared to see three innocent men go to prison rather than admit to ministerial errors over the arms-for-Iraq affair. Despite the facts becoming known and being widely published in the press, three of the four men continued to hold high government office while they awaited the findings of the long drawn-out Scott Inquiry.
- In the 1994 Budget the Chancellor lost a major plank of his financial legislation with the defeat of his measure to impose the higher rate of VAT on fuel bills. At one time defeat in a budget debate was as much an issue of confidence as a defeat in the debate on the Queen's Speech, but on this occasion resignation was not even mentioned.
- A succession of government ministers were exposed as indulging in conduct incompatible with high office. None of them, however, resigned of their own free will but waited to be forced out after prolonged pressure and a great deal of damaging publicity. The former Chief Secretary to the Treasury, Jonathan Aitken, went so far as to bring a libel action costing him nearly £2 million in legal fees to attempt to show that he was not lying or involved in unparliamentary behaviour: his action collapsed ignominiously when documentary evidence emerged contradicting evidence his teenage daughter was due to give on his behalf.

The Case of the Home Secretary

The change in expectations as to ministerial responsibility, however, was best typified by the case of Michael Howard, the then Home Secretary, who clung on to office despite a whole series of errors and misjudgments. On three successive days in one week in January 1995, an alleged mass murderer committed suicide in one prison, there was rioting in another, and three dangerous criminals escaped from a third. The response of the Home Secretary was to deny that there were any grounds for his resignation. He pointed out that the operation of the prison service was in the hands of the Prison Agency while he himself was solely responsible for policy and not operational matters. As many commentators pointed out, his response was like the criminal who tells the arresting officer, 'Nothing to do with me guv. It's all down to him'.

In October 1995 Michael Howard sacked Derek Lewis as Director General of the Prison Service. At once Lewis attacked Howard for improper interference in the day-to-day running of the prison service. Some indication of the extent of Howard's involvement was given in the Learmont Report into lapses of security in the prison service. According to Learmont, Howard had demanded that Lewis provide him with 1000 documents, including 137 'full submissions' in just four months. Lewis also offered to provide evidence that the Home Secretary had intervened in internal disciplinary matters; even attempting to determine the prison to which certain offenders should be sent. All of which seemed to contradict claims that the Home Secretary was accountable only for policy matters and had no interest in operational issues.

The most important charge against the Home Secretary was the accusation that Howard had overruled Lewis in dealing with the aftermath of the Parkhurst breakout. Lewis had wanted to transfer the governor, John Marriott, to non-operational duties pending a disciplinary hearing, but Howard had overruled Lewis, saying that Marriott was to be dismissed immediately. There was evidence that part of the blame for the problems at Parkhurst lay at the door of the Home Office but that Howard avoided the blame by claiming that he, as minister, was responsible only for policy decisions while the Prison Service was responsible for operational matters. Lewis continued to claim that his dismissal was wrong and this seemed to be upheld by Judge Tumim, the Chief Inspector of Prisons, who said that the Home Secretary's distinction between policy and operations was 'bogus'.

John Marriott, the former governor of Parkhurst Prison, retired at Christmas 1995. Free to speak now that he was retired, Mr Marriott used Radio 4's *World at One* to launch a bitter attack on the Home Secretary, accusing him of incessant meddling in prison affairs, indecisiveness and incompetent leadership. Papers were also leaked by Lewis which proved conclusively that while a disciplinary hearing into Marriott's conduct was proceeding at Parkhurst a telephone intervention by Howard had insisted on Marriott's immediate suspension: a clear case of an operational rather than a policy decision being imposed by a minister on an agency chief executive.

The Labour Party called a debate on the issue and the strength of the criticisms against the Home Secretary was such that it was widely expected that he would be forced to resign. But in the end a lacklustre speech by Jack Straw for the Opposition let Howard off the hook and the minister remained in office. Within two months, however, the Home Office was forced to concede that Derek Lewis had been wrongfully dismissed and to award him £125 000 in compensation. Howard continued to claim that he had done nothing wrong, although many on the Conservative benches conceded that if this judgment had been made before the debate on the issue the Home Secretary would have been forced to resign. The affair returned to haunt Howard in the form of a devastating attack on him by former Prisons Minister Anne Widdicombe which put paid to his chances in the Conservative Party leadership election after John Major resigned. The point, however, is that the possibility of resignation over a matter of principle concerning ministerial responsibility seems to have gone for ever. The true nature of the relationship between government minister and government agency, as it is now understood, was captured in a statement by Derek Lewis after his dismissal, '[it] gives the ministers authority without responsibility and the agency responsibility without authority' (*The Guardian*, 30 March 1996).

The Scott Report

The most severe test of government secrecy and ministerial accountability for many years was the enquiry by Lord Justice Sir Richard

Scott into the sale of arms to Iraq during the Iran–Iraq War. The significance of the inquiry was set out by Hugo Young,

> Whatever else Scott achieves, he will supply a unique public guide to the private, secretive, double-dealing world of unaccountable power which Whitehall created for the purpose of selling weaponry to Iraq. He will show just what ministers and officials are prepared to get up to and then either conceal or justify. He will lead many people to doubt not only whether present ministers were honest but whether the system, behind the screen of executive power, is any longer capable of integrity. (*The Guardian*, 8 February 1996, p. 17)

The reasons for the Scott Inquiry go back to 4 November 1992 when a former minister at the DTI, Alan Clark, was giving evidence in the trial of three executives from the firm of Matrix Churchill who were accused of selling war materials to Iraq. Under examination Clark admitted that the DTI had known all along that the equipment sold by Matrix Churchill was not for peaceful purposes. Asked about paperwork which suggested otherwise, Clark said, 'Well, it's our old friend being economical, isn't it?' – 'With the truth?' – 'With the *actualité*'. The case against the Matrix Churchill directors collapsed on 9 November 1992 and on the following day an enquiry was set up into the question of supplying arms to Iraq (McKie, 1993, pp. 232–4). The remit of the inquiry went beyond the Matrix Churchill case to take in the whole question of the government's policy on arms sales during the Iran–Iraq War, the secrecy with which the government surrounded their policy and the extent to which there was a cover-up. Among various lesser issues, there were four main questions to be answered:

- Did the government break, or turn a blind eye to, the guidelines laid down by the then Foreign Secretary, Sir Geoffrey Howe, in 1985?
- Were those guidelines changed in 1988 without parliament being informed?
- Why, if the guidelines had been changed, were the directors of Matrix Churchill prosecuted for breaking those guidelines; particularly when one of the accused was known to be working for British Intelligence?

• Why did a number of government ministers sign Public Interest Immunity Certificates to suppress evidence that was vital to the defence of the Matrix Churchill accused? And why did the Attorney-General tell those ministers that it was their duty to sign when this was not the case?

The enquiry lasted three years, during which time there were 276 witnesses delivering 430 hours of evidence, 61 witnesses being heard in public hearings and 19 including John Major and Lady Thatcher, being heard in private sessions: the remainder gave written evidence. The enquiry requested and received 200 000 pages of official documents. And at the end of it all the report itself stretched to 1800 pages, in four volumes, delivered to the government on Wednesday 7 February 1996, eight days in advance of the general release of the report. The total cost of the inquiry and report was £3 million.

During those three years there were constant impediments put in Sir Richard's way. At the start Sir Geoffrey Howe accused the enquiry as acting as 'detective, inquisitor, advocate and judge' rolled into one and wanted lawyers with the ability to cross-examine other witnesses to represent government witnesses. Such a time-wasting move was ruled out but, for the sake of fairness, Scott allowed every witness to have a list of questions in advance and the right to correct transcripts of what was said. Although the work of the inquiry was finished by the summer of 1995 there was a further delay because ministers who were criticised in the inquiry were sent copies of what was said about them and allowed to prepare replies to those criticisms. Finally, the government was allowed eight days to study the report before publication and thus had over a week to prepare the government's statement to the Commons. In contrast, Robin Cook for Labour and Menzies Campbell for the Liberal Democrats were allowed three hours in a closed room to study the report on the actual morning of the day it was published; while the rest of the Commons were only able to obtain copies a mere 30 minutes before publication.

As the rebel Tory MP, Richard Shepherd, put it, 'the underlying problem that Scott identifies [is] that considerations of embarrassment and administrative convenience are so routinely given precedence over the public's right to information' (*The Guardian*, 28 February 1996). The behaviour and attitude of the government concerning the report suggested that this continued to be the case.

The report was very long and Lord Justice Scott's language, with its superfluity of double negatives, was less than transparent. This combined with the time granted to the government for a trawl through the pages of the report for favourable quotations with which to defend their position, enabled them to survive the initial attacks of publication day.

The Scott Report found that:

- Ministers, including William Waldegrave, repeatedly misled parliament in breach of ministerial accountability and this failure to inform parliament properly was 'deliberate'.
- Sir Nicholas Lyell, the Attorney-General, mishandled the Matrix Churchill case which should never have been brought. Sir Nicholas had assured Michael Heseltine that the limited application of the Public Interest Immunity certificate would be drawn to the attention of the judge but this was not done.
- Whitehall officials and lawyers did try to prevent crucial evidence about arms sales being revealed and, although it could not be called a conspiracy, ministers did collectively conceal government policy from parliament.
- The view held by ministers that the guidelines on arms sales to Iraq had not changed but merely interpreted more flexibly, was 'not remotely tenable' (Richard Norton-Taylor in *The Guardian*, 26 February 1996).

The government was attacked on all these points by the combined opposition parties and even by some of their own backbenchers. Yet the government used the obscure wording of Sir Richard Scott's report to claim that:

1. William Waldegrave may be guilty of 'consistently misleading Parliament' but he did not do so with the intention to mislead.
2. Sir Nicholas Lyell may be 'constitutionally guilty' of mishandling the Matrix Churchill trial, but he was not 'personally guilty'.
3. Because arms-making equipment rather than actual weapons was exported to Iraq the guidelines were not really broken but merely interpreted liberally.

There was a widespread expectation that the Scott Report would seriously damage the government: certainly many people felt that the ministers involved, such as William Waldegrave and Sir Nicholas Lyell, were so tainted by the findings that they could not, in all honour, refuse to resign. Yet the government's careful management of the debate over the report was such that this did not happen:

> While the political futures of Waldegrave and Lyell hung in the balance for a few days, they were given the full backing of the Prime Minister, their Cabinet colleagues and an overwhelming majority of their own backbenchers. In these circumstances . . . ministerial miscreants can survive (and have always survived) virtually any criticisms of their policies and actions! (Adams and Pyper, 1997, pp. 170–4)

Conclusion

There was some evidence during the 1997 election campaign that the electorate's disillusionment with politics and politicians had led to abstention on the part of sections of the electorate on polling day. There seemed to be a mood at large, and certainly among the young, which condemned all politicians as untrustworthy and all government ministers as shifty. It was a mood which helped contribute to the declining membership of the political parties and the transfer of political activity from political parties to single-issue pressure groups, and to direct action such as was seen at the site of Manchester airport's second runway or those ports engaged in the export of veal calves.

There does, however, seem to have been a sense in which this disillusionment was bound up with the length of time the Conservatives had been in government. Many journalists and political correspondents noticed and commented upon a feeling of relief that seemed to attach itself to Labour's victory in the 1997 election. The honeymoon period was not likely to last: within weeks of the election the Labour Party was hit by allegations of sleaze in the Glasgow Govan constituency, Robin Cook split with his wife after an affair with his assistant, there were questions raised about Lord Simon, former boss of BP, who held on to his BP shares after being made Trade Minister, and there were murmurs of concern about the undue influence of Tony Blair's inner circle. Nevertheless, there did seem to be a lightening of mood while the Blair euphoria lasted, and a consequent lessening of the sense of disillusion.

Nevertheless, for all that the Blair administration is dedicated to cleaning up the political system after the misdemeanors of Hamilton, Aitken and others, the damage has been done to the integrity of British politics, as was acknowledged when Sir Gordon Downey published his report into standards at the start of July 1997. That report made it clear that a handful of men who had succeeded in rising to responsible positions in government had taken secret sums of money to give parliamentary representation to companies being investigated by the DTI; they received cash, gifts and holidays; they even charged firms who should have had free representation because they were in the MP's own constituency; they hid these gifts from parliament and their constituents and they lied about it all to parliament, the voters and their superiors in government. Add those factors to the findings of the Scott Report and it is no wonder that the public became alienated from the political culture.

Yet it is easy to make too much of it, as was made clear by Alan Rusbridger, editor of *The Guardian*, who had done more than most to shine a light into the darker corners:

> It bears saying again: British public life is amongst the least corrupt in the world. . . The great majority of MPs have always been honest, decent and hard-working. But this bears saying again too: there was in the late eighties the beginnings of a significant culture of corruption at Westminster. (Editorial in *The Guardian*, 4 July 1997)

What concerned the media and other commentators was not so much the scale of corruption and sleaze as the fact that there is no body to regulate the behaviour of MPs except parliament itself. If it had not been for the perseverance of media watchdogs such as *The Guardian* or Granada TV, no one need have known about what went on. Even after it was all brought into the open nothing happened to those shown to be guilty because no body has jurisdiction over a parliament that will always use self-regulation and parliamentary privilege to protect its own. The one issue above all others thrown up by these cases of sleaze and denials of accountability is the way in which the public at large no longer feel they can trust the politicians to police themselves.

12

Nationalism and the Governance of the United Kingdom

The British public outside London tends to identify the government with the south-east of England and feels alienated from that government as a result. This is particularly true of Scotland which was a separate country with its own parliament and government until 1707, and for Wales which has its own language and culture. It is even true for regions of England like the north or south-west where the inhabitants see London as a distant place which does not understand the problems of the regions. Such feelings were exacerbated by the process by which successive Conservative administrations marginalised local government, abolishing or removing power from whole sectors of local or regional democracy.

Any resentment that is felt at obeying orders from, and paying taxes to, Westminster is made all the worse by the fact that the Conservatives, a supposedly national party, have increasingly become no more than the party of England, and of a rural southern England at that. After the 1997 election there were no Tory MPs left in the whole of Scotland and Wales, nor in the metropolitan areas of England. Despite this, the Conservative Party is opposed to any weakening in the union of countries making up the United Kingdom, while still being opposed to the centralism of Brussels against which the party summoned up the argument of subsidiarity.

As a political concept, subsidiarity has been in use for some time but during negotiations on the Maastricht Treaty for European Union it came to have a specific application in order to counter British fears of what was seen as the committed pro-federalism of the Maastricht agreement. In Britain, unlike the rest of Europe, federalism was equated with a powerful administration in Brussels imposing its will on the member states, with no regard being paid to the wishes of national parliaments. What was developed at Maastricht was a form of the doctrine of subsidiarity, originally defined in the Treaty itself as being when 'decisions are taken as closely as possible to the citizen':

> In areas which do not fall within its exclusive competence, the Community should take action, in accordance with the principle of subsidiarity, only in so far as the proposed action cannot sufficiently be achieved by the Member States and can therefore, by reason of the scale or effects of the proposed action, be better achieved by the Community. Any action of the Community shall not go beyond what is necessary to achieve the objectives of this Treaty. (*Treaty on European Union*, Title II, article 3b)

The argument here is that Brussels is too remote from the people and that, for certain critical legislation, decisions need to be taken by competent authorities closer to the people – like national governments. Where the democratic needs of the people are concerned, action by a remote federal government are deemed inappropriate.

It is here that the Conservative proponents of subsidiarity made a rod for their own backs. Simply because a proposal is thought to be inappropriate for Community action does not necessarily mean that action by national governments is any more appropriate. It could well be the case that regional or local action might be even more suitable. Certainly the Scottish National Party has adopted the concept of subsidiarity with enthusiasm, with its slogan of 'Scotland in Europe', meaning that in matters of importance to Scotland there need be no intervening English body between Brussels and a Scottish Assembly or Council. And the anomaly is that although the Major government advocated subsidiarity to prevent centralisation in Brussels, it remained very ardently centralist in its management of the affairs of the United Kingdom. The Major government faced the possibility that in safeguarding the principle of national sovereignty they sacrificed the United Kingdom to the greater democratic goal of subsidiarity through devolution (Pilkington, 1995, pp. 112–13).

The sidelining of local government during the Thatcher years, to the benefit of central government, allied to the role of centrally appointed quangos in taking accountability away from local communities, led to an increased awareness in the regions of the gulf between the decision-makers in London and the general public in the rest of the United Kingdom – a gulf that is both geographical and ideological. That awareness re-awakened the devolution issue, not only for Scotland and Wales but as a possibility for the regions of England as well; not to mention its relevance to any settlement of the Northern Ireland situation.

English Regionalism

It is ironic that while the Conservative government under John Major continued to reduce the powers of local government, attempting to replace the old county–district two-tier council structure with a unitary single-tier system, a whole new tier of government was emerging which did not exist before, in the form of executive regionalism. There are a number of factors which have caused the introduction of this new tier, sometimes as the wish of central government, in other cases informally and without recognition from the centre.

In 1994 the government created ten integrated English regional offices (IROs) which have merged the regional offices previously maintained by the Departments of the Environment, Employment, Transport and Trade and Industry. These regional offices, with the population for the area covered by that office, are:

London	6.9 million	South East	7.7 million
Eastern	5.2 million	South West	4.8 million
West Midlands	5.3 million	East Midlands	4.1 million
Yorks & Humberside	5.0 million	North East	2.6 million
North West	2.6 million	Merseyside	1.5 million

These integrated offices are supposed to serve the same administrative functions for the English regions as the Northern Irish, Scottish and Welsh Offices do for the national regions.

The replacement of local authority bodies by quangos and the handover of certain civil service functions to government agencies has led to networks of semi-autonomous bodies, each of which has a strong regional structure. Taken together with the IROs this means that there is a level of government designed to supervise the regional implementation of government policy. It is, however, wholly subordinate to the central government and is not democratically accountable to the people of the regions concerned.

The European Union's structural aid funds are distributed on a regional rather than a national basis and the EU prefers to work directly with regional authorities. In the case of Objective One funding, which is the most generous assistance programme, help is given to areas whose GDP is less than 75 per cent of the EU average, originally there were no Objective One regions in England, although Northern Ireland and the Highlands and Islands of Scotland did qualify. The unilateral action of Liverpool in forming the Merseyside Task Force from local authorities in the area, declaring that Merseyside is separate from the rest of the North West region and entering into direct negotiations with the EU, has resulted in Merseyside gaining Objective One funding worth £1.28 billion over six years. Merseyside's success has led to other local authorities getting together to form regional action groups to handle negotiations with Brussels.

The Maastricht Treaty created the Committee of the Regions (COR) to act as a body which must be consulted during the EU legislative process on any matter which it is felt has regional implications. In most member states of the EU there are strong regional governments and administrations which can be represented on the COR. Since no such bodies exist in Britain the UK is represented on the COR by a representative delegation from regionally grouped local authorities.

The IROs and quango networks are examples of 'executive regionalism' and exist as an arm of central control. As these have grown, from the late 1980s on, they have been countered by regional associations of local authorities made up of nominated members and seconded local government officials. They exist to promote cooperation between local authorities to create regional integrated policies on matters such as transport, economic development and liaison with the EU. They cover much the same ground as the IROs and act as a defence of local government against encroachment from the centre.

As Jack Straw, then shadow Home Secretary, said in July 1995 '. . . the government regional offices, sub-regional and regional quangos, and numerous agency offices form a nascent administrative and governmental infrastructure for England's regions' (Stokes, Hopwood and Bulman, 1996, pp. 191–5). If such a framework exists, it suffers from the disadvantage of being largely formed by nominated rather than elected representatives. This aspect caused parliament to inflict an important defeat on the government during ratification of the Maastricht Treaty, when ministers wanted to send quango members to the COR but opposition parties successfully demanded that those representatives should all be elected councillors.

For those wishing to curb the centralising imperative of central government this development of regional structures is considered to be highly desirable. If the logic of the development was accepted and legitimised by introducing elected regional governments, then the enthusiasts would see this as a key factor in constitutional reform. Most enthusiastic is the Liberal Democrat Party, which would like to see devolution to the English regions just as much as it desires devolution for Scotland and Wales, and, as a logical conclusion, would like to see a federal structure for the whole of Great Britain.

The Conservative Party, while being responsible for the growth of regional bureaucracy, is opposed to any form of devolution which it sees as tending to the break-up of the United Kingdom. Therefore, any proposals for directly elected regional government are rejected on the grounds that:

- regional government would be an additional layer of government in an already over-governed state;
- it would be an additional burden on the taxpayer, being in effect a needless extra expense; and
- there is no evidence of any public demand for English devolution.

The Major government did all that it could to prevent regional representation on the EU's Committee of the Regions, believing that 'the prospect of British representatives in EU politics, acting for regions rather than the British state as a whole, undermines the very sovereignty of the state' (Bradbury, 1996, pp. 16–19).

The Labour Party, on the other hand, has taken a position virtually midway between the Liberal Democrats and the Conservatives. There is a faction within the party which favours regional government, largely because of Labour's concentration of support within certain regions but also as a by-product of Labour's support for Scottish devolution. However, Labour has recognised that there is not the same public demand for devolved government in the English regions as there is in Scotland or Wales, and the idea also meets with not inconsiderable opposition from the Labour-dominated local authorities who would have most to lose in terms of power and influence from the introduction of an additional tier of government. In July 1995, Jack Straw, then shadow Home Secretary, proposed a gradualist approach to the issue.

Straw's proposal was that the regional associations of local authorities should be given the control of IROs, quangos and agencies in their region and that the regulation of privatised utilities in the region should also be their responsibility. They would be strategic bodies responsible for planning across a range of policy areas, including the implementation of EU policy. Such bodies would be indirectly democratic in that a large proportion of their membership would be composed of elected councillors but, if public opinion demanded it, they could institute direct elections to regional assemblies later, thereby becoming fully devolved bodies. Since this would involve constitutional change, the move to directly elected assemblies would only be made as the result of a referendum and the transfer of power would only take place when the people so decided. As a result, Straw could foresee a future in which some regions of England would follow Scotland and Wales in accepting devolved power, while other regions might choose not to do so.

In one area, however, the Labour government elected in May 1997 showed itself more immediately ready to institute a form of devolution for England. Ever since the Thatcher government abolished the GLC the government of London had been in the hands of the 31 borough councils, with no coordinating authority to deal with the integrated transport and planning needs of the capital city. Labour proposed to deal with this lack by following the example of other major cities in the world and instituting a directly elected executive Mayor. Subject to approval by a referendum the London region will, by the autumn of 2000, elect its own chief executive officer who, aided by a small strategic assembly of 24–32 members, will run integrated programmes across all London boroughs, replacing many quangos. The details were left vague, particularly details as to how it will be funded and the extent of democratic control, but the framework now exists for an authority which would be suitable not only for London but also for other English cities and regions.

Devolution

The arguments for devolution are strongest where the people of a given region feel the sense of a common identity that is distinct from that of other regions and from that of the centralising power. This sense of identity is obviously strongest where there is a history of separate development as with Northern Ireland, Wales and Scotland and where rule from London is seen as not only figuratively but literally alien. Here the options are not confined to regional local government but to the alternatives of devolution of power or outright independence.

It must be recognised that the United Kingdom is neither a unitary state nor a federal state but is what is known more simply as a union state. Like a unitary state it has a single sovereign parliament but that parliament has grown from the merger of previously separate assemblies. The UK parliament was formed through the union of the English Parliament with the councils, assemblies or parliaments of Wales (1543), Scotland (1707) and Ireland (1800). In contrast to a federal structure, therefore, the component parliaments have surrendered their jurisdiction and sovereignty. Unlike a unitary state, on the other hand, the component nations of the UK continue to possess pre-union rights and institutions peculiar to themselves which maintain some administrative autonomy.

Northern Ireland

This is the one region of the UK which has had a devolved assembly in recent times. When the larger part of Ireland gained its independence in the 1920s, the six predominantly protestant counties in the north-east formed a separate province still subordinate to the British Crown and with MPs in the Westminster parliament. The UK government was, however, responsible only for major policy matters such as economics and foreign affairs; most executive and legislative matters concerning the province being dealt with by a Northern Ireland Parliament at Stormont which had its own executive, legislative and administrative powers, including the control of law and order. However, it was long recognised that Stormont was totally dominated by the Ulster Unionist Party and was used as a tool to maintain a protestant supremacy in the province. During the 'troubles' of the 1970s, Stormont was suspended and its executive and legislative powers were transferred in 1972 to the direct rule of Westminster. Northern Ireland continues to have its own institutions, however, and they are administered by the Northern Ireland Office rather than Whitehall Departments, so that a form of administrative devolution remains. Devolution in the form of a return of executive powers to Stormont was foreseen by the government when it imposed direct rule and various power-sharing solutions have been proposed, only to founder in the light of the continuing conflict. Nevertheless, some form of devolution is likely to be offered as the ultimate solution of the 'Northern Ireland Question'.

Wales

In one respect Wales has less of a claim to political autonomy than other national components of the UK, in that it was never a fully independent state in its own right. Under feudal law, unlike Scotland but rather like Ireland, it was not a unified kingdom but merely a collection of small principalities who, more often than not, accepted the overlordship of the English king. Much of the territory we call Wales was in the hands of Anglo-Norman marcher lords by the end of the twelfth century, and some areas such as Monmouth hardly regard themselves as Welsh today.

It was only the north-western principality of Gwynedd which held out independently of the English Crown until the late thirteenth century, and it is this north-western corner of the country which continues to exhibit Wales' strongest argument for separate treatment, which is the existence of the distinctive linguistic and cultural difference represented by the Welsh language, with its poetry and music. It is no coincidence that the four constituencies which elected Plaid Cymru MPs in 1992 and re-elected them in 1997 – Caernarfon, Ceredigion, Meirionydd Nant Conwy and Ynys Mon – are essentially Welsh-speaking and cover an area which corresponds almost precisely with the borders of ancient Gwynedd. Wales has had administrative devolution through the Welsh Office since 1964 but the mountainous and divided nature of the country means that for the people of North Wales the bureaucracy in Cardiff is often as remote from them as that in London.

Scotland

Constitutionally, Scotland has the strongest case of any region of the United Kingdom for devolution, if not complete independence. Scotland was a separate country with its own monarch, parliament, laws, economy and diplomatic relations until as late as 1707. Even then the union was achieved through negotiation between equals, rather than through one side imposing its authority on the other: however it may have appeared in reality since then. Since the union Scotland has retained its own very distinctive legal and education systems, the Presbyterian Church has remained the established Church of Scotland, Scottish banks have been allowed to print their own bank notes and there is an advanced form of administrative devolution in the institutions of the Scottish Office and the Scottish Grand Committee.

There has been a movement for Home Rule since 1886 and ten Home Rule bills were presented to parliament between 1886 and 1914. The Scottish National Party was founded in 1927 but made little headway until the 1960s, when a combination of alienation from the unionist parties and the realisation that North Sea oil could give Scotland economic independence led to an upsurge in interest and support for the nationalist cause. In 1979, the referendum on acceptance of the Callaghan government's plans for Scottish devolution actually gained a majority of the votes but, because there were many abstentions, the 'Yes' vote did not receive support from the majority of the Scottish population and the reform failed according to the rules governing the referendum.

Administrative Devolution

The Scottish Office was founded in 1885 with a remit totally unlike that of other government departments, in that it is a territorial rather than a functional department with responsibility for general government activity in Scotland. At the head is the Secretary of State for Scotland, a cabinet minister, with two Ministers of State and two Under-Secretaries of State in support. Also, since the Scottish legal system is very different from the English, there are two Scottish law officers, the Lord Advocate and the Solicitor-General for Scotland (Mitchell, 1996, pp. 16–18). The Scottish Office took on its present form when it was established at St Andrew's House in Edinburgh in 1939. At that time it was organised into four functional departments, but that has since been extended to five, dealing with agriculture and fisheries, education, environment, home and health, and trade and industry.

Within the Westminster parliament there has been, since 1894, a Scottish Grand Committee on which all MPs for Scottish constituencies have the right to sit. Two committees within the standing committee structure exist to examine the details of specifically Scottish legislation and, since 1979, there has also been a Scottish Affairs select committee. One difficulty with the last is that in recent years a Conservative government has not won sufficient Scottish seats to staff the select committee once Scottish Office ministers have been appointed. The Scottish Affairs Committee was suspended between 1987 and 1992 and was only able to resume by being allowed a Labour chairman and having the Conservative numbers made up by English MPs.

Some element of accountability is introduced into Scottish affairs by there being a Question Time in the Commons set aside for Scottish questions. But this is counterbalanced by the fact that party membership of the Scottish select and standing committees is proportional to the composition of the Commons as a whole and does not reflect the party balance in Scotland. This is a significant argument against those, like the Conservative Party, who say that a reformed use of administrative devolution is sufficient to meet the distinctive needs of Scotland. Critics reply that the Scottish Office and Scottish committees are subordinate parts of an overwhelmingly English parliament.

Naturally enough, there was no such office for Northern Ireland while the Stormont parliament existed. However, after direct rule was imposed in 1972, the Northern Ireland Office acquired many of the same characteristics of the Scottish Office. A Secretary of State is supported by two Ministers of State and two Under-Secretaries. The Office is responsible for functional departments like education but, of course, routine administration has taken second place in the past twenty-five years or so in the face of the continuing 'troubles' and security situation. Unlike Scotland, Northern Ireland did not have a select committee of the Commons dedicated to it until after the 1992 election, when one was promised by John Major in his bid to win Ulster Unionist support for his government.

The Welsh Office was only established in 1964 with a Secretary of State for Wales and an executive base in Cardiff. The Welsh Office is smaller than the Scottish, with just one Minister of State and one Under-Secretary, and there is less a departmental function than a remit to oversee the application of national policy to Wales in the areas of agriculture, education, health, labour, planning, trade and transport. There is a Welsh Affairs select committee but, as is the case for Scotland, the Conservatives have been so under-represented in Wales that, after 1992, the select committee had a Labour chair and English Conservative MPs in its membership. Indeed, for most of the period of Conservative government after 1979 the Secretary of State for Wales was either English, or a member for an English constituency, or both. After William Hague, a former Welsh Secretary, became leader of the Conservative Party he acknowledged the poor standing of the Tories outside England by failing to appoint shadow secretaries for Wales or Scotland, replacing them both with Michael Ancram as a single shadow spokesman on all constitutional matters. This also foreshadowed the fact that the near-inevitable introduction of a Scottish parliament and Welsh assembly will mean the end of the Scottish and Welsh Offices.

Devolution or Independence?

Generally speaking, in the run-up to the 1997 election there seemed to be three possible solutions for the future governance of Scotland; and, by inference, for Wales, Northern Ireland and perhaps the English regions as well. The Scottish local election results of 1995, which saw the Conservative Party virtually eliminated north of the border, awoke renewed interest in the plans being made by the various parties for the future governance of Scotland. For some time a special committee, the Scottish Constitutional Convention, had been meeting to discuss these matters in an unusually wide alliance of the Labour and Liberal Democrat Parties, the Scottish churches, the Scottish TUC and various civic bodies. On 30 November 1995, St Andrew's Day, the Convention met to publish their findings. Two days earlier the then Scottish Secretary, Michael Forsyth, had outlined government proposals for changes in the way Scotland is governed. Also, while the Convention was meeting in the Assembly Hall of the Church of Scotland, the SNP was at the Edinburgh City Chambers to outline proposals for an independent Scotland. Within the same week three alternative proposals for the future of Scotland, and by implication for Wales, had been announced:

1. Things could go on as they were, but with increased and improved administrative devolution which was the position of the Conservative Party.

2. There could be executive and legislative devolution, as advocated by the Labour and Liberal Democrat Parties.
3. There could be full sovereign independence within Europe, as desired by the SNP in Scotland and Plaid Cymru in Wales.

The landslide success of Labour in the 1997 election, supported by their partners in the Constitutional Convention, the Liberal Democrats, meant that a form of devolution for Scotland and Wales was the only real option to be considered; subject of course to the approval of referendums. White Papers issued on 22 and 24 July 1997 outlined proposals for both countries, although the proposals for Scotland were far more radical and wide-ranging than those for Wales. A parliament of 129 members was proposed for Scotland which, even though sovereignty would rest with the UK parliament in Westminster, would have considerable powers to pass primary legislation, including money-raising powers, as well as considerable powers of scrutiny over both British and European proposals. The proposals for Wales on the other hand were far more modest, merely suggesting the creation of a 60-member assembly that would have no tax-raising or primary legislation powers.

An issue which immediately arose was as to whether the Welsh would accept the much less generous package they had been offered. The difference in status between the two was heightened by the actions of the Queen who agreed to performing the state opening of the Scottish Parliament but refused to open the Welsh Assembly on the grounds that it was not a proper parliament. One spokesperson was guilty of referring to the Welsh Assembly as no more than 'a glorified county council'.

The issue of full, true independence remains, even though both the SNP and Plaid Cymru agreed to support the devolution proposals on the grounds that half a deal was better than nothing. The nationalist parties obviously saw devolution as merely a step on the way to much greater autonomy, thus underlining the Conservative argument that the granting of devolution would lead inevitably to independence and the break-up of the United Kingdom. However, even the Conservative leader, William Hague, agreed that a future Tory administration would not alter the devolution measures once they were in place. In the meantime they would campaign hard for a 'no' vote in the referendums and concentrate their fire on Scottish and Welsh representation in the UK parliament after devolution, through pursuing the so-called West Lothian question.

The West Lothian Question

> For how long will English constituencies and English Honourable Members tolerate not just 71 Scots, 36 Welsh and a number of Ulstermen but at least 119 Honourable Members from Scotland, Wales and Northern Ireland exercising an important, and probably often decisive, effect on English politics while they themselves have no say in the same matters in Scotland, Wales and Ireland? (*Hansard*, vol. 939, cols 122–3, 14 November 1977)

This question was asked by Tam Dalyell, MP for the Scottish constituency of West Lothian, during the second reading of Labour's Scottish devolution legislation in 1977, and has become famous since then as 'the West Lothian question'. It recognises the point that any devolution of power from Westminster would lead to a disproportionate presence of MPs from the devolved regions in the Westminster parliament.

Scotland has always had more representatives at Westminster than the size of the country would seem to warrant. In the 1707 Act of Union, Scotland was granted 45 MPs and 16 representative peers in the parliament of Great Britain, the over-representation being said to compensate Scotland for the loss of an independent parliament and to prevent the Scottish voice being swamped beneath the English majority. There is also the point that the two Highland constituencies north of the Great Glen probably represent nearly 50 per cent of the land area of Scotland but only a fraction of the population: in order to keep Scottish constituencies geographically manageable the average size of a constituency has to be around 50 000 rather than the 60–70 000 that is normal in England. By the time of the 1992 election, Scotland contained 9 per cent of the UK population but its 72 MPs represented 11 per cent of Commons membership. The same picture is reflected for Wales, where 5 per cent of the population are represented by 6 per cent of MPs (Adonis, 1993, p. 8).

This disproportionality, if it continued after the introduction of devolution for Scotland or Wales, leads directly to the West Lothian question, or rather to two related questions:

- If Scotland had its own parliament and Wales its own assembly, each dealing with Scottish or Welsh legislation, would either country need so many Westminster MPs? Would it not be the case that Scottish and Welsh electors would be twice as well represented as the electors of England?
- Would it be right for English MPs to have no say on legislation that was specifically Scottish or Welsh, when Scottish and Welsh MPs would be able to speak and vote on legislation that was specifically English in nature? This is, of course, the real West Lothian question.

The obvious answer is that the number of Westminster constituencies would have to be reduced for any part of the United Kingdom which became subject to a devolved assembly. The reverse was shown in 1972 when Stormont was suppressed. Before that time, while the Stormont Parliament existed, Northern Ireland had 12 Westminster MPs: after the abolition of Stormont the number of Northern Irish constituencies was increased to 17. The Labour government has agreed that the next Boundary Commission review will not be bound by the statutory requirement for a minimum number of seats in Scotland and that the number of constituencies will be reduced from the present 72 to around 60. A similar re-assessment may be applied to Wales.

There is one fly in this ointment and that is the heavy reliance of Labour on Scottish and Welsh seats for the party's representation in parliament. The party easily predominates in both countries: over half the votes cast in Wales are for the Labour Party, while about 20 per cent of all Labour MPs sit for Scottish constituencies. The dilemma for Labour is that they are a party committed to some form of devolution for Scotland, and yet to redistribute and reduce the number of Scottish seats in the wake of devolution could well reduce the size of any Labour majority in the Westminster parliament. This does not matter when the Labour majority is as large as it was in 1997, but with a smaller majority it could be crucial.

Nevertheless, the 1997 election saw the triumph of pro-devolution parties in both Scotland and Wales, and the complete eclipse of the unionist Conservatives. No matter what constitutional problems remained it was inevitable that the Labour government would press ahead with the immediate implementation of its devolution proposals for Scotland and Wales.

Northern Ireland

The issue of Northern Ireland is very complex and also unusual in that it is an issue about which there has been basic agreement between the main parties in parliament. Conservatives and Labour are united in offering a bi-partisan approach, and since there is no argument between the parties it is unlikely to affect voting behaviour in mainland Britain. It is also an issue almost impossible to discuss in a book such as this because the situation changes to such an extent and so frequently that any writer is unable to pin the situation down at any one point in its development: the whole nature of the problem can change in the space of a single week.

In the Anglo-Irish Treaty of 1921 the 26 southern counties of Ireland became an independent Irish Free State within the British Empire. In 1949 the Free State cut its links with Britain and left the Commonwealth to became the Republic of Ireland. In these settlements it was established that there were six counties in Northern Ireland which were dominated by a Protestant majority, compared to the rest of Ireland which was devoutly Catholic. Since the Protestants of the north were apparently ready to fight to remain British and stood by their right to be excluded from the Free State, the southern Irish had to accept the partition of Ireland, although only after a bitter civil war between those for and against the treaty. The Province of Northern Ireland was formed with its own devolved parliament at Stormont, which nevertheless continued to be subordinated to the United Kingdom parliament in London.

Irish nationalists never accepted the partition of Ireland and they continued to struggle to reunite Ireland. That struggle was partly political but there was also the 'armed struggle' in which the IRA used shootings and bombings against the British and Stormont governments. Not all the nationalist and Catholic population of Northern Ireland supported the IRA but they were all hostile to the political system imposed by Stormont, which manipulated the political and electoral system to maintain the Protestant majority in power and which discriminated against the Catholic minority in areas like housing, education, employment and law and order. To make matters worse the convention was established that matters within the competence of Stormont could not be raised at Westminster by any of the Ulster MPs.

Both sides in the Irish dispute had constitutional safeguards for their position. The Republic had a clause in its constitution dedicated to restoring territorial integrity to the 32 counties of Ireland, while Section 1 (2) of the Ireland Act setting up the Republic of Ireland stated that '. . . in no event will Northern Ireland or any part thereof cease to be part of His Majesty's dominions and of the UK without the consent of the Parliament of Northern Ireland' (Cunningham, 1992, pp. 30–3).

In the 1960s, encouraged by the success of the American civil rights campaign conducted by the blacks under Martin Luther King, a largely middle-class and Catholic-led movement in Northern Ireland began to campaign for Stormont to concede basic civil rights to the Catholic minority. Moderate nationalist, left-wing and Catholic opinion formed a new political party, the Social and Democratic Labour Party (SDLP), which was to represent the rights of the minority in a non-violent and democratic fashion. The civil rights movement also created an important political figure for the minority population in John Hume, later to become leader of the SDLP.

The Northern Ireland government made many concessions to the Catholic community but Catholics saw these concessions as being too little, too late, while any concessions at all were seen as being too much by the Protestants. The civil rights movement continued, with marches and protests, but they were increasingly met by a Protestant backlash. The old Unionist Party – which had ruled Northern Ireland as a one-party state since 1921 – split, with moderate leaders like Terence O'Neill being rejected by their rank-and-file supporters in favour of more extreme leaders like William Craig and Ian Paisley. More seriously, the exclusively Protestant special police force known as the 'B-Specials' acted very violently against Catholic protesters. With the Royal Ulster Constabulary (RUC) unable to contain the situation, Stormont called for military help from London and British soldiers were sent to the Province in 1969.

At first the British soldiers were welcomed by the Catholic community, who saw the army as coming to save them from the B-Specials. But the Stormont government increasingly called on the army for help, until the British army became firmly associated with Stormont in the eyes of most Catholics. At the same time an extreme nationalist grouping replaced the old IRA which had largely given up the armed struggle. This was Provisional IRA, and its political wing Provisional Sinn Fein. The Provos, as they were known, represented themselves as defenders of the nationalist/republican/

Catholic community against what they called the 'British colonial occupiers'.

For three years, faced by increasing violence from the IRA and other paramilitary groups like the INLA, and with counter-violence coming from the army and RUC, the London and Stormont governments argued over civil rights and control over security. In 1972 the Northern Ireland government resigned in protest at their lack of control over security matters. The Heath government immediately ended the devolution of Northern Ireland with the abolition of Stormont and the imposition of direct rule from London. In that same year of 1972 the Troubles really started, with the IRA and other republican paramilitaries waging war on the British presence in Ireland, and conducting a terrorist bombing campaign against British targets in mainland Britain and Europe. To complicate matters the Unionist/Protestant/loyalist community also produced its paramilitary gangs. Alongside the so-called armed struggle there was also a civil war of sectarian killings in which Protestant paramilitaries murdered Catholics and vice versa.

After 1972 there was continuous violence alongside repeated attempts to reach agreement in a political settlement. The latter process dragged on over the years and took the form of various proposals for an agreed renewal of devolved government. The two main stumbling blocks were that the nationalist community did not want any devolution that might restore the one-party rule of the Unionists, while the loyalist community refused any form of power-sharing devolution which might permit the Dublin government some say in Northern Irish affairs (Cunningham, 1991).

In 1973 an attempt to restore devolution was begun by William Whitelaw, the first Secretary of State for Northern Ireland. A 78-seat, multiparty assembly was elected in June 1973 and a power-sharing executive composed of the Official Unionists, the Alliance Party and the SDLP took office on 1 January 1974. Proposals for Dublin's participation through a Council of Ireland, however, provoked opposition from the less moderate unionist parties. The executive was undermined and finally brought down in May 1974 by a protestant workers' strike called by the Ulster Workers' Council.

In 1975 the Labour government's Northern Ireland Secretary, Merlyn Rees, called a Constitutional Convention in May. It was only a discussion group but collapsed without achieving anything in March 1976.

In 1982 under Margaret Thatcher, James Prior began a process of what he called 'rolling devolution'. A Northern Ireland Assembly of 78 members was elected in October 1982. It was hampered from the start by the refusal of the Unionist parties to share power with the Republican parties. As a result it was boycotted by Sinn Fein and the SDLP, the latter party entering into talks with Dublin in the so-called New Ireland Forum. The unionist parties continued in the Assembly as a form of scrutinising committee looking at Northern Ireland legislation coming from London. A unionist boycott of the Assembly in 1985 led to the venture being abandoned in 1986.

In 1985 the Anglo-Irish Agreement of 1985 between the London and Dublin governments was a major advance because Dublin openly recognised for the first time that there could only be change in Northern Ireland with the consent of the majority. The agreement provided for regular meetings between British and Irish ministers and a permanent staff of British and Irish civil servants based at Stormont to help negotiate agreements on cross-border disputes. The agreement was totally opposed by unionist parties who refused to allow that Dublin has any say in Northern Ireland, and it was ignored by Sinn Fein who claimed that the point about majority consent was irrelevant because a majority in Northern Ireland is a minority in Ireland as a whole.

A serious peace process began in the second half of 1994 with an IRA cease-fire, followed by similar announcements from the loyalist paramilitaries. However, the British government and Unionist parties refused to take part in talks with parties such as Sinn Fein, as long as paramilitaries kept their weapons and could threaten to restart the violence if talks failed. Sinn Fein, for the IRA, stated that they were willing to enter talks as equal partners, but to give up their weapons would be like admitting defeat. They would do nothing that might suggest surrender. In late November 1995, only days before President Clinton was due to arrive in Northern Ireland, a deal was fixed. A twin-track approach would be adopted by which the arms issue was separated from the question of talks. Negotiations for talks would continue on one track while the arms question would be examined separately by an international and independent commission under a former US Senator, George Mitchell.

In 1996 the IRA cease-fire ended with a bomb set off at Canary Wharf in London, Sinn Fein blaming the British government for bad faith and delaying tactics. Other bombs followed in Germany and Manchester and it began to look as though the peace process was breaking down. During the Protestant marching season in the summer of 1996 there were confrontations and renewed violence between the two communities.

In 1997, soon after his election, Tony Blair with his Northern Ireland Secretary Mo Mowlem made serious efforts to get the peace process back on course, taking a middle track that ran the risk of offending both extremes. For a time during the 1997 marching season it looked as though the whole process could break down again in communal violence. However, some of the Unionists and members of the Orange Order proved ready to compromise on some of the summer's marches and shortly afterwards the IRA announced the renewal of its cease-fire, Sinn Fein earning entry into the peace talks as a result.

That so many of the paramilitary groups from both sides were willing to declare cease-fires in 1994, even if temporary, was a sign of a general recognition that ultimately there would have to be a negotiated settlement rather than a military solution to the Northern Ireland problem. But it is hard to see how the various hard-line attitudes can ever be reconciled and it may be worth considering some of the alternative solutions that have been proposed (McGarry and O'Leary, 1990):

1. Integration would mean the complete abandonment of any form of devolution and the complete integration of the province within the UK. The most significant factor of integration would be the participation of mainline British political parties in the Northern Ireland process. There are those who believe that the difficulties of Northern Ireland are made worse by having political parties that are essentially sectarian and whose very reason for existence is the prolongation of the internal Irish struggle. A few Conservatives support the idea and the Conservative Party has actually contested Northern Irish constituencies, although without success. However, integration has no support in Dublin or in the international community as a whole. It is not a serious option.

2. Unification with the rest of Ireland is the aim of both Sinn Fein and the SDLP, although their views on methods are very different. However, it is no more likely as a solution than integration, even though the British government would probably accept it if the people of Ulster wanted it. But it is

vigorously opposed by all the unionist parties, who remain in a majority in the province. Nor would Dublin really want to acquire the problems that integration would bring if it acquired a hostile and vociferous protestant minority, while the people of both parts of Ireland, whatever their public declarations, would probably not want integration if they realised the increased taxation that would inevitably follow.

3. Independence for Northern Ireland is sometimes put forward by the Protestant community when they are most disenchanted with the London government. Naturally enough it is bitterly opposed by the nationalist community who see it producing the same Protestant domination and discrimination that typified the Stormont government. Even the unionist community can see the anomaly in a Unionist Party advocating independence, while pragmatically they realise they would lose massive government grants that are currently sent from London.

4. Re-partition is often taken to mean that those parts of the province that now have a near majority of Catholics, such as Fermanagh, Tyrone and the city of Derry, would pass to the Republic, leaving a smaller province as part of the UK. However, the distribution of the two communities is such that they could not be divided simply by re-drawing the border. Any change would leave large communities of both traditions on the wrong side of the line, with the possibility of forced movements of people and the horrors of ethnic cleansing as it was seen in Bosnia.

5. Joint sovereignty by both Britain and Dublin has been put forward on more than one occasion and has its attractions, especially for those who see it as a joint administration by two fellow members of the EU. On the other hand, the problems are too great even to envisage.

It has to be acknowledged that the likeliest outcome, when it ultimately comes, may be a form of devolved and power-sharing administration with close links to both London and Dublin, with a number of cross-border institutions dealing with problems common to all Ireland, as with tourism and agriculture. This in many ways is what was proposed in the Anglo-Irish Agreement of 1985. The problem for Northern Ireland is that any peaceful solution would have to be acceptable to all the many incompatible groups within the province.

Summary

The issues relating to the governance of the United Kingdom have been in the background for many years and have centred largely on the question of devolution, waxing and waning in importance according to the party in power and the political climate of the time. As of the 1997 election Britain has a government that is determined to force through the issue of devolution. The problem as far as this book is concerned is that we are standing at a major turning point. The problems of regional and national government are likely to remain as political issues for some time to come, but they are likely to be very different from the problems that have created the issues until now.

13

Gender, Ethnicity and Discrimination

A very potent issue in politics is formed by the very large number of people who feel unfairly disadvantaged and discriminated against simply because of who or what they are, rather than for what they do or have achieved. Of course the greatest sufferers from this are women, who continue in many respects to be treated as second-class citizens even though they represent more than 50 per cent of the population. On the other hand the most blatant forms of discrimination linked with prejudice are found in the treatment of non-white British citizens, in actions that range from unfair treatment under the law to outright racism. There are other sub-groups of society who also suffer from disadvantages, ranging from legal inequalities to job discrimination. Such groups include most disabled people, homosexual gay and lesbian groups and the old in general.

There are two main strands in the issue of discrimination. One is the action or lack of action that is being taken to ensure equality of treatment. The other is the issue of parliamentary representation for disadvantaged groups. This latter point is most clearly seen from the woman's perspective, particularly since the campaign for women's suffrage was such a high profile issue in the early part of the century: an issue which most people thought had been fought and won by the 1920s. And yet, even though women have had the vote for well over half a century they are still quite considerably under-represented in parliament at the end of the twentieth century. 52 per cent of the British population are female but, until the 1997 landslide swept in a total of 120 out of 659, less than 10 per cent of MPs were women. The question as to why there have been so few women in parliament has therefore been a major political issue.

The Women's Movement

Even though women may not be properly represented in parliament, women have always been active in politics. For nearly 200 years there have been campaigns on women's issues such as divorce, married women's property, the right for women to be educated and to work in the professions. Women have often been involved in community action and were allowed to take part in local government long before they were allowed to vote in parliamentary elections. In Britain there are nearly three million women in organisations like the Women's Institute and other women's clubs, all of which are involved in influencing local and national government on a range of political issues.

Many battles over women's issues were fought and won in the later years of the last century and the first two decades of this. Victorian women won the right to be educated, the right to enter the professions and the right to own property in their own right rather than being little more than a possession of father or husband. By the end of the First World War the suffragette movement with its direct action of protest, strike and riot – but helped considerably by the work women did during the war – had gained women the vote. Yet many of these gains 'affected only educated and professional women' (Cole and Howe, 1994, pp. 16–18). Many women, particularly working-class women, remained the victims of excessive child-bearing, were paid less than men, were trapped in loveless marriages and forced to live in a male-dominated culture that has seen women as fit only for domestic tasks as wives and mothers.

The fact that women's rights have failed to become as serious a political issue as the numbers involved would seem to suggest, is because working-class women particularly have 'been prey to sexist culture propagated by the media. . . As a result, many working class women are themselves fierce advocates of the "woman's role in the home" . . . [and] women's issues have tended to remain off the political agenda' (Kingdom, 1991, p. 112). After gaining the vote the question of women's rights lay dormant through the 1930s and 1940s and women tended to distance themselves from political matters. Many were seemingly content with their lot, although most radical feminist thinkers would say that they were brainwashed into this by men and the media. But part of that contentment meant that women were not politically active in a radical sense. Even working-class women were deferential to their male superiors, tending to support the Conservatives politically and far less unionised in the workplace than men. At that time, also, women got very little support from the unions who saw working women on low pay as threats to their members' jobs.

The civil rights atmosphere of the 1960s had its obvious impact on racist politics in Britain and, as was discussed in the previous chapter, it provoked a reaction against religious discrimination in Northern Ireland. But it also had an important impact on the new generation of women then growing up. This was the generation which had benefited from the 1944 Education Act and which had produced women who were better educated than their mothers had been. Naturally they wished to reap the rewards of their education and felt resentful when they found that they were underpaid, under-represented and less well-rewarded when compared with male counterparts who were no better qualified than they.

In 1970 a number of the radical and Marxist feminist groups that had been formed in the 1960s came together for a series of Women's Liberation conferences at Ruskin College, Oxford. This was the start of an identifiable Women's Liberation Movement covering a wide range of issues from battered wives to abortion clinics to peace camps to support for the miners. Some gains for women had been made during the 1960s with, for example, acts such as David Steel's Abortion Act of 1967 and the divorce reform of 1969. Now, Women's Lib demanded the extension of this programme into actions meant to regain control of their own bodies and free their lives from the domination of men, through such things as:

- free access to abortion and contraception;
- protection from sexual harassment and rape; and
- equal pay and equal opportunities at work.

The campaign very quickly produced important results in two pieces of parliamentary legislation:

1. The Equal Pay Act (EPA) of 1970, introduced by Barbara Castle after a strike for equal pay for women by female workers at Ford in 1968. The EPA ordered equal pay for equal work.
2. The Sex Discrimination Act of 1975 was intended to remove all inequalities felt by women in education, housing and employment. The Act also set up the Equal Opportunities Commission to oversee the workings of both the Equal Pay and Sex

Discrimination Acts. Lesser acts passed at about the same time were the Employment Protection Act of 1975, meant to secure a woman's job while she was absent on maternity leave, and the Domestic Violence Act of 1977, meant to assist in bringing successful prosecutions against men who were violent towards their wives, partners and children.

Critics of Women's Liberation have claimed that the benefits have all been for middle-class career women, and that there has been very little gain for the average working-class woman who often has a poorly-paid and part-time job. These same critics would argue that social class is a far greater source of disadvantage than gender, and much the same argument is sometimes used about race.

Despite the Equal Opportunities Act and legislation on equal opportunities, women still tend to be treated unfairly at work compared to men. Despite having a woman as prime minister, or perhaps because of this, the Conservative Party under Margaret Thatcher did not favour women's issues. The Thatcher government's claim to support old-fashioned Victorian values often appeared to include the Victorian attitude to women, including such values as 'a woman's place is in the home' and 'the primary role of a woman is as wife and mother'. There were those who believed that such attitudes were a thing of the past but the position was famously restated by Patrick Jenkin, then the Tory Shadow Social Security spokesman, who said during a television broadcast in 1977, 'If the good Lord had intended us all having equal rights . . . he really wouldn't have created men and women'.

The Conservative governments after 1979 were not kind to women's issues, particularly over such matters as unfair dismissal, maternity rights and poor pay. There were reforms to the Equal Pay and Sex Discrimination Acts but these were largely only introduced because of directives on equal rights originating in the European Union. Indeed, many women's groups made the important discovery that European Law is much more favourable to women than British law and, as a result, appealed successfully for better and fairer treatment in the European Courts, on things like maternity leave and benefit, equal pension rights and job security.

One of the main benefits to be gained from the Labour government's immediate acceptance of the EU's Social Chapter on taking office in 1997 was that a considerable proportion of that social programme was dedicated to helping the sort of part-time, temporary, poorly-paid and insecure positions that all too often are filled by women, and also meant that European rulings on women's rights became enshrined in British law.

Racism and Race Relations

Britain has long been a multicultural society, having provided a haven for political, religious and economic refugees for centuries. However, until the 1950s and 1960s most of these immigrants were culturally European and racially white and easily assimilated into the British way of life. Then, in the postwar economic situation a labour shortage developed which was so severe that it could not be satisfied by native British workers or even immigrants from poorer European countries. Attention was turned to countries of the new Commonwealth, countries like the West Indies or the Indian subcontinent, where the non-white population were ready to accept poorly-paid work in Britain to escape the Third World conditions of their homelands. In the late 1940s and early 1950s, employers such as London Transport and the National Health Service were actively recruiting in the West Indies and many Afro-Caribbeans settled in Britain at that time. Other immigrants came from India and Pakistan during this period, although the main influx of Asian immigrants came between 1967 and 1976 when the newly independent African countries of Kenya, Uganda and Malawi threw out their Asian residents and they, having British passports, came to this country rather than to the Indian sub-continent.

All through the centuries these groups of immigrants have suffered from discrimination and prejudice offered them by the native British, particularly the English. Over the centuries Flemings, French Huguenots, Irish, Jews, Blacks and Asians have all been persecuted in turn because they are different to the native British in speech, behaviour, culture and looks. This racial discrimination, however, is worst for the non-white immigrant because, while immigrants of European origin blend in to the native community within a generation, non-whites remain very visibly different. This is especially relevant to the children and grandchildren of immigrants. Grandchildren of European immigrants who are born in Britain differ from their fellow citizens possibly only through having a non-English name. Skin colour, however, marks members of the immigrant community as being different even when the family has been resident in Britain for more than half a century and the speech, dress and way of life of those families is often indistinguishable from those of their white neighbours.

Non-white Britons have suffered certain disadvantages:

- *Housing*   They have often been forced into ghettoes in areas of poor housing in the inner cities, overcrowded and with poor facilities. In addition, prejudice means that some white inhabitants move out of areas with a high immigrant population, thus tending to confirm those areas as ethnic enclaves. At the same time, non-whites have found it difficult to move out of the ghettoes, sometimes due to a prejudice-induced reluctance to sell houses to non-whites in areas that regard themselves as 'white areas'.

- *Employment*   Immigrants originally came to do the jobs that no one else would do, and it remains true that blacks are mostly employed in low-paid, unskilled manual jobs. It is also true that in a period of high unemployment blacks are more likely to be unemployed than whites. The trade unions have not done much to help, because one of the causes of racial prejudice is the fear at times of high unemployment that immigrants are a threat to the jobs of native Britons on the employment market. This has been true since the fourteenth century, when Flemish immigrants were thought to threaten the jobs of English weavers and were persecuted as a result.

- *Education*   Many non-whites tend not to do well in education, partly perhaps because of language difficulties if their home background is not English-speaking, partly because of prejudice by teachers who have low expectations of how well black students can do, and partly because of a curriculum which is possibly too deeply embedded in European culture for a multicultural society. The contrary position also has to be stated in that research in recent years has shown that certain ethnic groups, particularly some Asian communities, can be high achievers in education.

- *Position in society*   As is the case with women, even when there are apparent equal opportunities in career or promotion prospects, members of ethnic minorities are under-represented in senior or managerial positions.

- *Police harassment*   Rightly or wrongly, non-white young men, particularly Afro-Caribbeans, claim that the police are always 'picking on' them. Again, this is possibly largely due to the high visibility of non-whites but there is certainly evidence that racists exist in the police force. Unfortunately reaction against police pressure often leads non-white youths into crime, creating a self-fulfilling prophecy and allowing the police to believe that they were right all the time.

- *Racism* There are groups, especially in white working-class areas, who are associated with parties like the National Front and the British National Party which are openly and violently racist in their policies, using violence against members of ethnic minorities and their property. By the logic of their own beliefs these racists are defending the British way of life and urging these intruders 'to go back where they came from'. This attitude persists, even when it can be shown that the non-whites being threatened are second or even third generation British born.
- *Deprivation* Many of the problems of non-whites, such as bad housing and unemployment, are problems common to working class people of whatever colour. However, it is true to say that since non-whites are disadvantaged because of both their race and their class, they are doubly disadvantaged.

The main political parties are supposed not to be racist and would angrily deny any such accusations. Both Labour and Conservative governments have introduced equal rights legislation to prevent racial discrimination, just as they introduced legislation to counter sex discrimination, and there is a Commission for Racial Equality to monitor race relations. However, both parties have also introduced anti-immigrant legislation and it is often said that the Conservative government in recent years has been too harsh in its policy of deporting illegal immigrants. The opinions expressed by right-wingers such as Michael Portillo or Peter Lilley suggested that they believed queues of potential immigrants were waiting to enter Britain simply for what they could get out of the UK's health, education and social security systems. The anti-immigration measures introduced by Michael Howard when he was Home Secretary were so severe that the final irony came when it was shown that Howard's parents, who were refugees in the 1930s, would have been denied entry into this country under their own son's definition of undesirable immigrants. The Conservative government's record in detaining and deporting refugees, including those seeking political asylum, was so bad as to gain adverse judgments in the British High Court and a number of international tribunals.

To put race discrimination in context, it has to be said that it is a factor that has been common to all Western European countries in recent years. It is simply that Britain's imperialist past meant that more immigrants from the Third World had links with Britain than most other countries. There is also the point that, although the existence of ghettoes means that the ethnic population is concentrated in just a few locations and therefore appears to be quite high in those places, there are comparatively few non-white citizens if Britain is considered as a whole. At the last count, in the 1991 census 94.5 per cent of the population of Great Britain were classified as white, and only 5.5 per cent as non-white (Layton-Henry, 1996, pp. 21–4).

Just as is the case with women, there are non-white MPs and non-whites who hold important positions in business, administration and industry, but not in anything like the numbers that would be expected from this proportion of the population. There are those who claim that the situation can only be put right by positive discrimination.

Fair Representation of the People

In his survey of the British constitution for *Politics UK*, Philip Norton identified four different forms of parliamentary representation, one of which is described by him as 'a person or persons typical of a particular class or group of persons . . . as . . . when opinion pollsters identify a representative sample . . . in which members reflect proportionately the socioeconomic and other characteristics of the population as a whole' (in Jones, 1994, p. 296). Underlying this view is the belief that representatives need to share the problems of their constituents in order to understand them and before they can do anything about them. By inference the membership of an assembly should represent a demographic profile of the society which it serves as council or parliament. This form of representation is sometimes known as microcosmic representation because a parliament so formed acts as a microcosm of the nation.

Consideration of the House of Commons will show that on a national rather than local level our electoral system produces an assembly that is very far from being a microcosm of British society. In the 1992 election only three MPs fell outside the age range of

30–70 and two-thirds of all MPs were aged from 40–60. Nearly half were privately educated, with 62 per cent of Conservative MPs having been to public schools, while a good two-thirds of all MPs are university graduates, half of them graduates of Oxford or Cambridge. Despite the fact that something like 5.5 per cent of the British population belong to ethnic minorities, they are represented by fewer than a dozen MPs from ethnic communities, less than 2 per cent of the whole. Although, as a rule, local and county councils are slightly more representative of their constituent populations, the profile of the average MP reveals someone who is overwhelmingly a white, middle-aged, middle-class university graduate. He was also, until the 1997 election at least, almost certainly male (Butler and Kavanagh, 1992).

There is no doubt that women have formed the most seriously under-represented group in British politics. Until the potential breakthrough of 1997, only 171 women had been elected to the Commons since women were first admitted in 1918. Women form 52 per cent of the population, but of the MPs elected in the 1992 general election only 9.2 per cent were women, representing 60 of the 651 members: even the five women added later as a result of by-elections did not quite take the figures to 10 per cent. And yet, at the time, the 1992 statistics showed the highest proportion of women ever elected to Westminster at one general election; and a great improvement on the performance of women in recent years even during – perhaps especially during – the Thatcher governments. It is ironic that the 1979 general election, which saw the first woman prime minister take office, also saw a mere 19 women MPs elected, the lowest female representation since 1951. A report of the European Commission on 7 September 1993 showed that the United Kingdom had one of the worst records for representation of women in the whole of the EU. Britain's 9 per cent compared very unfavourably with 33 per cent in Denmark, or 22 per cent in the Netherlands (McKie, 1994, p. 132).

Many reasons have been advanced to explain the failure of women to gain adequate representation in parliament:

● Women are socialised not to be assertive. While the characteristics of successful politicians are thought to be aggression, ambition and self-confidence, these are seen as masculine rather than feminine characteristics.

- There is an inbuilt male chauvinism which suggests that women are not really up to the job. According to this viewpoint, women occupy a different sphere to men; they are mothers and carers, not decision-makers or administrators, and are too emotional for rational political thought. The running joke on the television programme *Spitting Image*, suggesting that Mrs Thatcher was a man in drag, only reflected a deeply-held belief that a 'proper' woman would not be capable of doing the job.
- Centuries of social conditioning mean that even a successful career woman is still expected to devote herself to the children and running the home. The dual needs of family commitments and a career leave little time for political involvement as well. Most women in politics tend to become involved rather later in their lives than do the men.
- The House of Commons is like a man's club; working hours and practices are not suited to a woman's lifestyle, and toilet and other facilities are meagre in a building where the expectation seems to be that the only women present will be secretaries and clerks.
- The most decisive factor, however, lies in the constituency committees which are called to select parliamentary candidates and which are notoriously reluctant to select women candidates for winnable seats (they are a little less reluctant in seats the party is not expected to win). This is not necessarily because of any prejudice or discrimination on the part of committee members themselves, but because they assume that the electors will not vote for a woman and therefore see no point in choosing one in the first place. On the whole, statistical evidence seems to suggest that this view is quite possibly correct. For example, 'this was clearly the case in 1987 when only 14 per cent of candidates were women, and their success rate was less than half that of men – one in eight women candidates was elected, compared to one in three men' (Adonis, 1993, p. 55)

As Coxall and Robins (1995, p. 422) say,

If a potential woman candidate expects there to be a slim chance of being selected by the party in the first place to fight an election, and then sees her sex as an electoral liability if the candidates put forward by rival parties are men, we cannot be surprised that there are so few women in Parliament and on local councils.

It must be said that, suitably modified, the reasons why women do not get elected are equally applicable to all minority groupings whether that minority involves class, age, occupation or ethnic origin. Candidates are said to be ruled out because the need to earn a living does not leave them sufficient time to cultivate potential support in their constituencies; they are said to be insufficiently educated or to lack experience; or it is claimed that their cultural background distances them from the majority of their potential constituents. Above all, the selection committees of all parties do not think that people in a particular constituency will vote for a working-class, non-graduate or black candidate any more than they would for a woman. There was the famous instance in the 1992 election of the black lawyer, John Taylor, who was selected to fight Cheltenham for the Conservatives against the protests of many within the constituency Conservative party. The main criticism made of Taylor was that he came from an alien culture outside the constituency and while, overtly, this was said to be because he came from Birmingham and similar criticisms would have been made against a white candidate originating from that city, there is little doubt that protests against his selection were racially inspired.

Positive Discrimination

The question of what to do about the under-representation of women began in 1980 with the formation outside parliament of the all-party 300 Group under the leadership of Lesley Abdela. The group had as its aim the election of a minimum 300 women MPs to the Commons before the year 2000. Throughout the 1980s the group pursued this aim but the only apparent result was that the number of women MPs actually went down, and it is now agreed that the group's original aim is no longer realisable. Many women lost faith in all-party ventures like the 300 Group and turned to attempting to influence the individual parties, as was the case of Emily's List, a group formed within the Labour Party to raise funds to support women candidates.

The Conservative Party has always been slow at addressing the issue but, finally, Emma Nicholson (who later defected to the Liberal Democrats, partly because she felt they gave a fairer hearing to women) was made vice-chairman of the party with a special responsibility for women members, and after the 1992 election the proportion of women on the party's list of approved candidates almost doubled. Nevertheless, when the National Conservative Women's Conference debated this matter in November 1995, it had to be stated that the Conservative parliamentary party contained only 18 women, two of whom would be standing down at the next election, and, of the first 146 Tory candidates selected for the next general election, only 15 were women, all but four in seats held by Labour or Liberal Democrats which the Tories seemed unlikely to win. After the landslide which decimated the Tory Party on 1 May 1997, a mere 13 women were left on the Conservative benches, only 5 of them new MPs.

The Liberal Democrats have always been more favourably inclined towards women, although it is an attitude that has not necessarily borne fruit. In the 1992 election the party had the highest number of female candidates – 143 compared to Labour's 138 and the Conservatives' 62 – but only two were elected and even by-elections and defections only took the number to four by the time of the 1997 election. Although not going as far as all-women shortlists, the Liberal Democrats did introduce the requirement that each shortlist of candidates' names must contain those of at least two women (Cole and Howe, 1994, pp. 17–18). However, despite this positive discrimination and in spite of the Liberal Democrats having doubled their numbers in the Commons, the party ended with only three women MPs since Diane Maddock and Liz Lynne lost their seats and Emma Nicholson retired.

In the Labour Party, however, opinion has slowly changed in favour of the belief that, if the change was not going to take place naturally, then it would have to be forced through the compulsion of positive discrimination. This already worked in some European social democratic parties such as that of Sweden, where the Social Democrats were committed to fielding equal numbers of male and female candidates in the 1994 elections.

Under the process of reform that began under Neil Kinnock and continued under John Smith and Tony Blair, the Labour Party moved slowly towards adopting positive discrimination in favour of women. Kinnock began the process in 1989 with a quota system requiring Labour MPs to cast at least three votes for women candidates in elections to the Shadow Cabinet. The quota was raised from three to four in 1993 but this resulted in a male backlash that cost Harriet Harman her shadow position.

However, the main aim became to increase the number of women candidates and, hopefully, MPs in parliamentary elections. Identifying the main opposition to change as being the attitude of selection committees that would not select a female candidate if they could avoid it, the proposal adopted was to impose all-women shortlists on certain constituencies. The 1993 conference at Brighton, at which all attention was focused on the 'one member, one vote' debate, also passed a resolution by which only women would be included on selection shortlists in 50 per cent of winnable constituencies and 50 per cent of seats where Labour MPs were retiring. The decision as to what constituted a 'winnable' seat, and which seats would be chosen to be subject to this rule, was supposedly left to 'regional consensus meetings'. Very quickly it became apparent that accepting the policy was very far from putting it into practice. It proved very difficult to arrive at consensus and, while agreeing to the policy in principle, very few constituencies proved willing to accept it as applying to them. Finally in January 1996 a tribunal in Leeds, faced by an appeal from unsuccessful male candidates, found that the policy of all-woman lists was unlawful under the Sex Discrimination Act and the process was quietly dropped, with 14 candidates left to select.

Nevertheless, the triumph for women in the 1997 election, when the number of women Labour members rose from 37 to 101, a quarter of the Parliamentary Labour Party, can only be explained in the light of positive discrimination:

This influx of women has not happened by osmosis . . . it is a triumph for quotas. Half the new Labour women were chosen from all-women short lists . . . An example: the sole woman MP in Wales, Ann Clwyd, has been joined by three others. Each was chosen from an all-women short list. (Milne, 1997, pp. 16–17)

During the 1980s the arguments over positive discrimination were also used in the Labour Party to deal with the growing problem of black representation. As the only part of Labour's traditional vote to remain loyal at a time when large sections of the working class were deserting them, the black vote became very important to the party and a committee was formed to examine the best way to gain and retain black partisanship for Labour. This committee recommended the setting up of black sections in the party, similar to the women's sections that had existed for some time. Despite overwhelming support from the unofficial black groups that already existed in some constituencies, the idea was rejected by the NEC and conference because the Labour Party claims to support racial integration in society and the setting up of black groups would suggest that there is something 'different' about people of disparate racial groups. The ironic implication was that the imposition of separate racial groups within the party would mean an acceptance of segregation and a form of apartheid.

Another form of positive discrimination in electoral reform was rejected outright. This was the suggestion that minorities, of whatever kind, could be formed into separate electorates each of which would vote for their own MPs. Those who argue for this solution point to the example of New Zealand where the Maoris have elected their own representatives for many years. But that is being phased out in New Zealand and the system has too many overtones of fascist corporatism or 'separate development' as practised in the days of apartheid in South Africa.

Minority Representation through Proportionality

Many people believe that the recipe for fairer treatment, whether for women or for under-represented minorities, lies in some form of proportional representation. With any form of list system, or a semi-list system like the Alternative Member System, the problem of under-represented groups is easily solved by the parties making up their quota of elected members by the requisite numbers in the category of candidate they feel to be entitled to proportional representation. If the Single Transferable Vote were used, the existence of multi-member constituencies would remove one of the main barriers to minority groups being represented. At the moment constituency parties are reluctant to select women or ethnic candidates when there is only one member to be elected: if a constituency has only one chance of getting their candidate into parliament they are not going to choose any candidate whose electability is in doubt. When a party can enter two, three, four or five candidates for the same constituency they are more willing to take a risk on one or more of those candidates, because they have hedged their bets, as it were, with other safer candidates.

It has been said that most proportional systems are every bit as undemocratic as majority systems, because the power to dictate who should become MPs or councillors is taken out of the hands of the electorate and passed to the political parties. This is even more true of any form of microcosmic representation, especially if that involves the imposition of quota numbers for designated categories. Which leaves the issue of discrimination centred on the question: what can be done to correct imbalance and unfairness, if the remedy is itself unbalanced and unfair?

Summary

There has been a concentration in this chapter on the inequalities of representation, as typified by membership of the House of Commons. The logic underlying this concentration is that discrimination is not going to just go away: change must be enforced by legislation. But that change will not come while the legislative body itself is subject to the prejudices and ethos of a discriminatory culture. Change the nature and make-up of parliament and something might be done. The women's movement is leading the way and other groups must follow.

A significant move for the cause of women was the institution under Tony Blair of a cabinet sub-committee focusing on women's issues. With Harriet Harman in the chair and with most other prominent Labour women as members, the committee would look at issues like childcare, pensions, employment and domestic violence. Its aim would be to improve communications between women's groups and the politicians from whom, according to Ms Harman, they often feel 'disconnected and alienated'.

As far as anti-racism was concerned, Jack Straw promised a range of measures, including an inquiry into the killing of Stephen Lawrence, new crimes of racial violence and racial harassment would be created, with relaxation of immigration rules and the appointment of a race advisory committee.

14

The Environment

Concern for the environment has been growing for a number of years. In 1973 environmental pressure groups in Britain attempted to venture beyond their extraparliamentary role through the foundation of a political party dedicated to environmental issues, known originally as the Ecology Party but soon renamed as the Green Party. For most of their period of existence the Green Party 'have been restricted to the fringes of UK politics' (Pattie, Johnston and Russell, 1995, pp. 21–5), but an apparent turning point in their fortunes came with the 1989 elections to the European Parliament. In that year the Liberal–SDP Alliance was finally breaking up in confusion and recrimination, while the Conservative government was at the height of its unpopularity over the poll tax. As a result the significant protest vote regularly given to third parties at times of government unpopularity transferred itself from the Alliance to the Green Party, who got 15 per cent of the vote.

Because of the British electoral system, no Green Party candidate was elected in the 1989 election, even though the British Green vote was higher than it was for those other European Green parties who did elect MEPs. The result, therefore, although very disappointing to the Green Party in some respects, was encouraging in boosting the morale of environmentalists and leading the party to believe it had finally come of age. Moreover, the high green vote persuaded the other parties that environmental issues were important to the electorate, and from then on all political parties produced policies on the environment and claimed to be 'greener than the Greens' (Curtice, 1989, pp. 217–30). This was not so much a departure for the Liberal Democrats, since the former Liberal Party had favoured the environment since the mid-1970s, but it was a significant new departure for the Conservative and Labour Parties.

Unfortunately for the Green Party the high tide of 1989 soon receded in party political terms. The creation of the Liberal Democrat Party as successor to the Alliance and the adoption of green policies by the major parties led to the Green Party losing its position as recipient of the protest vote. At the same time the growing economic recession that hit Britain after 1989 led to environmental issues taking a very poor second place among the electorate's concerns when compared to the more pressing and relevant economic issues. By the time of the 1992 general election the Green Party's share of the vote had dropped to 1.9 per cent. Even in the European elections of 1994 the Green Party could manage no more than 3.3 per cent, little more than a fifth of the vote they had received five years previously. By the summer of 1996, weakened by continual internal battles, the Green Party announced its withdrawal from future elections in an effort to save money. In the 1997 election the party fielded less than 100 candidates, each of whom had to meet their own electoral expenses, including their own deposits, and there was no advertising.

An important point to realise about environmental issues, therefore, is that they have very little to do with partisan politics and party allegiances. On the other hand, they are so much a concern for pressure and interest groups that matters involving the environment are to the fore in provoking personal participation in politics through direct action of the individual and group. According to reports which appeared in the national press about the influences on the leadership of the Green Party when they decided to abandon hope of the partisan political process: '. . . So many of its potential grassroots activists are involved in alternative direct action protests such as the Newbury bypass because they perceive the political route leading nowhere' (John Vidal in *The Guardian*, 27 August 1996).

The main problem with environmental issues is that they rely on the altruism of the public and this is not always available. In prosperous times, under the influence of the feel-good factor, the electorate has compassion to spare and can afford to worry about the fate of other people and about harm being done to the environment. In the harder climate of recession and economic insecurity the average voter is more concerned about personal and family worries, with no sympathy to spare for more impersonal matters.

Environmental Issues

The main environmental concerns are:

- *Pollution* of the air, water and soil.
- *Conservation* of finite natural resources such as fossil fuels.
- *Preserving* the natural world, including rare species of plant and animal life and the areas where these rare species live.
- *Control* of toxic and nuclear waste.
- *Reduction* in carbon emissions to prevent global warming.

There are many individual concerns within the overall umbrella term of the environment so that some groups are concerned with the pollution of rivers, others with the dangers of the nuclear industry and yet others with endangered species of animals. Yet they are often interlocking issues and even diverse groups feel a sense of common cause and will combine in alliance to fight any environmental issue. A scheme to build a new road like the Newbury bypass, or the construction of a new runway at Manchester Airport, will initially attract those groups who are concerned about interference with the natural environment through the digging up of the countryside, the clearing of woodland and the destruction of wildlife habitat (a rare snail in the case of Newbury), but even after the actual construction process is finished the environmentalists are worried about pollution from traffic or aircraft noise and exhaust emissions, not to mention the potential waste of natural resources through the unimpeded growth of transport networks.

Some action groups restrict themselves to specific sections of the environment but the larger, often international, groupings like Greenpeace or Friends of the Earth are concerned with the full range of environmental issues and their ability to damage the Earth itself. At other times various groups will come together in formal and informal alliances to work for a common end. For example, a private member's bill of autumn 1996 introduced by the Plaid Cymru MP, Cynog Dafis, to reduce the volume of road traffic had the backing of a tripartite alliance between Friends of the Earth, Transport 2000 and the National Society for Clean Air. This is to recognise that environmental pressure groups should not only be concerned with direct action over high-profile projects like the Manchester runway, but must maintain a constant watchdog role over the environmental effects of governmental or industrial action.

There is a sort of glamour about the media interest generated by ecological protest but equally, if not more important, work is done in quiet negotiations with councils, politicians and civil servants.

Environmental Ideology

Many environmental activists act because of concern over some specific worry such as the pollution of bathing beaches, but underlying most environmental groups and Green parties is an eclectic ideology which forms a reasoned world view of the future. The main strands of that ideology are:

- A global approach. In all activity the finite nature of the world's natural resources should be borne in mind, as well as the fragile nature of world ecology.
- Think of our children and our children's children. We should realise that we are only temporary guardians of the planet and it is our duty to avoid passing on to future generations an exhausted and polluted Earth.
- Conserve our resources. We should recognise the finite nature of raw materials and energy sources and we should not squander these in a never-ending search for growth.
- Planet Earth. We must realise that environmental problems are the problems of all humanity and we should encourage the sharing and fair distribution of resources for all (Coxall and Robins, 1995, p. 427).

This ideology places the environmentalists and the Green Party in direct ideological opposition to all other political parties in Britain today. Explicitly or implicitly all the main political parties are dedicated to the idea of growth. Government policy and party rhetoric assumes that industrial production, commercial and financial activity and the general standard of living will and must continue to grow and expand indefinitely. The ideologues of the green parties would answer that indefinite growth is impossible and that a halt has to be called at some point if we are to conserve resources. This is a major factor which has limited the electoral success of green issues, since it is very difficult to get people to vote for a halt or reversal to any improvement in their standard of living.

In truth, however, it is more a case that there are several different levels of support for environmental matters, not all of which are ideological. At its simplest, Dobson divided the environmental lobby into the 'light greens', who argue that the environment can be saved if the existing system is reformed, and the 'dark greens' who believe that if the ecology is to survive at all it will require a total radical change in the nature of society (Dobson, 1993).

Legislation

Over the years, and increasingly since the profile of environmental issues started to rise in the 1970s, the government has introduced a certain amount of legislation intended to deal with the pollution of the environment. Responsibility for administering and overseeing the application of this legislation partly falls on two government agencies:

- Her Majesty's Inspectorate of Pollution (HMIP). Formed in 1987 by merging the various inspectorates for air pollution, radio-chemical, hazardous waste and water pollution.
- The National Rivers Authority (NRA). Set up in 1989 by the Water Act which privatised the various water authorities. The responsibilities of the NRA, other than pollution control, include flood defences (both inland and coastal), control of water resources (including abstraction for use) and control of fishing, navigation and recreational uses of waterways and coastal waters.

A great deal of direct control over environmental matters is given to local government authorities who are empowered by national government legislation such as the Clean Air Acts of 1956 and 1968, the Control of Pollution Act of 1974 and the Environmental Protection Act of 1990. The most important factor governing local authority involvement in environmental matters is the collection and disposal of waste, both domestic and industrial. The 1990 Act also obliged local authorities to devise strategies for recycling waste, with a target for recycled waste set at 25 per cent to be achieved by the year 2000. These various bodies were brought under the supervision of the Environment Agency in 1996.

Local authorities are also given a considerable say in planning, thus controlling the physical environment through determining land

use, the erection or demolition of buildings, the building or extension of roads and preventing development from encroaching on
rural areas or designated green belt zones. The government has also
provided measures to protect the environment through a number of
conservation agencies. These include the Countryside Commission,
English Nature, English Heritage, Scottish Natural Heritage and the
Countryside Council for Wales. These in turn can deploy special
weapons to aid conservation, very often through their ability to
nominate areas of the countryside as sites of special scientific
interest (SSSIs) or as areas of outstanding natural beauty (AONBs).

In the Major government, John Selwyn Gummer as Environment
Secretary was treated with respect by green groups because of a
series of initiatives which seemed to favour the environment, and his
foundation of the Environment Agency in 1996 was one of the few
widely recognised success stories of that government. He is himself
an organic farmer and encouraged a scheme for farmers known as
Environmentally Sensitive Areas. In May 1996 he launched a bio-
diversity action plan along lines suggested by Brussels. In August
1996 he received praise from environmentalists for announcing air
quality targets for eight key pollutants, recognising also that road
traffic is the chief source of air pollution. These measures seemed to
bear out the justice of the award to Mr Gummer of the BBC Wildlife
Green Ribbon for political support of the environment. In Denver,
at the United Nations Earth Summit of June 1997, Tony Blair paid
tribute to John Gummer as one of the few members of the former
Tory administration to understand environmental issues.

Yet, although Gummer seemed in some respects to have been the
answer to the environmentalists' prayers, in others he showed
himself unwilling to break with his own party's support for the
motor car. He was willing for the Newbury bypass to cut through
open countryside, damaging more than one SSSI in the process, and
he was noticeably unwilling to set targets for the reduction of road
traffic. This in fact is one of the main issues concerning the
environment. Politicians are very ready to speak in support of the
environment but they are often unwilling to take action if they feel it
is contrary to the interests of their supporters. For example, when
privatised water companies were unable to meet European-directed
standards on water treatment, it was John Gummer who redefined
the Severn and Humber estuaries as seas rather than rivers to take
them out of the scope of the legilsation (*The Observer*, 25 August
1996, p. 7).

It is perhaps unsurprising that green groups place far more trust in legislation and support from Brussels and the European Union, than from British politicians at Westminster.

Europe and the Environment

At the Dublin European Council of June 1990 a declaration was signed by all 12 heads of state or government:

> The environment is dependent on our collective actions; tomorrow's environment depends on how we act today. . . We intend that action by the Community and the Member States will be developed on a co-ordinated basis and on the principles of sustainable development and preventive and precautionary action. (European Commission, 1992)

The Treaty of Rome contained a commitment to improve the quality of life for member states, but that this might apply to the environment was not accepted until the late 1960s and it was 1973 before the first Action Programme on the Environment was announced. The environment is very much a Community affair because pollution pays no heed to national boundaries. Pollute the upper reaches of the Rhine and the pollution will affect France, Germany, the Netherlands and ultimately the seaboard of the North Sea. Air pollution in Britain can create acid rain over wide stretches of Northern Europe. Concerns such as these led the Community to take preventative measures, leading to a total of 280 environmental legislative measures, 200 directives issued and four Action Programmes approved between 1973 and 1991.

Two factors led to a change of emphasis in 1987. One was the work involved in setting up the Single European Act. There was the need for a coordinated approach by all governments to environmental requirements on factories and industrial plants to provide a level playing field for the various member states involved in the Single Market. Also in 1987 the World Commission on Environment and Development (WCED) produced what is known as the Brundtland Report, drawing attention to the way in which economic growth was leading to the destruction of finite resources. The WCED called for 'sustainable' growth. These two factors together produced the communiqué of the Dublin Summit, the establishment of a European Environmental Agency in 1990 and the introduction of a fifth Action Programme, named *Towards Sustainability*, to run from 1993 to the year 2000 (Young, 1993, pp. 6–8).

The main targets of environmental legislation, for the EC as much as anyone else, have always been pollution of the air, water and soil, together with the problem of waste, particularly toxic waste. Since the emphasis has shifted to sustainability the Community has laid great emphasis on issues such as the conservation of finite energy sources such as fossil fuels, saving energy through insulation and other means, and the generation of energy from renewable sources like wind, sun and tide. There has also been a growing interest in the protection of wild life, both flora and fauna. One ruling of the EC has been to say that any major engineering project must take into account its effect on the environment, particularly on the habitat of wild life.

Community directives have laid down strict emission standards for the release of pollutants into the air and water. Directives have concerned the release of sulphur dioxide (1980), lead in exhaust gases (1982), nitrogen dioxide (1985) and ozone levels (1992). There has also been a continuing programme curbing the emission of carbon dioxide, held responsible for global warming. Key directives have also been issued concerning the quality of drinking water, the pollution of rivers and waterways and the quality of bathing water at seaside resorts (Department of the Environment, 1992).

A major environmental initiative was the 1992 Habitat Directive which built on a 1979 directive on the protection of birds and was intended to preserve or restore the habitat for species of flora and fauna whose existence is threatened by intensive farming or pollution. The scheme, as reported by the environment correspondent of *The Guardian*, was launched in Britain by the then Agriculture Minister, Gillian Shepherd, and sought to persuade farmers to restore the natural environment in three areas:

1. Any set-aside land which is managed for the nurture of endangered species of plants, butterflies, birds and so on will be subsidised at the rate of £275 per hectare.
2. Along the fringes of certain key waterways farmers would be paid to maintain a strip 20 metres wide from the water's edge within which farmers would not use artificial fertilisers and pesticides. This will allow safe areas for the colonisation by wild life while preventing the pollution of the water by nitrates and

other toxic substances, with their consequent effects upon fish life and the food chain of water-birds. Farmers will be paid for these water fringes at a rate of £360 a hectare if the land is used for crop production, or £240 if the land is under grass.

3. Certain areas of land reclaimed from the sea or marsh and maintained by expensive and potentially damaging coastal defence or drainage schemes will be allowed to revert to natural water-meadows, marsh or wetlands at a subsidy of £525 per hectare if withdrawn from crop production or £196 if under grass (*The Guardian*, 16 May 1994).

Environmental schemes are expensive and therefore unpopular with governments and industry. As a result there have been many disputes between national governments and the Commission about non-compliance with Community directives on the environment. The British government's first attempts to privatise the water industry had to be abandoned because the Community refused to accept the suggestion that the privatised water companies should regulate themselves. It was only after the institution of the National Rivers Authority to police the activities of the water companies that privatisation could go ahead. There are still continuing disputes over drinking water quality.

One long-standing dispute has been about the standard of bathing water on British beaches. This dates back to a directive of 1975 which demanded that national governments should designate bathing beaches which would be required to meet strict guidelines on water quality by 1985. The British government was first in trouble because they wanted to designate no more than 27 beaches for this purpose: after discussion this number was raised to 446. The British government then pleaded for more time to comply with the set standards and was granted an extension until 1995. Yet a report by the National Rivers Authority in 1994 showed that 55 beaches in Britain could well fail to meet the required standards by the 1995 deadline, and might remain with waters unsafe for bathing because of raw sewage and other pollutants (*The Guardian*, 16 May 1994).

Another high-profile dispute between Britain and Europe has been over the directive requiring civil engineering projects to have regard to the environment. In 1991 the then Commissioner for the Environment, Carlo Ripa di Meana, officially warned the UK government that it was in breach of Community regulations in seven engineering projects, the most famous of which was the building of the M3 across Twyford Down, an area of natural beauty and of historical and scientific interest near Winchester. The Commission was persuaded to withdraw its objections to Twyford Down in 1992 but disputes over the government's road-building programme have continued with the M11 extension in London, the Newbury bypass and other schemes.

The Commission receives more complaints about Britain than any other member state: in 1990 there were 125 complaints registered (Young, 1993). It should not, however, be assumed that Britain is the worst offender. In 1991, in terms of non-compliance with Community directives, Britain with 23 offences was the fourth most compliant, with only Denmark, Luxembourg and the Netherlands having a better record. The figure 23 compares favourably with Greece's 50, Italy's 53 and Spain's 66 (*The Economist*, 20 July 1991).

Environmental Pressure Groups

The main British parties all have environmental policies and some 'green' legislation has been passed. All the same, the environment remains one issue where the battle is not principally joined between the political parties. For, despite some party involvement, the politics of green issues in Britain remains very much an area where people put more trust in direct action through pressure groups than they do in the promises of political parties:

- Membership of environmental pressure groups is large, growing and is often greater than the membership of some political parties. In 1991, for example, membership of Friends of the Earth stood at 111 000, Greenpeace at 408 000, the Royal Society for the Protection of Birds at 852 000, while the National Trust could claim a membership well over two million (Central Statistical Office, 1994).
- The present-day growth in pressure group activity dates from the late 1960s when the heyday of the two-party system was largely over. In a survey of the environmental lobby carried out by Lowe and Goyder in 1983, over half the groups had been formed since the late 1960s (Lowe and Goyder, 1983). It represents a trend that was contemporary with the Liberal revival and upsurge of Scottish and Welsh nationalism: all the indications in fact of disillusionment with confrontational party politics.

- Membership of environmental groups is particularly strong among young people who want to become involved in politics but who do not trust politicians. Environmental issues are also strong with the educated and prosperous, thus representing a difference from the disadvantaged or dispossessed who support pressure groups over poverty or similar issues. Environmental pressure groups have mobilised thousands of protesters, often middle-class men and women not usually associated with protest movements, to fight against environmental issues like the building of the bypass at Newbury.
- Factors like these have led Baggott to believe that the increased involvement of the middle classes in environmental pressure groups, especially in direct actions of protest and demonstration, has been the product of social changes similar to those of the early nineteenth century that gave rise to the great moral crusades against slavery, drink and child labour (Baggott, 1995, p. 170).

The environmental pressure groups can be divided into four broad categories (Grant, September 1995, pp. 31–3):

1. The animal protection groups. These can have a wide-ranging concern for the welfare of animals both wild and domestic, such as the RSPCA or the World Wildlife Fund, or they can be more narrowly focused on one species or field of interest, like Save the Whale or the League against Cruel Sports. The groups are very diverse and some have become enthused by the ideological belief that animals have rights like any minority group, leading to animal liberation groups who are prepared to use violence and illegal methods to further their ends. Part of the effectiveness of these animal protection groups has been dissipated through disputes over strategy, between those who are content to use propaganda and reasoned argument and those who break into kennels housing experimental animals, sabotage fox hunts or place bombs in laboratories or supermarkets. Protest over animal welfare is at its most effective when the disparate groups can be encouraged to work together, as was the case over the live export of veal calves in 1995.

2. Groups to protect amenities such as the Council for the Protection of Rural England, the Keep Britain Tidy group or the Woodland Trust. They form a vocal opposition to many schemes promoted by national government or multi-national

companies and tend to proliferate at local level which is where they are at their most effective. This is when external action is liable to have an effect on a local community, whether it is the great disruption in Kent caused by the Channel Tunnel or the concern of parents at the presence of toxic waste on a local tip. Critics of such local groups dismiss them as not-in-my-back-yard (NIMBY) groups who are happy enough to see much-needed progress and development as long as it does not affect them personally. It is true that many such groups are indeed selfish and guilty of blocking schemes that otherwise are for the public good. Even worse, the delays and disruption created by NIMBY protests are expensive; the *Sunday Times* estimating in 1989 that NIMBY action could cost the economy as much as £1.5 billion a year (*Sunday Times*, 8 January 1989).

3. The anti-road lobby is a movement that has gained pace in recent years and which has gained a considerable degree of support. Under a general umbrella, represented by a coordinating body in London known as Alarm UK, a great number of causes have come together. There are amenity groups who protest at the building of roads through local areas of beauty and interest, protection groups who protest at the destruction of wildlife and its habitat, and those ideological protesters who are opposed to the destructive impact of the motor vehicle on the environment, the air and the consumption of scarce resources. In 1994 it was estimated that there were no fewer than 250 different local anti-road groups in existence. The diversity of the groups involved and the differences between them over methodology mean that they do not always present a united front. There are always those who are prepared to go as far as violent resistance to the road-builders and sabotage of their earth-moving equipment, but many of them are more law-abiding and are willing to go no further than passive resistance, even if it is as spectacular as building and living in tree-houses in woodland that must be felled or tunnelling deep into the foundations of the new construction. The divisions in the movement rob it of some effectiveness, and while the road-builders have law and the police on their side the law-abiding protesters must always give way.

4. Large, broad-based groups or consortia of groups which are ready to campaign on all manner of environmental issues. Such groups are Greenpeace or Friends of the Earth who are ready to

tackle a range of issues running from opposition to nuclear testing, to opposing the hunting of whales, to stopping the pollution of the oceans. Such groups are often worldwide in their interests and membership and action by them is often carried out through the cooperation of various national groups. For example, in 1995 the British, Dutch, German and other European branches of Greenpeace combined to defeat the Shell Oil company and several European governments over the disposal at sea of a North Sea oil-drilling rig, *Brent Spar*.

The effectiveness of these pressure groups is questionable. Some high-profile protests such as those on the site of the Newbury bypass, the M3 at Twyford Down, the M11 link road at Wanstead, the widening of the M25 at Runnymede and many other protests over motorways, have gained a great deal of press coverage and public interest but ultimately they have failed inasmuch as the projects against which they were protesting have gone ahead. The difference between success and failure was usually dependent on whether work had actually started on the schemes. When work had actually started on the site, with large sums of money committed, protests usually failed: where the protests were most intense at the planning or policy-making stage, the pressure groups were often more successful.

There are two main routes to success for environmental pressure groups:

- By the groups becoming 'insider' groups, consulted by government and with easy access to civil servants. Some of the larger groups, such as Friends of the Earth or the RSPB, are consulted by the Ministry of Agriculture and other government departments. Many of the environmental groups are divided as to the strategy they should adopt. Many activists see direct action as useful in terms of the media attention and publicity it produces for the group's ideas. But more moderate members feel that such action is only likely to alienate official opinion and that a more reasoned and moderate approach will encourage official circles to take them more seriously. According to that view far more can be accomplished through consultation than could ever be gained through confrontation.
- Through using consumerism. Many companies – and Body Shop was a leader in this field – stress that their products are envir-

onmentally friendly and the 'green factor' is actually used as a marketing strategy. Other companies are forced to moderate their policies for fear of an adverse consumer reaction: the success of Greenpeace over the *Brent Spar* incident in 1995 was largely due to a consumer boycott of Shell petrol stations throughout Germany.

The political climate in Britain, certainly during the years that Margaret Thatcher was in power, was often hostile to environmental groups, inasmuch as over-great concern for the environment was judged to militate against free market forces. In face of that opposition there were many pressure groups who found that a far more open and promising road to progress was open through the European Union.

Environmental Pressure Groups in Europe

One indication of the way in which an increased share of policy-making has moved from national governments to the European Commission is the way in which pressure and interest groups are coming to focus their attention at a European level in Brussels. The removal by the Single European Act of the national veto in the Council of Ministers on all matters relating to the single market meant a massive shift of influence over policy to the Commission and, increasingly, the Parliament. Any British pressure group which continues to rely exclusively on lobbying Whitehall and Westminster is at a disadvantage, because on a large range of issues policies are now being determined in Brussels (Mazey and Richardson, 1993, p. 20).

The European Union was committed to the protection of the environment by the Maastricht Treaty and has a programme of environmental action in hand. What distinguishes the Community from most national governments is the apparent openness of its institutions to those promoting sectional interests, and the willingness of officials to talk to a wide range of lobbyists rather than just a few favoured groups. As Mazey and Richardson say, 'The very willingness of officials to talk to groups and individual firms means that the market for policy ideas is much more broad and fluid than in the UK'. The result has been a fair degree of success for environmental groups in getting their ideas framed by the European

Commission as directives: being particularly successful in fields such as water pollution. The problem remains that the EU may issue directives but it is up to national governments to enforce them.

Summary

In Europe, as elsewhere, the problem for environmental groups is that they are not only divided in purpose among themselves but that there are conflicting pressure groups, representing industry or business for example, who are quite as influential as the environmental groups and which can negate their influence. This represents the real heart of the problem and the paradox which is the real environmental issue. People may dislike what industry and commerce is doing to the environment but they are unwilling to give up the benefits which industry and commerce bring to their standard of living. On a smaller scale the same paradox exists for the person who hates the destructive effect on the environment of the motor car and deplores the impact of the internal combustion engine on air pollution, but who would find it impossibly inconvenient to give up driving their own motor car.

As Robin Cook said at the G7 summit in Denver, on 23 June 1997, '[the government] will find it difficult to deal with a domestic audience which is still very much in a culture of large extravagant private cars and generous consumption of energy as a cheap commodity'. He was speaking largely about the American administration but he was speaking for all governments that are faced by the basic unpopularity of legislation intended to help the environment. The incoming Labour government of 1997 was faced with a commitment to abandon the VAT levy on gas and electricity imposed by the Conservative government. Yet, that tax had been introduced as an energy-conservation measure and the Chancellor was well aware that abolition of VAT on energy would have to be replaced by some other disincentive to energy-use, such as increased taxation on petrol.

15

The Politics of Events

Harold Macmillan, when he was prime minister, was once famously asked what he found was the most difficult issue to deal with in government. 'Events, dear boy,' he said, 'Events!' The issues we have dealt with so far in this book are, in a sense, always with us. They may change in form and seriousness but they are a continual presence and political parties develop policies and strategies to deal with them. Yet they are not always nor necessarily what concerns the public and electorate most. Quite unexpectedly, as a result of an event overseas perhaps, or the irrational behaviour of a disturbed individual, something will cause the public to become concerned enough to become politically involved. In recent years that event has, with disturbing frequency, been the result of a serious policy mistake or misjudgment on the part of government. As Patrick Dunleavy has put it, 'Britain now stands out amongst comparable European countries . . . as a state unusually prone to make large scale, avoidable policy mistakes' (Dunleavy et al., 1997, p. 335).

The concern generated by these events is often amplified by opposition parties seizing on yet another way of harassing the government, or by the media sensationalising the matter for their own ends, or by pressure and interest groups following their own concerns. The concern then becomes an issue, often part of or associated with another wider issue, but nevertheless an issue in its own right about which the electorate expects the government and opposition parties to devise a strategy or policy. Very often the very fact of government involvement helps to amplify the importance of an issue, particularly if it is badly handled and even more particularly if it has to do with public health. According to Rob Baggott,

255

. . . one can identify a range of issues – food additives, pesticide pollution, salmonella poisoning, lead in petrol, smoking and alcohol abuse. In all these cases governments have been reluctant to take action to protect health, even where the consequences are potentially disastrous. (Baggott, 1996, pp. 2–8).

As a contributing factor, Wyn Grant also mentions, 'a self-confident administrative élite lacking knowledge of the field in which they are operating but reluctant to make use of the full range of outside expertise' (Dunleavy *et al.*, 1997, p. 335).

It is impossible to deal fully with such issues in a book like this. By their nature those events which cause most public concern are unforeseen and unplanned. Some persist in the public mind and become long-lived political issues, concerning which the parties will have to formulate an attitude and for which there will be a place in the party manifesto, in which case they come within the remit of this book and have probably been dealt with in the preceding chapters. Other event-inspired issues may be more ephemeral and, having hogged the headlines for a few months, or even years, will fade away and often be forgotten as rapidly as they first arose: more than a nine-day wonder, but not much more.

A particularly clear example of this kind of issue is provided by the BSE crisis which overwhelmed the farmers and food processors of the British beef industry, a crisis which mirrored and foreshadowed other instances of public fear about the safety of food, such as listeria in cheese, salmonella in eggs and E-coli in cooked meats.

These various food scares have one common element: there was a massive mobilisation of public opinion on the part of consumers and intense involvement by the media in the name of the consumer, but there were equally powerful forces representing the producers who were directly opposed to the causes which had found favour in the public's eyes. Moreover, the groups opposed to public opinion, although smaller in number, carried more political clout. For a start it is probable that they had access to more resources and had wealthier backers than those groups supporting the public will: they were certainly more influential in government circles. Baggott has mentioned this aspect of pressure group dynamics when he discusses the extent to which pressure groups can counterbalance each other, 'neutralising to an extent each other's campaigns' (Baggott, 1995, p. 35). Campaigns to stop smoking are typical of this effect: the anti-smoking organisation ASH, although supported by doctors, health workers and medical opinion in general, is opposed by the pro-smoking FOREST, supported by the big money of the international tobacco companies and by an awareness in government circles of the importance of tobacco duty to a government's tax revenue take.

Food and the Consumer

In July 1993, when he was Minister for the Public Services and responsible for the Citizen's Charter, William Waldegrave gave a lecture to the Public Finance Foundation in which he claimed that a consumer-oriented view of accountability, as exhibited by quangos and government agencies, was a democratic gain rather than a democratic deficit. In answer to those who complained about the undemocratic nature of these unelected groups, he replied that the crucial issue was not, 'whether those who run our public services are elected, but whether they are producer-responsive or consumer-responsive'. When it arose to prominence the BSE crisis was seen as important because it ran directly counter to the principle as expounded by Waldegrave, inasmuch as a combination of manu-facturers, farming interests and government ministers representing the producers appeared to conspire together to ignore the wishes, interests and even the health and safety of the general public as consumers.

Bovine spongiform encephalopathy (BSE, or Mad Cow Disease), is a terrible disease in which the cow's brain turns to a spongy jelly, losing its capacity to control the body and limbs and leading inevitably to death since there is no known cure. Although BSE only came to light in 1986, spongiform diseases have been known for some time. Scrapie, a spongiform disease of sheep, was clinically recognised as long ago as 1732 but was probably introduced into Britain with new breeds of sheep as far back as the fifteenth century. The existence of human spongiform diseases, such as Kuru which afflicts the brain-eating cannibals of Papua New Guinea, has been known for almost a century and the human form most closely related to BSE, Creutzfeldt-Jakob Disease (CJD), was first diag-nosed in 1921. The problem with spongiform diseases is that they are not transmitted by means of viruses or bacteria but through proteins called prions. Therefore very little is known about them, even about so simple a matter as how the disease is passed on from one animal to another of the same species. For a very long time no one suspected that the condition could be passed from one species to another, let alone that it could be passed from some animals to humans.

Since it was not thought to affect humans nobody paid much attention to BSE after its discovery in 1985 and the official confirmation of that discovery in 1986. Two years later, however, in 1988, a committee set up by the Ministry of Agriculture, Fisheries and Food (MAFF) under Sir Richard Southwood discovered a link between BSE and scrapie in sheep. Manufacturers had been putting animal protein into the types of cattle food prepared for the intensive factory-farming industry and this meant that meat from sheep that had died from scrapie was being fed to cattle and thus finding its way into the food chain. If scrapie-infected meat from sheep could cause BSE in cattle then there were fears that beef from cattle with BSE could cause humans to develop CJD.

As a result of these findings, animal protein in cattle food was banned in 1988 and a selective cull of BSE-affected cows began in 1989. Unfortunately for the success of the cull, the government set the rate of compensation for the slaughter of beasts at only 50 per cent of the value of a healthy animal. Most farmers failed to declare the full extent of the disease in their herds for fear of losing too much money and the effectiveness of the culling programme was seriously weakened because so many infected beasts were slipping through the net. In early 1989, first Germany and then the United States banned the import of British beef.

In February 1990, rather late in the day, the compensation rate for the slaughter of cows was raised from 50 to 100 per cent and the breeding of calves from BSE-infected mothers was banned. These moves which were meant to defuse the situation did not do so, particularly in May when a link was proved between BSE in cattle and a spongiform disease in cats, transmitted through tins of pet food. Panic broke out again, with most local education authorities in Britain banning beef from school meals menus, while France joined the number of countries worldwide to ban the import of British beef. In an attempt to counter the panic the safety of beef was reiterated in an official statement and, in a famous publicity gimmick, John Gummer, then agriculture minister, appeared on television feeding his little daughter Cordelia with a beefburger in front of the cameras in an attempt to get the message across that there was nothing to worry about and that beef was safe.

In March 1996 the BSE issue came back to life, even more dramatically than before! A government research team in Edinburgh discovered a link between BSE and a new, more virulent form of CJD which had been reported as affecting 10 young people whose average age was 27. Until then the incidence of CJD was normally associated with older patients, the previous average age being 63. The connection between these 10 worryingly early deaths and BSE was admitted by the Health Secretary, Stephen Dorrell, in a statement to the public made on 20 March. The result could well be described as panic-stricken.

- Beef sales to the public collapsed.
- The European Union imposed a worldwide ban on the sale of British beef.
- McDonalds and other outlets announced that they would only use imported beef.
- British farmers began to demand better compensation from the government, a call that was resisted by the Treasury until the EU agreed to provide 70 per cent of that compensation. Unfortunately, this 70 per cent was offset against the British rebate from the EU and the true value of the compensation payments was probably nearer 25 per cent.
- A programme of selective slaughter was started, eliminating cattle over 30 months old. The government found it very difficult to put this plan into operation since the capacity of abattoirs to handle this volume of throughput was limited and bottlenecks were created. It was also difficult to assess whether the culling procedure was appropriate. The EU's agriculture commissioner, Franz Fischler, was not alone in saying that if the findings announced on 20 March were correct then the slaughter programme was not enough; if the findings were at all suspect then, 'a more careful reaction might have been preferable' (Dunleavy *et al.*, 1997, p. 345).

Putting the Blame on Europe

The government's answer to the discoveries of 1996 was to argue that there was nothing wrong and to summon up teams of veterinary experts to argue with the European Commission for agreement to lift the ban. When that was refused 'the government decided to attempt to shift the blame for what had happened onto the European Union' (Dunleavy *et al.*, 1997, p. 340). The British government announced a programme of non-cooperation in decisions of the Council of Ministers until the EU agreed to withdraw the ban: as a result, European business was disrupted for three weeks and 80 different European measures were blocked by a British veto. At the Florence European Council in June a small concession was made on beef products in return for a British policy of culling 125 000 cattle. It was a very small concession and no more than Britain could have won through negotiation but it was enough for Major to claim a victory in his 'war' with the Council and Commission. The anti-European and xenophobic actions of the government may have helped John Major in the internal disputes about Europe within the Conservative Party, but it did nothing for Britain's status in Europe and it finally destroyed any willingness on the part of the Europeans to help Britain, 'The residue of ill feeling left by the British tactics was everywhere apparent . . . as they look to Europe's future, others have decided they can no longer accommodate their awkward island neighbours' (*Financial Times*, 24 June 1996).

Britain moderated the policy of non-cooperation but repeated that there was nothing to worry about and that there was no evidence of a BSE connection. In August the government produced a report which said that BSE would die out quite naturally by the year 2001, without any need for the cull. Europe remained adamant in its refusal to lift the ban and there were many advisers who told the government that, whether or not the threat from BSE was real, the public worldwide had lost confidence in British beef and the only way to restore that confidence was by continuing or even intensifying the cattle cull.

Towards the end of the year the government was challenged by a debate on its handling of the beef crisis. At first the Agriculture Minister, Douglas Hogg, tried to claim that everything that possibly could be done had been done but, after attacks from all parties, he had to concede that mistakes had been made and there was no guarantee that government action would solve the problem. The government won the debate by just 303 votes to 302. Early in 1997 the relevant committee of the European Parliament – to whom Douglas Hogg refused to speak on the grounds that he might compromise British sovereignty – produced a report that was extremely critical of the British government's handling of the situation. Their line was very similar to that of the editor of the

New Statesman, 'A panicking government first refused to cull dairy cattle, then over-enthusiastically slaughtered the beef herd, then mismanaged the scheme and overpaid the abattoirs [while John Major] launched his absurd "beef war" against the EU' (*New Statesman*, 21 February 1997, p. 5).

This meant that the BSE crisis stumbled on to the end of the Conservative government and beyond. The more conciliatory attitude towards Europe exhibited by the Blair government had its impact on those concerned with the beef argument and there was talk of a relaxation of the ban, certainly as it related to the beef cattle of Scotland and Northern Ireland. Then, in early June 1997 the Agriculture Minister Jack Cunningham seemed to go on the attack by reversing the criticism, expressing himself as very bitter that 'although Britain cannot export beef to the rest of the EU, other EU countries have continued to export beef here' (*The Guardian*, 6 June 1997). Rather than continue simply with demands for the ban on beef to be lifted, Cunningham insisted that other EU countries should now follow the same stringent regulations as had been placed on the United Kingdom. As the minister was quoted as saying in the same issue of *The Guardian*, 'I thought it was an absurd situation that, with all the rigorous controls on beef in this country, we are importing beef that was not subject to the same safeguards'. The veterinary committee of the EU issued a report stating that there could well have been 1700 cases of BSE in Europe rather than the 290 officially reported, and the agriculture commissioner Franz Fischler expressed disquiet at the fact that abattoirs in only four other countries apart from the UK – Ireland, Netherlands, Portugal and France – remove the suspect spinal cords and brains from the carcasses of sheep and cattle.

The political significance of the BSE crisis is that it is in line with a whole sequence of public health crises – food additives, salmonella in eggs, pesticides in drinking water, lead in petrol – where the government has first of all denied that there is a problem, then been forced to admit that some problems do exist. The admission creates panic among the public, leads to possible financial ruin for the producers in question, and the measures to try and correct the problem are usually too little and too late. Whether or not there really is a BSE problem and whether or not the EU Commission was right in its actions, there is no doubt that the Conservative government mishandled the crisis and once again shook the public's faith in their competence in the dying months of an 18-year administration.

BSE as an Issue

There is no doubt that BSE itself was a political issue, although it was very much a transitory one that may not survive in the public mind once the EU ban on British beef is withdrawn. Where it does have an impact is in the implications thrown up by the BSE crisis for other, more long-term issues:

- *Europe*   The way in which the Major government handled the beef ban was indicative of the way in which the Conservative government, riven by internal disagreements over Europe, tended to use the EU as a handy scapegoat for unpopular government actions. As with arguments over fishing, the introduction of any agricultural measure that upset the farmers met with the handy excuse that the government's hands were tied by European legislation. The EU's ban on the export of British beef was represented in the British press as an example of the bureaucracy in Brussels interfering unfairly in British affairs. What was not mentioned was that the EU only took action to meet the justifiable concerns of residents in countries to which British beef was exported after the British government had failed to take suitable action itself. As for the so-called 'beef war', the threat to paralyse European legislation seemed all too much like treating the EU like little Cordelia Gummer who would be forced to eat British beef whether she wanted to or not. One important by-product of the BSE affair was the way it highlighted the problems faced by the Common Agricultural Policy, making it certain that reform of the CAP was an urgent imperative for the future development of the EU.
- *Government competence*   The British government, and its representatives such as Douglas Hogg, failed to realise that a worried public would not be content with simply being told there was nothing to worry about: there had to be some evidence that the government was doing something. When the government apparently overreacted and started to slaughter more cattle than had been asked of them, this did not reassure the public that nothing was wrong but rather convinced them that the scale of the action proved there was indeed something seriously wrong. It may well be that Europe did not handle the matter as competently as they might have done either, but the attempt to put the blame on Europe was seen as yet another example of a tired administration

seeking to blame anyone other than itself for its mistakes, as well as an increasingly weak and indecisive John Major attempting to mollify the Eurosceptics in his own party.

- *Devolution* Many of the problems faced by farmers, including the sense of unfairness they felt at their treatment, were due to the British government's insistence on treating the problem on a UK-wide basis. Throughout the crisis it was known that certain parts of the UK, such as Scotland and Northern Ireland, were relatively free of BSE, and farmers in those areas with totally healthy beef herds could have been exempted from the ban much earlier if agricultural policy decisions had been devolved to regional level. There was another element present in Northern Ireland in that for all practical purposes their beef industry is integrated with that of the Republic of Ireland. If food policy had been treated as an all-Irish issue in Europe there would have been no need for Ulster cattle to have faced the ban. But Unionist politicians and Conservative politicians wishing to keep the Unionists happy, would not allow political accommodations with Dublin under any circumstances and Northern Ireland suffered accordingly.
- *Advice and information* The BSE crisis was typified by the role of technical experts in animal husbandry, veterinary science and food safety in giving advice and technical assistance to those dealing with the crisis. The nature of this advice and of the persons giving it has an important part to play in the development of the crisis as a political issue. This aspect mostly relates to the management of information by the government to present the case in a light favourable to them. Government scientists and advisory committees are bound by measures such as the Official Secrets Act and this enables the government to conceal or suppress unwelcome information. The media-amplified public panic over food scares like BSE is largely a result of the public being kept in the dark, feeling confused and open to the wildest speculation. 'Politicians and civil servants find it useful to hide behind the veil of scientific advice, while controlling the flow of information . . . they can discredit and damage those who disagree with the majority view' (Baggott, 1996, p. 5). A micro-biologist, Professor Richard Lacey, was highly critical of the government's handling of food scares and even more so of their treatment of so-called independent scientists who could be 'manipulated and sometimes even threatened by civil servants' (*The Observer*, 24 March 1996).

- *Producer versus consumer* Part of the issue in question is the accountability of the Ministry of Agriculture, Fisheries and Food. MAFF is responsible for food safety, even if sometimes in association with the Department of Health, and in that respect is answerable to the consumer. Yet MAFF's primary responsibility is to look after farmers, fishermen and their respective industries, and therefore it is a ministry for whom the interests of the producers must necessarily come first, to the possible detriment of the interests of the consumers. As the *New Statesman* asked (21 February 1997), 'Should a ministry established to supervise an industry be given responsibility for matters that are so crucial to consumers?' This lack of an independent food safety body that would not be subordinate to the producers was recognised by Tony Blair while in opposition and he authorised an enquiry under Professor Philip James of Aberdeen University. As a result of the report made by Professor James, one of the first acts of the Blair government was to set up an independent Food Standards Agency free of ministerial control, and therefore free to represent the interests of the consumer.

Along with a more conciliatory attitude towards Europe and the government's plans for devolved government, the Food Standards Agency should help the Labour government to avoid the pitfalls of food safety scares into which the previous Tory administration had fallen. Not all the procedures are yet in place, however, and the Blair government will remain as vulnerable as all its predecessors to the unexpected event that is then taken up by the media and turned into an issue of public concern.

Conclusion: Issues, Elections and the Political Process

It was once believed that an individual's voting intentions were learned through political socialisation – from family, friends, school and neighbourhood – as part of the process of growing up. In the form of partisanship which ensues, party loyalties are so strong and so much a part of the individual's sense of values that it is unthinkable for them to vote for any other party. This is known as normative voting because their support for a particular party is seen by the individual as normal behaviour. Because normative voting is learned from people of the same social background, partisan voting tends to be based on social class and associated with areas that are safe seats for one party or another.

In the 1970s the strict two-party loyalties of class-based normative voting behaviour began to break down in the processes called de-alignment and re-alignment. Electoral behaviour became far more volatile and political parties found that they could no longer count on ideas such as 'Labour is the party of the working class' providing them with an automatic majority in some constituencies: voters switched parties between elections and there was increasing support for third parties. Voting behaviour moved from being normative to being thought of as 'instrumental', which means that when individuals come to decide how they should cast their votes they make their decision on the basis of what would be in the best interests of themselves and their immediate family, rather than some abstract idea of the common good. And instrumental voting is best expressed by issue-based voting, or the 'consumer model of voting' as it is sometimes called.

This is the form of voting that political parties like to think happens. It is thought that the voter decides what the most important issues are and then votes for the party with the best

265

policies for dealing with those issues, as if choosing from a shopping list. That is why parties lay such stress in their election manifestos on issues such as those which have been discussed in this book. Yet there is some doubt as to their importance. Research before the 1987 and 1992 general elections into the issues regarded as important by the electorate, and into public perceptions of the parties' ability to cope with those issues, showed that the National Health Service, unemployment and education were considered the most important, and Labour was regarded as well ahead of the Conservatives on all issues except the economy. Yet the Conservatives won in both elections. After the 1987 election Ivor Crewe had written, 'Had electors voted solely on the main issues Labour would have won', and that verdict had not changed in 1992 (Crewe, 1992).

For most people their judgment about political issues is based almost entirely on what they are told by the media. The political information communicated by the media, and the way in which it is communicated, is of the greatest importance in influencing political opinion and in deciding which issues are seen as being the most important for the electorate. After the Conservatives' unexpected success in the 1992 general election the former Treasurer of the Conservative party, Lord McAlpine, famously said, 'The heroes of this campaign were . . . the editors of the Tory press' (*Sunday Telegraph*, 12 April 1992), giving credit for the Conservatives' victory to the newspapers, and the tabloid newspapers in particular. The *Sun* newspaper put it more succinctly in the headline 'IT'S THE SUN WOT WON IT'.

The extent to which the *Sun* did in fact win the 1992 election for the Conservatives is still a matter for debate, but what is indisputable is the growing importance of the mass media as the old normative certainties of political support decline and are replaced by the rival merits of different political issues. Politics may well revolve around the importance of political issues, for politicians and electorate alike, but it is the media which are responsible for defining the nature and importance of those issues. The importance given to the media by the politicians may well be leading towards what one commentator has described as, 'the "public relations state" engaging in a more or less permanent publicity campaign for all its activities' (Negrine, 1997, p. 26). But Negrine, in fact, foresees the existence of a more or less permanent election campaign which increases in intensity during the three to four weeks of the official campaign, but which is nevertheless continuous between elections. Political activity has become a form of 'political marketing' in which 'the citizen becomes more like a consumer – forced to choose between political parties in the same way as he or she would choose between products'. In this process of projecting a party and its policies through the media the place of the marketing manager is taken by the press secretaries or 'spin doctors'.

Simon Hoggart defines spin doctors as 'people employed by politicians and their parties to put a favourable "spin" on political events and speeches' (in Linton, 1997, p. 22), and, as Hoggart points out, spin doctors are not new in British politics – 'before spin doctors were called spin doctors, they were known as press secretaries'. The first press secretary to become a spin-doctor in the modern, American sense was Bernard Ingham who acted as Margaret Thatcher's press secretary for many years, so successfully that there were those who claimed that in a press release they could never tell whether the words were those of Bernard Ingham or those of Mrs Thatcher.

The rise of New Labour and the unparalleled grip that Tony Blair had on his party was the product of a new generation of spin doctors and two men in particular, Alastair Campbell and Peter Mandelson. Campbell has been known to telephone the BBC and attack them for leading the 9 o'clock news bulletin with a news story other than a speech Blair had made that evening. Mandelson, as MP for Hartlepool, helped mastermind the 1997 campaign from the Millbank campaign headquarters, imposing an almost Stalinist grip on what Labour MPs and candidates felt free to say and do. After the election Mandelson was made minister without portfolio with a position within the Cabinet Office, and a brief to employ his spin-doctoring skills for the government rather than the party.

It is the duty of spin doctors to manipulate the media and, as we have established, it is the media who present and explain political issues to the public. Therefore it is within the power of the spin doctors to determine the political agenda, deciding which issues will be discussed and controlling that discussion so as best to favour the party for whom the spin doctor is 'spinning'.

The role of the spin doctor in general, and Peter Mandelson in particular, has been much criticised by members of all parties but it would seem that the role is here to stay, again for all parties. It is therefore perhaps salutary to recognise that, despite all their efforts to control the political agenda, the spin doctors are still powerless in face of the interest and concerns of the public.

During the 1997 election campaign there were two issues that monopolised public interest at great expense to other issues that the spin doctors really wished to promote. During the early part of the campaign the refusal of Neil Hamilton to stand down in Tatton, and the failure of the government to allow the Commissioner for Public Standards to report his findings on accusations against Hamilton, meant that the media were dominated by the sleaze issue. It was only after Martin Bell was established as the anti-sleaze candidate in Tatton that the media could turn to another matter. And then the media settled on Europe and the single European currency, not from the viewpoint of Europe's importance to Britain in the election campaign but on the question of the Conservative Party's policy on Europe. The spin doctors, especially those belonging to the Tory Party, tried desperately to bring the discussion back to the economy or taxes or education, but without success. The media, right up to polling day, concentrated on stories about Europe and attitudes towards Europe despite the fact that the Eurocentred nature of the debate only succeeded in two things. Firstly, it made it very clear to the public that the Conservatives were totally divided over Europe and that John Major could do nothing to heal the divisions in the party. And secondly it was equally apparent that although the British public were suspicious of Europe and, perhaps assisted by the media, were hostile to the EU, that hostility was not enough to turn European membership into a prime issue as the Tory Euro-sceptics seemed to want.

Therefore we can conclude by saying that political issues are now a principal determinant in voting behaviour, that the media and the press machines of the various parties will attempt to manipulate the public's perception of issues, but that in the last resort the electorate will make up its own mind about how those issues instrumentally affect individual electors, their families and their way of life.

Bibliography

Abel-Smith, B. and Townsend, P. (1965) *The Poor and The Poorest*, LSE Occasional Papers on Social Administration, no. 17, London School of Economics.

Adams, J and Pyper, R. (1997) 'Whatever Happened to the Scott Report?', *Talking Politics*, Spring.

Adonis, A. (1993) *Parliament Today* (Manchester: Manchester University Press).

Baggott, R. (1995a) 'Putting the Squeeze on Sleaze?', *Talking Politics*, Autumn.

Baggott, R. (1995b) *Pressure Groups Today* (Manchester: Manchester University Press).

Baggott, R. (1996) 'Where is the Beef? The BSE Crisis and the British Policy Process', *Talking Politics*, Autumn.

Barnett, A. (1994) *Power and the Throne: The Monarchy Debate* (London: Vintage).

Barnett, A. (1995) 'The Constitutional Crisis and the Monarchy', *Politics Review*, September.

Barnett, A. (1997) 'Yes, the Revolution Really is Here', *New Statesman*, 23 May.

Barnett, C. (1986) *The Audit of War* (London: Macmillan).

Belton, T. (1997) 'Beyond Quangocracy', *New Statesman*, 18 July.

Beveridge, Sir William (1944) *Full Employment in a Free Society*, Government White Paper (London: HMSO).

Bradbury, J. (1996) 'English Regional Government', *Politics Review*, April.

Butler, D. (1985) 'Electoral Reform', in J. Jowell and D. Oliver (eds), *The Changing Constitution* (Oxford: Clarendon Press).

Butler, D. and Kavanagh, D. (1992) *The British General Election of 1992* (Basingstoke: Macmillan).

Central Statistical Office (1994) *Social Trends: 24* (London: HMSO).

Childs, D. (1992) *Britain since 1945: A Political History*, 3rd edn (London: Routledge).

Cole, M and Howe, J. (1994) 'Women and Politics', *Politics Review*, November.

Cope, S., Starie, P. and Leishman, F. (1996) 'The Politics of Police Reform', *Politics Review*, April.

Cowley, P. and Dowding, K. (1994) 'Electoral Systems and Parliamentary Representation', *Politics Review*, September.

Cox, C. B. and Dyson, A. E. (1971) *The Black Papers on Education* (London: Davis-Poynter).

Coxall, B. and Robins, L. (1995) *Contemporary British Politics*, 2nd edn (Basingstoke: Macmillan).

Crewe, I. (1992) 'Why did Labour Lose (Yet Again)?', *Politics Review*, September.

Cunningham, M. (1991) *British Government Policy in Northern Ireland 1969–89* (Manchester: Manchester University Press).

Cunningham, M. (1992) 'British Policy in Northern Ireland', *Politics Review*, September.

Curtice, J. (1989) 'The 1989 European Election: Protest or Green Tide?', *Electoral Studies*, vol. 8.

Department of the Environment (1992) *Protecting Europe's Environment* (London: HMSO).

Dobson, A. (1993) 'Ecologism' in R. Eatwell and A. Wright (eds), *Contemporary Political Ideologies* (London: Pinter).

Doig, A. (1994) 'Scandal, Politics and the Media', *Politics Review*, November.

Dunleavy, P., Gamble, A., Holliday, I. and Peele, G. (eds) (1993) *Developments in British Politics*, vol. 4 (London: Macmillan).

Dunleavy *et al.* (eds, see above) (1997) *Developments in British Politics*, vol. 5 (London: Macmillan).

European Commission (1992) *Protecting our Environment*, European File series, Luxembourg.

Field, F. (1995) *Making Welfare Work*, Institute of Community Studies, London.

Finer, S. E. (1956) 'The Individual Responsibility of Ministers', *Public Administration*, vol. 34, no. 4.

Foot, M. (1973) *Aneurin Bevan: A Biography*, Vol. 2 (London: Four Square).

Gilbert, M. (1988) *Never Despair – Winston S. Churchill 1945–1965* (London: Heinemann).

Grant, W. (1995) 'Are Environmental Pressure Groups Effective?', *Politics Review*, September.

Gregg, P and Wadsworth, J. (1995) *The Oxford Review of Economic Policy*, vol. 11, no. 1 (Oxford University Press).

HMSO (1994) *Public Bodies, 1993* (London: HMSO).

Hattersley, R. (1995) 'Opposition Will Heal all Wounds, Right? Wrong', *Observer*, 19 March.

Hogg, Q. (1947) *The Case for Conservatism* (London: Penguin).

Howe, G. (1961) 'Reform of the Social Services', in *Principles in Practice* (London: Conservative Political Centre).

Hugill, B. (1995) 'Tax: A Vicious Circle that Won't be Squared', *Observer*, 9 April.

Hutton, W. (1995) *The State We're In* (London: Jonathan Cape).

Hutton, W. (1997) *The State to Come* (London: Vintage).

Jenkins, R. (Lord Jenkins of Hillhead) (1989) *European Diary 1977–1981* (London: Collins).

Johnson, Joy (1997) 'The Weak Link Takes the Strain', *New Statesman*, 31 January.

Johnson, R. (1991) 'A New Road to Serfdom? A Critical History of the 1988 Act', in Education Group II, *Education Limited: Schooling, Training and the New Right in England since 1979* (London: Lawrence and Wishart).

Jones, B (ed.) (1989) *Political Issues in Britain Today*, 3rd edn (Manchester: Manchester University Press).

Jones, B (ed.) (1994) *Politics UK*, 2nd edn (Hemel Hempstead: Harvester Wheatsheaf).

Jones, B and Kavanagh, D. (1983) *British Politics Today*, 2nd edn (Manchester: Manchester University Press).

Jones, G. W. and Stewart, J. (1993) 'A Law Unto Themselves', *Local Government Chronicle*, 14 May.

Kavanagh, D. (1990) *British Politics – Continuities and Change*, 2nd edn (Oxford: Oxford University Press).

Kingdom, J. (1991) *Government and Politics in Britain* (Cambridge: Polity Press).

Layton-Henry, Z. (1996) 'Immigration and Contemporary Politics', *Politics Review*, February.

Leigh, D and Vulliamy, E. (1997) *Sleaze: The Corruption of Parliament* (London: Fourth Estate).

Linton, M. (ed.) (1997) *The Election: A Voter's Guide* (London: Fourth Estate).

Lloyd, J. (1997) 'Into the Ethical Dimension', *New Statesman*, 25 July.

Lowe, P. and Goyder, J. (1983) *Environmental Groups in Politics* (London: George Allen & Unwin).

Mazey, S. and Richardson, J. (1993) 'Pressure Groups and the EC', *Politics Review*, September.

McGarry, J and O'Leary, B (eds) (1990) *The Future of Northern Ireland* (Oxford: Oxford University Press).

McKie, D. (1993) *The Guardian Political Almanac 1993/4* (London: Fourth Estate).

McKie, D. (1994) *The Guardian Political Almanac 1994/5* (London: Fourth Estate).

Milne, K. (1997) 'Labour's Quota Women', *New Statesman*, 16 May.

Mitchell, J. (1996) 'Reviving the Union State?', *Politics Review*, February.

Moran, M. (1985) 'The Changing World of British Pressure Groups', *Teaching Politics*, September.

Moran, M. (1995) 'Reshaping the British State', *Talking Politics*, Spring.

Negrine, R. (1997) 'Politics and the Media', *Politics Review*, April.

Norton, P. (1994) 'The Constitution in Question', *Politics Review*, April.

Pattie, C. Johnston, R. and Russell, A. (1995) 'The Stalled Greening of British Politics', *Politics Review*, February.

Pilkington, C. (1995) *Britain in the European Union Today* (Manchester: Manchester University Press).

Powell, E. (1976) *Medicine and Politics: 1975 and After* (London: Pitman).

Puddephatt, A. (1995) 'The Criminal Justice and Public Order Act and the need for a Bill of Rights', *Talking Politics*, Autumn.

Public Information Office of the House of Commons (1991) *The House of Commons and European Communities Legislation,* Factsheet no. 56.

Pyper, R. (1994) 'Individual Ministerial Responsibility: Dissecting the Doctrine', *Politics Review,* September.

Reeve, A and Ware, A. (1992) *Electoral Systems – A Comparative and Theoretical Introduction* (London: Routledge).

Rosamond, B. (1994) 'The Labour Party and European Integration', *Politics Review,* April.

Rose, R and McAllister, I. (1986) *Voters Begin to Choose* (London: Sage).

Shell, D. (1995) 'The House of Lords', *Politics Review,* September.

Shell, D. and Beamish D. R. (eds) (1993) *The House of Lords at Work* (Oxford: Clarendon Press).

Stewart, J. (1995) 'Change in Local Government', *Politics Review,* November.

Stokes G., Hopwood, B. and Bullman, U. (1996) 'Do we Need Regional Government?', *Talking Politics,* Spring.

Stott, T. (1995–6) 'Evaluating the Quango Debate', *Talking Politics,* Winter.

Taylor-Gooby, P. (1991) *British Social Attitudes, 8th Report* (Aldershot: Dartmouth Publishing).

Timmins, N. (1995) *The Five Giants: A Biography of the Welfare State* (London: HarperCollins).

Weir, S. and Hall, W. (1994) *EGO Trip: Extra-governmental Organisations in the UK and their Accountability,* Democratic Audit and Charter 88, London, May.

Wincott, D. (1992) 'The Conservative Party and Europe', *Politics Review,* April.

Young, H. (1989) *One of Us* (London: Macmillan).

Young, S. C. (1993) 'Environmental Politics and the EC', *Politics Review,* February.

Index